To Jen, getting a film buff a present is easy, as long as they have not got it already
Janus

JACK LEMMON:
His FILMS and
CAREER

JACK LEMMON: His FILMS and CAREER

by JOE BALTAKE

Tribute by WALTER MATTHAU

Foreword by JUDITH CRIST

THE CITADEL PRESS • SECAUCUS, N.J.

To the memory of J.B.

Acknowledgments

To Victoria Brooks, secretary to Mr. Lemmon; Beau Bridges; Jane Biberman; Richard Carter; John Griggs; and of course, Mr. Matthau and Mrs. Crist: Thank you.

—Joe Baltake

Library of Congress Cataloging in Publication Data

Baltake, Joe.
    Jack Lemmon: His films and career.

    1. Lemmon, Jack.   2. Moving-picture actors and actresses — United States — Biography.   I. Title.
PN2287.L42B3   791.43′028′0924 [B]   77-636
ISBN 0-8065-1001-3

Designed by William R. Meinhardt

Published by Citadel Press
a division of Lyle Stuart Inc.
120 Enterprise Ave., Secaucus, N.J. 07094
In Canada: Musson Book Company
a division of General Publishing Co. Limited
Don Mills, Ontario

Queries regarding rights and permissions should be addressed to: Lyle Stuart, 120 Enterprise Avenue, Secaucus, N.J. 07094

Manufactured in the United States of America

Al Hirschfeld caricature of Jack Lemmon as Scottie Templeton in the play *Tribute*.

Contents

An Ode to a Lemmon

Walter Matthau.

A Tribute in verse by

WALTER MATTHAU

Jack Lemmon

is a clean cut well scrubbed Boston choir boy
with quiet hysteria seeping out of every pore to bolt
the banal Boston beanpot middle class drudgery
succeeds by dint of sweet faced determination to
scamper through to goal not touching one hair
of any hair about not wrinkling one's sensitive
geiger counter not tampering with a single solitary
soul's ego going full steam ahead with courage
generosity and decent tact and able along the way
take time to smell the flowers and help others
about to see and smell them too and simmer down
to satisfaction from a good cigar and mellow
glass of wine to be a good fellow of splendid
instincts and deeds.

Playing Oscar to Lemmon's Felix in
The Odd Couple, 1968.

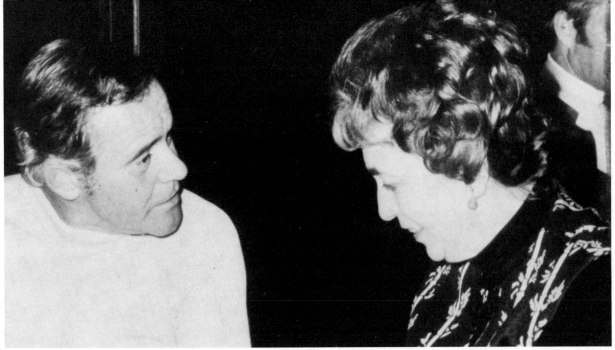

Lemmon chatting with Judith Crist.

(Photo courtesy of Harriet Norris, Tarrytown Conference Center)

On Jack Lemmon

A Foreword by JUDITH CRIST

There are stars—and there are stars beyond stars in the Hollywood heavens, for those of us who are the astronomers of the region, movie nuts who have devoted their years, for pleasure and/or profession, to studying that factory town's galaxles. There are the flashers, the durables, the professionals who are stars—and beyond them are the flashing durable professional stars who edge their way onto the screen and glow and grow in ever-increasing, always-more-dazzling intensity, ever beyond the magnitude we once assigned them.

Small doubt that Jack Lemmon is in the forefront of that all-inclusive star category, the actor whose professionalism is his hallmark, whose versatility is his crown and whose persona is the key to the affections of his audience. For much as Chaplin's clown in his time embodied the commonality of the common man, so Lemmon's white-collar everyman has provided the empathetic symbol for the mid-twentieth-century man in his uphill struggle against the bogeys of the affluent Fifties, the sour Sixties and the uncertain Seventies. Whether he's the smooth operator or the schnook, the crafty con-

niver or the victim thereof; whether he's out for the laughter or tearing at the heart—he's one of us, the all too human people in the middle who get it from top and bottom alike.

Lemmon is, above all, a craftsman, devoted to his acting art, and that, I suspect, explains the surprise with which even Lemmon devotees look back at the varieties of his performances, the risks taken in the course of a career that spans more than two decades. Symbolically, consider the range in his two Oscar-winning roles, eighteen years apart. His 1955 Ensign Pulver, which won him the Motion Picture Academy's Best Supporting Actor prize, combined all the brash, braggingly lecherous sass of young manhood with the laziness, the timidity, the callowness and the essential decency that are equally the characteristics of youth. At the other end of the scale, his 1973 Harry Stoner, which won him the Best Actor Oscar, was the desperate middle-aged spokesman for Pulver's generation, the ensign grown up and ground down, a decent man whose decency can't survive in a world without rules, without a memory of the past, with a reverence only for the material present and no hope or

Lemmon celebrating his 50th birthday with his wife, Felicia Farr, at a party in New York on February 19, 1975.

dream beyond another season of economic survival.

And fore and aft and in between Lemmon gave us a constant variety, initially as pure nice-guy in a spate of Fifties fun, with time out to portray a warlock or prove that he could be hilarious in girls' gladrags while proving irresistible to men and women alike. Proof of his triumph over sleaziness lies not only in that *Some Like It Hot* role but also in his portrait of a cog in the big-wheel success struggle in *The Apartment*, making a quasi-pimp not merely palatable but actually appealing and proving himself not only an actor of sensitivity but a master of taste.

And barely had one classified him as serious master of comedy than along came *Days of Wine and Roses* to prove him a dramatic actor of the first rank in a performance that grows in intensity with each re-viewing, one that starts with the familiar glossy man we expect and recognize and carries him to the very depths of physical horror and spiritual torment. And then back to the flip and the hip and the glossy.

The mark of the man is, perhaps, that he has worked with a number of directors a number of times, consistent in that mutual professional admiration, or admirable professionalism, that distinguishes Lemmon's career on and off stage.

8

A happy reunion with two of his leading ladies, Shirley MacLaine (left) and Maureen Stapleton, at his 50th birthday party.

Just as friendships from 'way back are honored, so are associations—a rare quality in a star whose "clout" has been acknowledged for more than a decade. There have been the ups and downs with Billy Wilder, from *Some Like It Hot* to *The Apartment* to *Irma La Douce* to *The Fortune Cookie* to *Avanti!* to *The Front Page;* win some, lose some, but it's the collaboration that counts. The partnership with Walter Matthau, with its particular chemistry under Wilder's directorial hand in *The Fortune Cookie* and *The Front Page* and still another under Gene Saks's in *The Odd Couple,* led to further creativity, with Matthau starring in *Kotch* in 1971 under Lemmon's direction; Matthau's portrait of the seventy-two-year-old widower was perfection but it was Lemmon's sure directorial touch that made the charm outweigh the sentiment in this touching and meaningful consideration of old age. And in turn, Lemmon is willing not only to perform for aspiring student directors—but sponsors showings of their works to help their careers. He is not one to leave behind the days of his own struggles and aspirations: an added zest to his finally appearing on stage with Maureen Stapleton (and Matthau) in a Los Angeles production of *Juno and the Paycock* early in 1975 was the shared memory of back when—when he was the piano-playing m.c. and Ms. Stapleton a song-and-dance girl in a barnlike nightclub that was going broke while they were both hoping for that big break onto Broadway.

While the Lemmon "character"—the ha-rassed man, outflanked, outranked and outmaneuvered, slipping on the invisible banana peels that beset the paths of us all—has its mannerisms, it's the particular Lemmon touch that individualizes each performance. The best example, perhaps, is in his Felix Unger, the role in *The Odd Couple* that for me will always be particularly his. Lemmon made Felix a revolting mass of tics and twitches and fussbudgetry but—and this is the triumph of craftsmanship—with all the priggishness and domesticity, his Felix is all male, without even the suggestion of camp or hint of a limp wrist. It's that fine precision of stopping—not on anything as gross as a dime—on the thin rim of the dime. It is, I suppose, what we call good taste.

One wouldn't, presumably, expect less of a Harvard man. Lemmon's of the gentleman breed of actors, the college graduates with a serious interest in acting—as opposed to the truckers and cowboys and drifters who became manufactured glamor boys in the days when movie stars could be stamped out on the assembly-line of the Hollywood factories. It is that seriousness that has provided the flash of inspired performance, the infinite variety of accomplishment, the steady growth. Only a serious performer, after all, could provide us with the joyous laughter of Lemmon's comedy—and only an actor of many humors touches our emotions so deeply in his dramatic moments. How fortunate for us all that some twenty years and more than thirty films seem to mark only the beginning of a career!

Lemmon, "a guy you're gonna like," circa 1953.

A Guy You're Gonna Like

A Biography of Jack Lemmon

When Jack Lemmon winged his way to Hollywood in 1953, the place was swarming with Rorys, Rocks, Tabs, Tonys and Ricks.

There was no doubt about it. The surrounding competition was pretty tough stuff: All male-model handsomeness with capped teeth of gleaming white and a veneer of studio-produced suavity.

Jack stood as an extreme digression from the then-popular norm. There wasn't any gloss on this New England boy.

Hollywood's latest discovery boasted such dubious assets as a slight build, sagging shoulders, slouching posture and a wide-open face filled with basset-hound anxiety, quizzical alertness and high-strung energy.

"A look of neutrality" is the way one writer elected to describe Jack's appearance. Looks, however, can be deceiving. For beneath the skin of this Lemmon lurks a soul of complexities and contradictions.

His transparent hazel eyes reveal the rinky-tink heart of a man who favors Dixieland and jazz, of a man who goes crackers over W. C. Fields, Buster Keaton and Walter Matthau, of a man who chatters away in the sharp, salty slang of musicians.

Within the confines of a fifteen-minute conversation, Jack manages to do mimes, tell jokes and philosophize to no end. He'll sound off on everything—from pollution to producing—punctuating each opinion with a corny W. C. Fields impression.

His calm "look of neutrality" is also cracked by his high degree of nervous energy. He fiddles. He faddles. He fidgets. And his hands are always preoccupied—with either a piano, a pool cue, a cigar, a fishing rod or gardening tools.

Columbia Pictures—the studio which discovered Jack—was well aware back in '53 that it had an actor of immense personality on its hands. Immense personality, but terribly average looking—especially alongside Rock and Tab and Rory.

The immediate problem then was how to peddle this spanking new commodity named Jack Lemmon. Would the escapist-conscious moviegoing public be willing to invest time and money in a fellow who looks uncannily like the young accountant living in the next block?

Columbia wisely decided not to be preten-

At Phillips Andover Academy, 1943.

With Ardelle and Arlene Turner as host of CBS' bi-weekly *Toni Twin Time*, 1953.

tious about Jack. They played it simple and straight. Having cast the young actor in his first film, a very funny Judy Holliday comedy titled *It Should Happen to You!*, Columbia quite simply introduced Jack as "a guy you're gonna like."

The public has closely identified with his perplexed, Chaplinesque screen heroes ever since. Jack's talent and versatility have played a big part in his success, but his genuine affability has been the titanic supporting structure.

Jack never planned to be an actor; he simply assumed he'd become one from the very start. "I always 'was' an actor," is the way Jack is apt to explain it, "so how could I ever decide to 'become' one?"

He became interested in theatrics at a very early age, entertaining his parents and their friends with imitations, teaching himself to play the piano by ear and composing some 400 ditties.

His acting debut came at age four when his father volunteered him for an amateur stage production of *Thar's Gold in Them Thar Hills*. Father and son, it seems, scored a personal success, so much so that son got hooked.

"From then on," reminisces Jack, "I wanted to be an actor—anywhere."

Of Scotch-Irish disposition, Jack was born John Uhler Lemmon III in the Back Bay area of Boston, Massachusetts, on Sunday, February 8, 1925.

He was born prematurely with acute yellow jaundice. "Just wanted to get a little attention, I guess," quips Jack. "Actors are impossible, you know."

The only child of John Uhler Lemmon, Jr.,

With Ralph Dunn, Bartlett Robinson, Horace Cooper, Georgiann Johnson, Stanley Prager and John Randolph in the 1953 Broadway revival of *Room Service*.

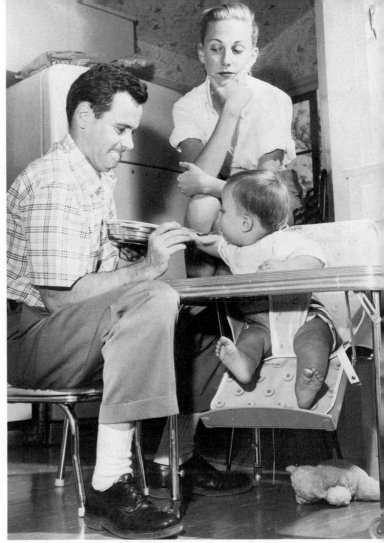

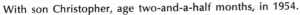

With son Christopher, age two-and-a-half months, in 1954.

With wife Cynthia and son Chris in 1954.

general sales manager and vice-president of the Doughnut Corporation of America, and his wife, the former Mildred LaRue Noel, Jack was continually besieged with ill health as a child.

Described as "scrawny," he had had three mastoid and seven adenoid operations by the time he was thirteen. "Jackie," his mother Millie once laughed, "popped in and out of hospitals like a cork on the Great Salt Lake."

The Lemmons resided in a quiet, sunny suburb named Newton, where his father—described by Jack as "a frustrated entertainer"—participated in amateur barbershop singing and soft-shoe dancing.

"My father," recalls Jack, "was always singing and dancing at benefits, although he wasn't very good at either.

"Whatever balance and good sense I bring to my life, I owe to my father," he adds. "He was a very simple, honorable man. He saw life clearly, and didn't try to complicate it."

Jack attended select New England schools,

including Rivers Country Day School, in Chestnut Hill, Massachusetts, and Phillips Andover Academy, in Andover, Massachusetts. He graduated from the latter in 1943.

He was still sickly and puny while attending Andover and, on doctors' orders, he had to forgo afternoon classes for workout sessions in the gym.

These exercises helped him to earn the reputation of being the first fourteen-year-old at Andover to run a mile in under five minutes.

Jack entered Harvard at eighteen, during the war years. Being eligible for the Navy's V-12 officer-training program, he majored in what was then called "war service sciences" (physics, chemistry, etc.).

"Taking war service sciences as my major was mandatory," notes Jack. "I was in the R.O.T.C. at that time and I had no choice. I was eighteen when the war broke out and had already been accepted to Harvard. I must say, I was extremely fortunate that I ended up there

13

Duffy, Jack, Cynthia and Chris, circa 1954.

instead of some other of the hundreds of accredited colleges in the R.O.T.C. program.

"Anyway, I had to take a number of naval courses in communications, engineering and the like. Just what every young actor needs, right? At that time, I should add, there were very few courses being given concerning the creative or interpretive arts. Harvard has since remedied this situation greatly and has also added the Loeb Theater—a great one."

As a Harvard student, Lemmon freely admits to having earned low grades. "The only reason I know French is because I flunked the course so many times that it sunk in by osmosis!"

He did, however, distinguish himself in college theatrics and, during his senior year, was elected president of the Hasty Pudding Club.

"I became president of Hasty Pudding in '45, and I'm convinced only because my name was Lemmon and another guy was named Appel, and those jokers thought it'd be very funny to run us against each other. I think I won by one vote."

Once, while on probation at Harvard ("Too much drama club and not enough studies"), Jack had concocted a depression-era musical revue titled *The Proof of the Pudding* and billed himself as Timothy Orange. "So that the faculty wouldn't know it was me."

One of the tunes for the show was a Lemmon original called "The Bottom's Fallen Out of Everything But You."

Also during his undergraduate years, Jack participated in the Harvard Dramatic Club and acted in a production of *Playboy of the Western World,* staged in Boston by "a splinter group from the Abbey Players, headed by a lovely lady named Maude DeWitt-Howe."

In 1946, Jack interrupted his education to serve a three-month hitch in the Navy as an ensign aboard the aircraft carrier, USS *Lake Champlain.* He was communications officer for the carrier.

"All in all, something like three years had been spent in trying to make an ensign out of me," he jokes, "and I spent all of an hour and a half at sea.

"I was a disaster of a signal officer. On my one sea trip, I left all the signal equipment on shore. Why, I might have sunk the Navy!"

Back at Harvard, Jack completed his studies and received his B.A. and B.S. degrees in 1947.

"When I left Harvard and borrowed three hundred bucks from dad so that I could hurry up and become an actor," Jack relates, "my dad told me something and I've never forgotten it.

"Dad said, 'I'm not going to give you any advice, but I hope you like what you're going to

At 1956 Oscar celebration with wife Cynthia, at which time he won a supporting actor award for 1955's *Mr. Roberts*.

do.' I said, 'All I know is that I have to do it.'

"My dad was in the flour-mix business and he said, 'That's fine. The day I don't find romance in a loaf of bread I'll quit.'"

The next stop was New York, where he took a five-dollar-a-week room ("actually, a windowless linen closet") over Isaac Gellis's delicatessen on West 54th Street, signed up for acting classes with Uta Hagen and managed to land a job playing the piano in Old Nick, a beer-hall on Second Avenue (now the site of El Morocco).

Old Nick, as described by Jack, was "a combination beer garden, restaurant, variety hall and movie theater," where he played the piano for the silent flicks for thirteen dollars a week.

"I got the job through a Harvard friend," Jack reminisces. "I played piano for the old silent movies because I don't read music, so I could play in the dark. I did some burley sketches and acts and at all times I was a waiter between shows. It was invaluable experience.

"I hardly made anything; in a way, it was a very black period. But watching Chaplin and Keaton night after night was like a Harvard education in comedy technique."

The Old Nick management also expected Jack to participate in a nightly singing competition with the customers. Anyone who could sing "By the Sea" the fastest would win ten dollars. No one ever beat him. How could they? Jack would have been fired.

Meanwhile, back at his windowless linen closet over Isaac Gellis's deli, situations were amusing and bizarre—not unlike some of the situations Jack would encounter in his film comedies.

With Lana Wood in Goodyear Theater's *The Victim*, televised Monday, Jan. 6, 1958 by NBC.

"I was actually *living The Apartment* back then," smiles Jack. "It was a darling room. I could watch the world through my transom."

One day, Jack went down the hall to shower and shave and accidentally locked himself out of his room. The only other key was in the delicatessen.

"Hell, I can go right by the people, I thought," says Jack, "by closing my eyes and walking fast. The main thing was not to act like the blithering idiot I felt like."

So dressed in only his shorts, Jack tramped his way through some gray winter slush and made a grand entrance into the crowded store.

"Hello," said Jack, "I'm Mr. Lemmon. I have Apartment 5-A and I'm locked out. Do you have a passkey?" Quick exit.

"My father tracked me down once," says Jack, "to see how I was getting along. By this time, he and mom had separated. When he saw the inside of that apartment, his mouth just fell open.

"I think he felt he'd gotten me through all those schools by the skin of *his* teeth. All he could say hoarsely was 'Harvard?!'"

Radio and television, however, changed matters for Jack. One of his earliest full-fledged professional acting jobs was as a lovelorn character named Bruce on the NBC radio soap opera, "Brighter Day."

"Jack obviously learned a lot from watching all those old movies," the show's director, Arthur Hanna, once commented. "He mugged all over the place, which was of no use on radio, but his timing and emotional range were great in the audition."

"I stayed in that show for a year," says Jack. "While I was still in it I got a job in another soaper, 'The Road of Life.'

"All of a sudden I was making big money, like a hundred and a quarter a week. Then I heard that the producer, Worthington Miner, was doing a TV show for his 'Studio One' called *Shadows and Substance*.

"I walked in and said, 'I'm from the Abbey Players in Dublin, y'know.' I had been practicing a Jimmy Cagney accent for the interview. Tony Miner was supposed to be quite impressed by the Abbey Players.

"Miner listened to me, asked me some

On the town with actress Felicia Farr in 1957.

Kroll caricature of Lemmon as Jerry in *Some Like It Hot*, 1959.

deadpan questions about my experiences with the Abbey Theater and about some Irish families he knew.

"Finally he looked at me and said, 'I just saw you on "Kraft Theater" a couple of weeks ago in *Charley's Aunt*, you phony, and you were about as Irish as Eddie Cantor, but I'll give you a part anyhow.'

"Time passed, and I must have done five hundred live shows in New York in two or three years—'Studio One,' 'Robert Montgomery Presents,' 'Suspense' and 'The Web,' among others. I even hosted a biweekly summer replacement show called 'Toni Twin Time' for CBS.

"Now they only hire stars; even off-Broadway is big business. But in those days we had a chance to learn. Why, Tony Miner didn't even have a door on his office at CBS. That's how I got to do that Irish play on 'Studio One.'

"I got fifty dollars for that. Chuck Heston got fifty dollars. And Maggie Phillips got seventy-five. Oh, those were wonderful days! It was immediate. No budget. No scenery. You just had

Making merry with Joe E. Brown in *Some Like It Hot*, 1959.

to come in on the faces. You had to concentrate on script and acting."

Jack's first professional stage role was in a brief off-Broadway revival of Tolstoy's *Power of Darkness*.

"Way off," says Jack. "It was at a place called the Ethnological Dance Hall on East 58th Street where it was so hot most of the audience fainted.

"It was summer; there was a heat wave on, and outside on the street there was pneumatic hammering even at night. So we had to close the windows. As a result it was a hundred and ten inside.

"I walked out on stage, said five sentences, and a guy in the front row fainted. I was sure that my acting had moved him so that it knocked him over. But when other people began to keel over, and I got woozy myself, I decided that wasn't the complete answer."

Jack's co-star in the play was blonde Cynthia Stone, then a radio actress and also an Uta Hagen student. She was a banker's daughter from the Midwest and a Finch College graduate.

Together, they collaborated on, produced (via their own company, Jalem) and co-starred in four fifteen-minute television series: "Wonderful Guy," "Heaven for Betsy," "The Ad-Libbers" and "The Couple Next Door."

"That may damn well have been the best time of all," Jack flatly states. "No star stuff then. Nobody was important and nobody had anything to lose, which is very, very important. We had just one fifteen-minute rehearsal. God, that was good! That was the best. I miss it. It was so exciting!"

Cynthia and Jack were married in her home town of Peoria, Illinois, on May 7, 1950. Their son, Christopher Boyd, was born four years later on June 22, 1954, in Hollywood.

With the experience of radio, TV and marriage under his belt, along with a smattering of summer stock performances in New England,

Jack at long last was ready for Broadway, making his debut in the role of Leo Davis, the hapless playwright, in the 1953 revival of *Room Service*.

Also in the cast were John Randolph, Everett Sloane, Ralph Dunn, Georgiann Johnson, Bartlett Robinson and the late Stanley Prager. Mortimer Offner directed.

The famed John Murray–Allen Boretz play opened at the Playhouse Theater on Monday, April 6, 1953, was severely panned and closed after sixteen performances on Saturday, April 18.

"It just wasn't funny," Jack mourns. "The jokes of depression days made no dent on the audiences."

The play's "fast sixteen-performance run," however, was enough time for Jack's performance to be noticed by Hollywood scouts: Columbia's Max Arnow saw the play, liked Jack and passed his name on to director George Cukor, who was busy preparing a new Garson Kanin screwball screen comedy for Judy Holliday.

"Actually, Jack had been offered studio contracts by Hollywood many times prior to *Room Service*," reveals Jack's long-time associate, Richard Carter, "but the illusion of a nonexclusive pact plus starring roles and Columbia lured him away from the 'honesty' of New York TV and legit."

Like it or not, Jack's days as a "drugstore

Goofing with George Raft on the set of *Some Like It Hot*, 1959.

actor" were over—the days when he and his fellow thespians "would all sit in Walgreen's, stretching a cup of coffee and telling each other how wonderful we were."

And so, in May of 1953, with a fat Columbia contract in tow, Jack and Cynthia drove to California in an old station wagon and set up housekeeping in Brentwood with a terrier named Duffy and a Finnish maid named Impy.

As a screen actor, Jack was fortunate in that he experienced almost immediate success and failure during his first few months on soundstages. His first two films are extremes, complete opposites. Their only common quality is that both experienced last-minute title changes.

A Name for Herself, the Cukor film, eventually emerged in theaters as *It Should Happen to You!,* while *The Pleasure's All Mine,* a Betty Grable musical, was released as *Three for the Show.*

The Cukor film—a success—is pure New York, highly clever and very urbane and funny; the Grable tuner—a failure—is all Hollywood, superficial, familiar and stale.

Dining out with mother Mildred Lemmon and actress Felicia Farr in 1959.

Jack worked smoothly with Judy Holliday on *It Should Happen to You!,* and liked and respected her.

"Judy was a consummate professional actress," says Jack. "She was extremely intelligent and erudite—not at all like the 'dumb blonde' she so often depicted.

"She was serious about her work and investigated all scenes and her character in great depth. She didn't give a damn where a camera was, how she looked, or about being a 'star.' She just played the scene and acted 'with,' not 'at.'

"She was also one of the nicest people I ever hope to meet in my life."

Everything that Jack says is clearly evident in *It Should Happen to You!,* a wistful and appealing little comedy which has remained incredibly ageless over the years. (So ageless, in fact, that author Garson Kanin once contemplated the idea of redoing it as a musical.)

There's something touching about the crazy relationship depicted in the movie—the relationship between an unemployed model, a nobody who wants to be somebody (Holliday), and the

Action shot of Lemmon during the climactic (and antic) chase sequence in *The Notorious Landlady.*

Philadelphia ad for Lemmon's 1960 stage play,
Face of a Hero.

little documentary filmmaker (Lemmon) with a penchant for nobodys.

The New York Times' Bosley Crowther received Jack's debut in this way: "Jack Lemmon has a warm and appealing personality. The screen should see more of him."

Jack was busy at work on *The Pleasure's All Mine/Three for the Show* when Columbia executives responded to his initial reviews by announcing plans to pair him again with Judy in an original George Axelrod comedy titled *Phfft!*

Phfft!, directed by Mark Robson, ultimately beat *Three for the Show* to the box office when the latter became bogged down with gnawing censorship problems over its light handling of polygamy.

The Axelrod–Robson comedy—an amusing to-do about an unsuccessful divorce—also underwent a title change.

Here's the way Jack explains it:

"One afternoon in the middle of filming at Columbia, Mark Robson was summoned up to Harry Cohn's office. He seemed to have been gone an interminable length of time, at least an hour and a half to two hours, while we all sat on the set wondering what was happening.

"Finally, he came panting onto the set, apologized for being gone so long, and explained that it was an extremely important and fruitful meeting.

"It seems that for weeks the studio heads had been concerned about the title of the film and everybody and their mother's uncle had been trying to think up a new one. No one came up with a satisfactory solution until Mark, having wasted several valuable hours of shooting time, made a facetious suggestion.

"They took him seriously and added another 'f' to *Phfft!*, making it officially *Phffft!*

"It's still the worst title I've ever heard."

Throughout all this, Jack also found time for occasional battles with Columbia's colorful head, Harry Cohn, most of which were on the light side.

Once, they fought over Cohn's plans to change "Lemmon" to "Lennon."

"I told him," says Jack, "that it had taken me most of my life to get over the traumatic effects of being called Jack U. Lemmon—pronounced Jack, you lemon—and that I was used to it now and I wasn't going to change it.

"I stood up to start to leave, and to sort of soften the argument, I said facetiously, 'Besides, if I changed it to Lennon, people would think I was a Russian revolutionary.'

"He jumped up and ran around this mile-square desk, grabbed my lapels and yelled, 'No! No! That's L-e-n-i-n. I looked it up!'"

There were also some lively discussions about the names of some of Jack's films. "I've always been dogged by massive titles like *It Should Happen to You!*" says Jack. "Do you know how they came up with such titles?

"They'd have studio contests. All the secretaries would compete. They'd win fifty dollars and we'd end up with titles like *You Can't Run Away From It.* It's ridiculous!"

Another time, Jack and Cohn battled over the actor's overanxious desire to play the Tyrone Power role in John Ford's *The Long Gray Line.*

Jack's screen test was a mess—so poor that he tried to dupe Cohn by having the mogul sit

With Betsy Blair rehearsing *Face of a Hero*, 1960.

through four reels of The Three Stooges before unveiling his stuff.

But there was genuine affection and admiration between the two men, with Cohn proudly referring to Lemmon as "my Harvard man." Jack found Cohn to be "tough, rough, sometimes crude but honest and never devious."

Jack's next big battle was over the role of Ensign Frank Pulver—a plum if there ever was one — in John Ford's film version of *Mister Roberts*.

He had attempted to test for the original New York stage production, but "never got inside the door." He eventually saw the play on a pass and drooled over the Pulver role.

But there were problems. First, Warner Bros. was producing the film, not Columbia, which would mean a loanout. Secondly, there was still the bitter aftertaste of Jack's last attempt to crash a Ford movie, worsened by the report that Ford had refused to look at his test.

An accidental meeting with Ford himself solved both problems. One day, while disconsolately roaming through Warner Bros., Jack was approached by "some old bum with a beat-up hat, torn trousers and dark glasses."

"You should play Pulver," the old man said. "I think so, too," responded Jack. "But no one has the sense to realize it!"

The old man then invited Jack to join him in an old Irish custom. "You spit on your hand, I'll spit on mine, and then we'll shake." Jack obliged him. "All right, you've got the part. I'm John Ford."

"At the time I worked with John Ford," Jack reveals, "I was still fairly new to films, highly impressionable, and I guess completely in awe and apprehensive about working with the great 'Pappy' Ford.

"I also only worked with him for half a film, as you know—Mervyn LeRoy replaced him when he took sick. So it's a bit difficult for me to draw many definite conclusions about Ford, the director.

"He commanded a tremendous respect from those who worked for him, on both sides of the camera. In fact, at times this respect would border on downright fear.

"Even if actors at times felt intimidated, I have never known of any to lose their great respect for him, or their admiration for his abilities.

"He was—is—a great and unique man, and working for him, even though it was all too brief, was one of the highlights of my career."

Jack won a Best Supporting Actor award in the 1955 Oscar race for his memorable performance in *Mister Roberts* and was, as Hollywood press agents are apt to put it, on his way to "stardom."

Upon completing *Roberts* at Warner Bros., Jack returned to Columbia to star (again) with Judy Holliday in Jule Styne and Leo Robin's attractive and peppy musical remake of *My Sister Eileen*.

It was Jack's first film with director Richard Quine, who helmed Jack's initial screen test and, eventually, five more Lemmon films.

Immediately prior to production, however, Judy Holliday did something that was almost atypical for her: She became temperamental and was released from the film. Betty Garrett, a woman whose potential has yet to be realized on screen, was her last-minute replacement ·and proved to be an excellent choice.

Director Quine, who started out as an actor and who, in fact, played a supporting role in the original Rosalind Russell film of *My Sister Eileen*, remains one of Jack's best (and oldest) friends in Hollywood. Professionally, Jack regards him as "a much more talented director than his career would indicate—even though he's had an extremely fine career to date."

Two years and five films into his screen career, Jack already had a solid identity with the moviegoing public—that of the common man. The guy next door. The young accountant living in the next block.

"A guy you're gonna like." The ads were right.

"Actually," confesses Jack, "I've been lucky. I'm not overly or under-bright. I'm not a particularly funny fellow. It depends on the script. I have a nice, likable personality, I guess. I'm fallible, flappable and unextraordinary.

"If I were five-foot-four, I'd be a character

With father John Uhler Lemmon II on the set of *The Notorious Landlady*, 1962.

actor, period, not a leading man. I'm not overly handsome, not good looking enough to set hearts to fluttering—I don't exactly ooze animal magnetism, so I can play parts I really like which are *character* leads.

"I don't have an identifiable accent. I don't have physical traits that limit me. I'm just kind of average, a very square simple guy, thus easy to identify with. I can be a Wall Street broker or the milkman."

And of course, added to all this is the fact that Jack is extremely (and rather casually) talented and his brand of humor is unique and human. "A farceur supreme," declares Quine.

Perhaps, Billy Wilder—who has directed Jack in six films, some of which are Jack's biggest hits—puts it best:

"He's the hardest worker in films. Whatever role he attempts, he will research to the bone, worry it to the nub, do the best possible job— and somehow make his expertise look instruc-

23

tive. He is a thinking, highly instructive actor who comes up with all sorts of goodies.

"He's somewhere between Chaplin and Cary Grant, but completely original. Audiences can tell by looking in his face what goes on in his heart and brain, and have their greatest rapport with an actor since Chaplin."

Jack is a little less enthusiastic about himself.

"If I had to sit through one of my films twice, I'd go mad. I tend to munch on popcorn, saying 'No, no, you fool, you're playing the scene all wrong. You're lousing up the picture. Come on, Lemmon, ACT!'"

And acting is what it's all about for Jack.

"It really bugs me," confesses Jack, "when someone thinks of me as a comic. If I read 'comedian Jack Lemmon,' I gag. That means that I'm not an actor—which I am. Good, bad or indifferent, I'm an actor.

"If you're a comic and somebody comes up to you and says, 'Be funny. Make me laugh,' you're supposed to knock him in the aisle. I couldn't do that if my life depended on it. Only if the material is written for me.

"I must admit, though, that when I read a script, I tend to look for one or two scenes where my character will really take off ... go to the moon ... be memorable. Like the soap-bubble scene in *Mister Roberts*.

"It's not bravura acting; its quintessence, a scene of great substance dominated by that character so he really comes to the fore in a memorable way.

"A scene like that not only gives the audience something to latch onto and remember vividly, it also gives an actor a chance to feel satisfied.

"I'm not a Method Actor per se, but I do have my own method of playing comedy. Mine is to look for an obstacle, then play a scene against it."

Obstacle, indeed. If Jack has any sort of an image, it's as a frenzied Everyman, a human Charlie Brown, a modern-day Chaplin. He firmly

With co-star Kim Novak and director Richard Quine on the set of *The Notorious Landlady*, 1962.

established this fact in his first five films and concocted brilliant variations of it in the thirty that followed.

"Lemmon has become the perfect personification of all harassed mankind," claimed the *Saturday Review* in its review of one of his later films, "—the outranked, outnumbered, outmanipulated little fellow with sound instinct and bad judgment. He is the one who is always taken advantage of. And, if in the end, he emerges triumphant, it's because of a basic decency rather than superior cunning or sudden inspiration."

Jack's screen specialty is not so much that he battles daily adversity, but that he scarcely seems to fight back at all. Chaplin gave out with wild protests in his films; Jack is a bit more downtrodden, pessimistic and—well—contemporary about it.

By 1956, Jack was somewhat of a commodity. Columbia recognized this fact and elected to star him opposite June Allyson in a big, splashy, CinemaScope musical remake of Frank Capra's *It Happened One Night*.

Dick Powell signed on as director; the title was changed to another "massive" job, *You Can't Run Away From It*, and Jack had his first all-out cinematic flop.

Meanwhile, back in Brentwood, Jack's marriage was—as the Hollywood gossip columnists put it—"on the rocks."

"It (the marriage) was never right," confesses Jack. "We split up four times before we finally got divorced. I don't know what happened to us. It's just that we were dead with each other.

"It was like that with my parents. They were separated for years. They parted after my college days. They lived five minutes away from each other and would see each other all the time. They just couldn't live together. Neither could we, I suppose."

Jack and Cynthia were divorced in December of 1956.

Earlier in '56, Jack returned to TV—briefly—

With writer I. A. L. Diamond, wife Felicia and director Billy Wilder on the set of *Irma La Douce*, 1963.

Doing the autograph bit with actress Shirley MacLaine at Grauman's Chinese Theater on July 4, 1963.

in a ninety-minute CBS color special titled "The Day Lincoln Was Shot." It was his first time back on the tube in four years.

Jack was hailed for his masterful, highly individualistic portrayal of John Wilkes Booth and for introducing the human quirk of having Booth primp himself every time he passed a mirror.

In 1957, Jack was represented on screen by Robert Parrish's *Fire Down Below,* a helping of trite tropical trash (for which he penned the "Harmonica Theme"), and Richard Quine's hilarious GI comedy, *Operation Mad Ball.*

Operation Mad Ball—very much the *M*A*S*H* of the Fifties—is a milestone of sorts in Jack's career.

For example, it was the first time he received top billing (something he wouldn't experience again until 1960's *The Apartment*).

What's more, also for the first time, his role in the film was clearly the leading one, the starring one, the pivotal one.

Thirdly, *Mad Ball* was to attract the attention of Jack's future Mentor, Billy Wilder—and thereby lead to *Some Like It Hot.*

But this wouldn't happen until 1959. So resounding was the success of "The Day Lincoln Was Shot" that Jack was prompted to "moonlight" and participate on an NBC-TV anthology series.

Under the banner First Anthology Inc., Jack joined forces with David Niven, Robert Ryan, Jane Powell and Charles Boyer to present "The

Goodyear-Alcoa Theater—A Turn of Fate," a weekly half-hour drama series.

The stars appeared on a rotation basis, with Jack starring in such titles as "Lost and Found," "Marriageable Male" and "The Victim," the latter with (then) child actress, Lana Wood.

"A Turn of Fate" ran only one season on NBC—the 1957-58 TV season.

The year 1958 kept Jack busy. In addition to the TV series, he made two more movies, Delmer Daves' *Cowboy* (excellent) and Richard Quine's *Bell, Book and Candle* (so-so); worked on another TV special, John Frankenheimer's *Face of a Hero* (on "Playhouse 90" for CBS), and fell in love.

Jack met striking Felicia Farr on the Columbia lot while he was making *Cowboy* with Glenn Ford. She was a struggling starlet and a fellow contract player—and perhaps most importantly, beautiful, feisty and intelligent.

Felicia understood his problems and thought Jack was the greatest actor in the world. Jack flipped the minute he met her. They became close friends.

Although the TV special, *Face of a Hero,* and Jack's performance in it attracted favorable response from public and critics alike, Jack was now disillusioned by and disgusted with TV.

"When less money was being shoveled out," says Jack, "and there were fewer experienced people in TV and you didn't have to be a name actor, there was a tremendous excitement

Relaxing over coffee on the set of
Under the Yum-Yum Tree, 1963.

and immediacy about it. It was like being let in
on the creative ground floor of something."

In *Face of a Hero,* adapted by Robert L.
Joseph from a Pierre Boulle novel, Jack essayed
the role of a prosecuting attorney in a small
town who's made ruthless by ambition and ultimately seeks to convict an innocent young man.

"It was a tough thing to do on TV," Jack
comments, "to study a man's mind. We merely
scratched the surface. That's one reason we took
it to Broadway—hopefully to develop it. The TV
performance was, more or less, a tryout."

Also in 1958, Jack recorded his first album,
aptly titled "A Twist of Lemmon" (Epic BN 523),
on which he displayed his singing and piano-
playing abilities and often did both at the same
time.

"A Twist of Lemmon" features reliable
standards ("You'd Be So Nice To Come Home
To" and "Let's Fall In Love"), one Lemmon original ("With All My Love") and a wild, especially
funny rendition of "The Kiss That Rocked the
World."

In his notes for the album, Steve Allen
wrote: "The sound is most pleasant but more
importantly the performances are in line with
what we have come to expect from Jack as an
actor. He brings an added quality of the creatively dramatic to his vocals whether in the style
of his handling a tender ballad or his playful
approach to novelties."

Billy Wilder's classic *Some Like It Hot* was
released in 1959 and brightened a film year
which otherwise leaned heavily on drama.

With co-star Walter Matthau on the set of *The Odd Couple*, 1968.

As two prohibition-era musicians forced to dress up as girls in order to escape a gang of thugs, Jack and Tony Curtis deftly underplay what most other actors would have overplayed, with Jack earning his first Best Actor Oscar nomination.

The late Marilyn Monroe was on hand, too—and her waiflike charm and presence provide the movie with an intangible quality which no critic has been able to successfully describe.

"Marilyn never conformed to 'group-behavior characteristics,' " reminisces Jack. "She simply wasn't like other people. If we were all in the same building, say, and it began to fall down, we'd all run, right? But Marilyn would probably have run in a totally different direction.

"Yet she wouldn't get hurt—because she was very smart."

Jack recorded a second album in 1959, this one inspired by the Wilder film. Titled "Jack Lemmon Plays and Sings Music From *Some Like It Hot*" (Epic BN 528), the album features songs of the Roaring Twenties.

Jack's next film, also released in 1959, has a most curious history. Writer Max Wilk came up with a rough draft, written with Jack in mind, about a young New England widower with two children who works full-time as a lawyer and part-time as a lobster farmer.

Old 97 Goes to Market—note the titular relationship to Frank Capra's *Mr. Smith Goes to Washington* and *Mr. Deeds Goes to Town*—eventually attracted director Richard Quine's attention and preparations for filming began.

At Columbia's insistence, Wilk and Norman Katkov reworked the original script, dividing the lead character into two—a widow and her lawyer-boyfriend. Now titled *Miss Casey Adams*, the comedy went before the cameras with Doris Day and Jack in the leads.

While in production, the film's title was changed twice—first to *That Jane from Maine* and finally to *It Happened to Jane*.

The resulting movie is a miracle—a fine example of Frank Capra-like Americana, a film style which has more or less been abandoned by today's art-minded moviemakers. Director Quine captured a wonderfully authentic "small town" atmosphere in the film and worked two pleasing performances out of Doris and Jack.

But *It Happened to Jane* was neither a financial nor a total critical success and remains one of Jack's (and Doris's) lesser known efforts.

Columbia eventually released a cut version of the film in 1960—this time under the title "Twinkle and Shine"—in an attempt to cash in on the then newly-acquired box-office power of its two stars.

The Apartment of 1960 provided Jack with a beautifully written character (an ambitious little office shnook); the perfect female counterpart (Shirley MacLaine), and a plot which balanced the comic and the near-tragic very well indeed.

A bittersweet movie about love and office politics, *The Apartment* earned Best Actor and Actress Oscar nominations for Jack and Shirley, firmly established Jack's star status ("surely the most sensitive and tasteful young comedian now at work in Hollywood," wrote *Time*) and cemented a lasting relationship between Jack and director Billy Wilder.

"Billy is, without question, one of the two or three writer-directors who are capable of doing both extremely well," says Jack. "Starting with the screenplay of *Ninotchka*, he has written and/or directed some of our greatest films over a tremendous span of time.

"And, he has not only managed to keep up with changing times, he has managed to cause them to change. For instance, a film like *The Apartment* probably could not have been done a few years before it was filmed. It would have been considered much too radical.

"Before it was completed and released, *Some Like It Hot* was considered a joke in the industry—many people thinking it was a ludicrous endeavor with an asinine plot, a sure failure. *Ace in the Hole* is now considered by many

With step-daughter Denise Farr (left) and her friend Debbie Freedman, 1969.

On the set of *The Out-of-Towners*, 1970.

to be a minor classic, but at the time it was shown, it touched too many sore spots too incisively and many rebelled against it.

"Billy's talent is truly immense, but I firmly believe that it takes a great talent to fail completely. When he is on his 'shtick,' he can give you magic, but when he misses, he really misses.

"He goes for the home run every time and sometimes he strikes out. So did Babe Ruth. But, Ruth was the greatest of them all and, in my opinion, so is Billy."

If anything, Jack's relationship with Billy made the actor more aware of quality screenplay writing ("Billy's scripts with Izzy Diamond have *everything* in them," boasts Jack) and also a bit more discriminating in that area.

"I'm interested in scripts that can expose in an enlightening way human behavior to the audience," contends Jack. "In other words, I hope the audience will be able to see themselves in the characters in my movies.

"When I read a script, if I don't know how to play the part, I'll get excited and want to do it. Good writing is harder to play because there are more depths, and it's delicious hell to decide which depths you're going to bring out.

"Eighty percent of acting," continues Jack, "is that delicious hell of finding out who the guy is. The rest is execution—letting somebody else

know what you know already. I think that talent is the least important part of being an actor. So that, in a sense, acting is the last step in acting.

"Usually it's two, three, four weeks into a movie before you really find the guy. All of a sudden you come out of a scene and you say, 'I've got him.' You know him. Then you paint on the rest of the face and say, 'There he is.'

"But if I know how to play it, then it's very surface stuff, very simple. It's 3B, 4H; I've done it a dozen times."

In the fall of 1960, having fulfilled his commitment to play the lead role in the long-delayed sea comedy, *The Wackiest Ship in the Army*, Jack took *Face of a Hero* to Broadway, where it promptly failed.

The production—this time under the direction of British filmmaker Alexander Mackendrick —opened Thursday, October 20, at the Eugene O'Neill Theater and played thirty-six performances. Also in the cast were Betsy Blair, George Grizzard, James Donald, Edward Asner, Ellen Holly, the late Albert Dekker and a newcomer named Sandy Dennis.

"It wasn't a   handicap," Jack theorizes. "It was good to get out of Hollywood for a while. If you've been used to working on movies, doing a sustained role in a Broadway play is like going to the gym and working out.

30

With Anthony Caruso in the stage revival of *Idiot's Delight*, 1970.

"It gets an actor back into shape, as training does an athlete. It doesn't matter whether the play hits or misses. He has been helped."

The closing of *Face of a Hero* was followed almost head-on by the box-office failure of *The Wackiest Ship in the Army*. And to add injury to insult, Jack lost the 1960 Best Actor Oscar to Burt Lancaster's *Elmer Gantry*.

"There are some actors you know can win the Academy Award only once," concluded Billy Wilder at the time. "Lemmon is not one of them. He's capable of winning the Oscar four or five times."

"Credit a clever little story by British nutmeggy Margery Sharp and a comic performance by Jack Lemmon that twinkles like a mischiefmaker's eye for the unexpected good humor that generally crackles and pops in Columbia's *The Notorious Landlady*, which came to the Criterion and the Beekman yesterday."

So wrote Bosley Crowther in his July 27, 1962, review of Richard Quine's *The Notorious Landlady*, Jack's first film after the *Face of a Hero* failure.

The Notorious Landlady was somewhat of a family affair: Jack's father played a bit part in the film, just prior to his death in 1961; so did costar Kim Novak's mother and sister, and director Quine's son.

At this point in his career, Jack became more

31

active in the production end of moviemaking. His old Jalem company was resurrected and used to import and present an American language version of the French travelogue, *Stowaway in the Sky,* with Jack serving as narrator.

Next, Jack and director Blake Edwards tried to get *Days of Wine and Roses* off the ground. A reported two years were spent in trying to get backing for the drama.

Jack's old friend, Harry Cohn, was no longer around at the time. Too bad; he enjoyed gambling. "If it weren't for him," Jack once said, "I might be selling ties today. He gambled and Columbia's now making a profit on his investment."

It was Jack L. Warner who finally gambled and decided to film J. P. Miller's moving drama about alcoholism. "Nobody would touch Jack Lemmon in a drama but him," recalls Jack, "nobody would touch *Days of Wine and Roses* but him."

The film was a total success—both financially and critically—and, as topping on the cake, won Jack another Best Actor nomination in the Academy Awards race. He lost to Gregory Peck, who won for *To Kill a Mockingbird.*

His film activity became almost ceaseless after *Days of Wine and Roses* and all Jack would ever do is smile and say, "This is the nicest way I know to have a nervous breakdown."

In 1962, Jack also traveled to Paris to co-star with Shirley MacLaine in Billy Wilder's songless version of the Marguerite Monnot stage musical, *Irma La Douce.*

He took time out on August 17 to attend a wedding ceremony—his own—with Felicia. "We spent six unsuccessful years," says Jack, "trying to convince each other why we *shouldn't* get married."

Billy Wilder and Richard Quine served as his best men. "They are both my dearest friends," said Jack. "I couldn't choose between them."

When the Judge popped the question, both Jack and Felicia answered "oui." The couple has been married ever since and has one daughter, Courtney Noel, born January 7, 1966. Billy Wilder is her godfather.

Miss Farr also has a grown daughter, Denise, by her first husband, Lee Farr.

Both *Irma La Douce* and the film that followed it the same year, *Under the Yum-Yum Tree,* were immensely popular at the box office,

Posing with a colleague on the set of *Kotch,* 1971.

so much so that Jack was named Number One Male Box Office Star of 1964.

Both were also criticized by reviewers for being smarmy and for catering to the public's thirst for sensationalism. What's worse, however, Jack's image was beginning to tarnish and he started to get a reputation (on screen) as a lecher.

"Funny," recalls Jack, "I had no criticism from fans or critics on *Irma La Douce,* a very adult film. But it worked out that I did three sex comedies in a row (the third being *Good Neighbor Sam*). I think if *Wine and Roses* had come between *Irma* and *Yum-Yum,* I wouldn't have gotten the criticism I did.

"I must say, however, the character I played

in *Yum-Yum* came out as an unpleasant, nasty voyeur. Usually, I have a better overall idea about a film.

"But I can't say I didn't know it was going to add up this way. Hell, I played it! But it'll never happen again with Lemmon, I'll tell you."

Jack's third album, recorded in conjunction with the release of *Irma La Douce* (Capitol ST 1943) consists entirely of piano selections from the score of the stage musical and André Previn's score for the Wilder film.

About a year later, he recorded a dramatic reading of E. B. White's essay, "Here Is New York" (Riverside RLP 849), a showcase for his most expressive voice.

Next, Jack concentrated on doing two 1930-40s Lubitsch-style comedies—David Swift's delightful *Good Neighbor Sam* and Richard Quine's adroit, suave *How to Murder Your Wife*. The characters he played are reminiscent of the kind of roles Cary Grant might have carried off during his heyday.

"Movies," Jack has been quoted as saying, "ought to be fun, not sociological messages or weird surrealistic things."

Jack's next movie—Blake Edwards' lumbering *The Great Race*—certainly wasn't a weird surrealistic thing; but it wasn't much fun either.

Shortly after the filming, Jack came down with hepatitis, which put him out of action for a while. His next flick, which came nearly fourteen months later, in 1966, was Billy Wilder's offbeat but brilliant black comedy, *The Fortune Cookie*.

In the meantime, Jack contemplated his career:

"I'd love to keep my film career alive as long as I can and on as high a level as I can, but that isn't easy right now.

"There's terrible economic pressure, less money available, fewer films produced. It's very difficult to work knowing that dark cloud is overhead. The fun has gone out of it, especially comedy. Something has happened to the product; the bubble of joy, madness, whatever you want to call it, isn't there any more, and that kind of feeling can sap you.

"Looking back, there are four or five performances I'm particularly happy with: Pulver in *Mister Roberts, Some Like It Hot, The Apartment, Days of Wine and Roses*—playing an alcoholic scared me and really made me dig—and, for some peculiar reason, *Irma La Douce*.

"Sure, there are roles I regret doing, but in God's honest truth, I can't think of any that I regret having missed."

While Jack's beautiful low-keyed playing in *The Fortune Cookie* didn't earn him another nomination, it did avail him the opportunity to meet and mingle—professionally and personally—with Walter Matthau.

Jack spontaneously refers to Walter as "the best actor I've ever worked with." They are the best of friends.

Meanwhile, Jalem—Jack's company—was busy producing two movies for 1967 release—Stuart Rosenberg's *Cool Hand Luke*, starring Paul Newman, and Clive Donner's *Luv*, starring Jack.

"I'm producing for a lot of reasons," said Jack at the time. "Mostly because it's a kick to be involved in something aside from acting. There's a feeling of accomplishment in something that you've helped create.

"Producing also allows a man to do things of his own volition. You experiment with ideas over which you have control in the future. You gotta take a chance or you end up with tired films. Take *Luv*. Either we'll have a hit or we'll miss by a country mile. That's the way it's gotta be.

"This gives you a chance to fall on your own fanny. You don't stay awake nights blaming the boss, because you're the boss.

"My own contribution to *Cool Hand Luke* is really just another voice that's sympathetic to the executive producer and director—Gordon Carroll and Stuart Rosenberg. I keep my nose out of it unless I think something is wrong. Then I just voice an opinion.

"Admittedly, I'd have loved doing the picture myself. But that's an instinct I have to suppress or else I'll be doing three films at once."

Luv, as Jack had predicted, missed by a country mile, emerging as perhaps the biggest failure of his screen career; the actor redeemed himself, however, the following year with his participation in Paramount's highly commercial and popular film version of Neil Simon's *The Odd Couple*. He reteamed here with Walter Matthau.

While *The Odd Couple* was in post-production, late in 1967, Jalem and CBS Theatrical Films signed a four-picture, $21-million deal which would include two Lemmon films, the first being *The April Fools*.

The April Fools, directed by Stuart Rosenberg and released in 1969, stands as a stylish (al-

With Diahann Carroll and the late
Cass Elliott on NBC's special, *Get
Happy*, 1973.

beit highly offbeat) throwback to Preston Sturges' film comedies—a fluffy, romantic love story replete with two nice and attractive leading players (Jack and Catherine Deneuve) and a bevy of screwball supporting players (Jack Weston, Harvey Korman, Sally Kellerman).

Hal Dresner's original screenplay is a leisurely and rambling to-do about two neglected married people who meet, fall in love and run off to Paris together—all within twenty-four hours.

Arthur Hiller's *The Out-of-Towners* followed next, in 1970, and would be Jack's last film until mid-1972. Based on an idea by Neil Simon, the movie proved amusing, much too frantic and high-pitched and, ultimately, disappointing.

Garson Kanin's classy 1970 stage revival of Robert E. Sherwood's *Idiot's Delight* at Los Angeles's Ahmanson Theater lured Jack back to live theater once again. He played Harry Van to Rosemary Harris's Irene.

The production—which played a limited en-gagement from March 17 to April 25—received enthusiastic notices and (as listed in the program) made use of "interpolated music by John Uhler Lemmon III."

Jack proudly refers to the engagement as "my longest run yet."

"For years I've had films that I really wanted to do, and I haven't been able to make a deal anywhere," pouted Jack back in 1970. "Today in Hollywood, there's nobody alive over thirty who can do a film he really wants to do just on his name. Not any more."

Nevertheless, Jack decided to pursue his next pet project—his long-time dream to direct a feature. In this case, it would be the film version of Katharine Topkins' novel, *Kotch*, with Walter Matthau in the title role of an old man who needs to be needed.

The studios? No dice. It was turned down by nearly every studio. Finally, ABC-Cinerama agreed to back it.

"I elected to do *Kotch* because it raises a lot

of questions that I think need to be raised," explains Jack. "In all the problems we're facing today—civil strife, unemployment, inequality—the plight of old people has been put down more than it should. It touches all of us.

"God knows, *Kotch* isn't a message picture—not with Matthau playing the old man. If it points anywhere, it says we should look beyond our instinctive selfish reactions to our own problems and maybe see them in a broader frame of reference.

"If the film isn't good, it's my fault, because the writing is there. There's something about this old man that is terribly majestic, a statement about the spirit of all men. He refuses to feel sorry for himself, but he lives constantly with the problem of so many elderly people today: rejection."

A highly acclaimed concertcast of the music of George and Ira Gershwin, handsomely staged and alive with carefully selected talent, was hosted by Jack on NBC early in 1972 and efficiently reminded viewers of Jack's triple-threat versatility.

" 'S Wonderful, 'S Marvelous, 'S Gershwin,"

a ninety-minute musical special telecast in early January, had Jack dancing with Fred Astaire; singing with Leslie Uggams, Linda Bennett, Larry Kert and Robert Guillaume; playing the piano with Peter Nero, and miming on his own.

Ethel Merman also appeared in a special segment. Writer-producer-(co)director Martin Charnin was the genius behind this truly special special.

It was embraced by the critics, the voting membership of the Emmy Awards and the general public alike, and has recently been acquired in edited one-hour form by the Public Broadcasting System.

A soundtrack album of the concertcast (DR-2009) was released by Daybreak Records, a subsidiary of RCA Records.

Although perhaps not directly, but rather in a spiritual way, the success of the Gershwin TV special triggered two years' worth of nonstop work on three back-to-back films.

Jack jumped enthusiastically from work on Melville Shavelson's *The War Between Men and Women* to John G. Avildsen's *Save the Tiger* to Billy Wilder's *Avanti!*—although the films them-

Receiving the 1973 Best Actor Academy Award for *Save the Tiger* from Gregory Peck and Liza Minnelli at the 1974 Oscar celebration.

selves were not necessarily released in that order.

The War Between Men and Women, the second of Jack's films under the CBS contract, was released during the summer of 1972. More or less a tribute to the ideas and drawings of the late James Thurber, the film is generally offensive and redeemed only by some clever animated bits.

Paramount, already riding high with *The Godfather* and anticipating an Oscar nomination for its star, Marlon Brando, didn't want to compete with itself at Oscar time; so the company wisely decided to push back the release of its *Save the Tiger* until early 1973 (since Jack's performance also was clearly Oscar material).

Meanwhile, United Artists—hopeful and perhaps overly optimistic over the Wilder movie—rushed it out before the year's end for Oscar-qualification purposes.

Wilder's *Avanti!* garnered generally patronizing responses from the critics—no all-out raves, no all-out pans.

Cut from the same bolt of cloth as Wilder's *Love in the Afternoon*—a relaxing, pastel-tinted tale set amidst romantic surroundings—the film improves with each viewing. Jack turns in a thoroughly "movie star" performance and his co-star, Juliet Mills, demonstrates that she's a criminally neglected, multifaceted actress.

Just prior to the national release of his big one, *Save the Tiger,* Jack appeared on another musical TV special, NBC's hour-long tribute to Harold Arlen, "Get Happy," produced by the old "Gershwin" gang.

Teamed with two particularly talented ladies, Diahann Carroll and the late Cass Elliot, Jack performed with his usual ease and expertise, but the show never seemed to take off. Which is curious. It had all the right ingredients.

To observe Jack's foremost performance in Shagan's and John G. Avildsen's *Save the Tiger* is to witness and share the actor's joy in having reached the pinnacle of his career.

Written and produced by Shagan with single-minded determination and directed by Avildsen with an eye for raw anguish, the film is an emotion-draining portrayal of a man trapped by the past and afraid of the future.

Jack plays the man—one Harry Stoner—and his performance provides a valuable lesson in what great screen acting is all about. The performance earned Jack still another Oscar nomination. This time, he won.

"In recent years especially," said Jack on accepting his award on Tuesday, April 3, 1974, "there has been a great deal of criticism about this award, and probably a great deal of that criticism is justified.

"I would just like to say that whether it is justified or not, it is one hell of an honor and I'm thrilled."

A little earlier in the year, Jack received another honor; he was invited back to Harvard on February 28 to concurrently celebrate the kick-off of the 125th Hasty Pudding Theatricals production and receive Harvard's Man of the Year award.

"French Chef" Julia Child also participated, preparing a potful of Hasty Pudding for the guest of honor, as well as Ms. Gloria Steinem, who was selected Person of the Year.

"You know, success presents an actor with the most peculiar paradox," reflects Jack. "When you are beginning, you'll take any kind of part, hoping for bigger speaking parts and then dreaming about good character parts. And then, 'Oh, God, if I could just get a nice, fat lead!'

"Finally when you begin to get the really good parts, the parts with substance, you begin to get terribly careful. Each part becomes terribly important—probably more important than it should be.

"Suddenly, you can only afford to accept the best scripts offered to you, and you find you're giving only two performances a year. You're a success as an actor, but vast limitations have been placed on your work.

"If you try defying the system—try taking smaller character roles as many fine actors in England tend to do—then you're no longer a 'star,' and the best pictures, the best scripts won't be offered to you any more.

"Success, unfortunately, is always somebody else's image of you. You spend your whole cock-amamie life trying to make an impression on somebody else.

"The terrible thing about 'success' is that instead of doing more and more, I have to do less and less. There's a terrible tendency now to be too cautious. I try not to be."

Practicing what he preaches (and obviously feeling reborn from the personal triumph of *Save the Tiger*), Jack returned to a busy filmmaking schedule, working on screen adaptations of three plays.

Beginning late in 1973 and working through

mid-1975, Jack essayed the leading roles in Melvin Frank's film of Neil Simon's *The Prisoner of Second Avenue*, Billy Wilder's remake of the vintage Hecht–MacArthur piece, *The Front Page* and Donald Wrye's Americanized version of John Osborne's *The Entertainer*, for NBC-TV.

He took a breather late in 1974 to return to the stage again, this time to star with Walter Matthau and Maureen Stapleton under George Seaton's direction in Sean O'Casey's venerable *Juno and the Paycock* at the Mark Taper Forum in Los Angeles.

Jack played the pixilated "Joxer" Daly, the obliging drinking crony of Captain Jack Boyle (Matthau) and rival of Mrs. Boyle (Stapleton).

The production, reportedly sold out months before it opened, debuted Thursday, November 7, 1974, and played a limited engagement through Sunday, December 22. It received mixed notices (*Variety* called it "a disappointment").

Lemmon donned an attractive moustache for his next two film roles—1976's dark morality comedy, *Alex and the Gypsy*, and 1977's decidedly silly *Airport '77*. Neither film did much to advance his art or his career (although *Alex* remains one of those fascinating failures), and after filming *The China Syndrome* in great secrecy during 1978, the actor opted to return to the stage.

The play, Bernard Slade's *Tribute,* was an original and it was such a resounding personal success for Lemmon that it put his career into yet another phase. He was far away, light years away, from being that young contract player who could do (and did) everything and anything. And he was no longer Hollywood's Golden Boy, a fashionably 40ish mainstream performer who got roles because of his bankability.

Tribute put Lemmon in the enviable position of an elder statesman who could pick and choose his roles, doing fewer films but inarguably special ones, socially aware ones. *Tribute* and the film *The China Syndrome* opened nearly a year apart, but started reaping awards practically in tandem. He earned a Tony nomination and an Oscar nomination, respectively, for the play and the movie, with the latter, *The China Syndrome*, bringing Lemmon the best actor award at the 1979 Cannes Film Festival.

The film of *Tribute* and another movie-made-in-secret, *Missing,* quickly followed, in 1980 and 1982, and with them came two more Oscar nominations—Lemmon's seventh and eighth.

"*Tribute,* the play, had a rather strange history," Lemmon recalls. "I was working on *The China Syndrome* at the time its script was left at the office, and I was not willing even to read it because when I am

shooting a film it is difficult if not impossible for me to concentrate on anything else. Berne Slade had sent the script from Canada where he and his wife, Jill, were doing *Same Time, Next Year*—and it arrived wrapped in a brown, waxy garbage bag with string around it. There was no way I could bring myself to read it...and as a result, it sat around the office for a few days and probably would have been even longer getting my attention if it hadn't been for Dick Carter.

"Fortunately, Dick opened the package, read the play and hounded me until I read it too.

"Incidentally, Dick, who has since died, had been operated on for cancer about seven or eight years prior to the time *Tribute* arrived, so when he read it, he had great empathy for the character. He also felt that it would be a wonderful part for me, and that I would just love to play it.

"It's a blessing that Dick hounded me as he did because if he hadn't, and I failed to read it when I did, Berne probably would have had to make a move elsewhere and I could have missed the entire experience. Dick certainly was right: I read it and went head over heels about it. I loved the play not just because I thought it would work, but primarily as an actor reacting to what I thought was a delicious part. I thought the character of Scottie Templeton was a consummate blend of comedy and drama which I am constantly looking for but which is so elusive (good examples being *The Apartment* and *Mass Appeal*).

"In any event, as soon as I read the play I committed to do it immediately upon completion of *The China Syndrome*. (As a matter of fact, I finished shooting the film on a Friday night, packed on Saturday, and left for New York on Sunday—rehearsals for *Tribute* started on Monday.)"

Every now and then, Lemmon gets a call from an actor who is playing the *Tribute* role somewhere and is going by the printed script. Something seems out of sync, but the actor in question can never quite figure out what it is. Graciously, Lemmon will send him a list of the cuts he made for his performance.

"Slade was a stubborn joy to work with. I say 'stubborn joy' because like most playwrights he was more than a bit reluctant to make cuts, but I overcame that problem once we opened in Boston. There were only minor necessary changes in the overall play. However, the monologue at the end of the second act needed heavier cuts. Because most of the changes were minor, it was not necessary for Berne to stay during the entire Boston run so he would take off for California at various points and then return to see how the show was progressing.

"During his absence, and with the full cognizance of the cast, I would cut some of my lines, but only a few at a time. Consequently, when Berne would see the show after a four- or five-day absence, he'd come back to my dressing room and say, 'Gee, it's going terrific but didn't you skip some lines tonight?' I would say, 'Absolutely not, Berne, I would have been told by the assistant stage manager who is on the book.'

"He would answer with a puzzled, 'Oh yes, of course.' The entire company, I might add, was in cahoots with me. In this fashion, I slowly whittled my part down to the performance that was seen. Berne never did know about it until after we had opened in New York."

Tribute opened on June 1, 1978, at the Brooks Atkinson Theater and was an immediate solid hit, with perhaps its most apt review coming from John Simon, of *New York* Magazine, who wrote that "only a nice man could have written *Tribute,* and to spend a

couple of hours in his company is a privilege and a pleasure."

Of Lemmon, Simon said: "His Scottie is all anyone could ask for—charming with the right undertones of slightly sleazy slickness, expert at squeezing the last juicy drop out of a dryly witty line, magnificently mercurial, and a wizard at rapid changes from the heartbreaking to the heartwarming. In the last scenes, he conveys exquisitely partial revagement by illness: the body dented, the mind undaunted. No one is better than Lemmon at presenting the strengths of a weakling, and this part gives him his head."

The play ran as long as Lemmon was willing to appear in it. It closed when he grew tired and was eager to rethink it for the screen.

"One of the problems an actor faces is the paradox of wanting the show to be a hit, and then facing the challenge of keeping his performance fresh night after night for months on end. It's very difficult,

With Maureen Stapleton and Walter Matthau in *Juno and the Paycock,* 1974.

naturally, but I found a silly little device which helped get my adrenalin going just before every performance.

"Each dressing room has a speaker that picks up dialogue from the stage so that when an actor is off stage, he can know exactly what is happening and therefore runs no danger of missing his cue. These microphones also pick up the buzz from the audience prior to the curtain going up. When they would call 15 minutes (meaning 15 minutes to curtain), I would start to slightly raise the gain on the speaker in my dressing room. A few minutes before the curtain, I would turn it up full. The hubbub made me realize more than ever that to that particular audience, it was opening night. I could hear and feel their excitement and that, in turn, excited me."

The release of *The China Syndrome* was buoyed by overall excellent reviews, some damning slings and arrows from the U.S. Nuclear Regulatory Commission and the auspicious timing of the "accident" at Three Mile Island, but Lemmon lost his Oscar to Dustin Hoffman and *Kramer Versus Kramer*.

He was beaten out for his performance in the film version of *Tribute* in 1980 by Robert De Niro (who won his Oscar for *Raging Bull*) and, in 1982, Lemmon's work in *Missing* was topped by Ben Kingsley's *Gandhi*.

Not all has been days of wine and roses and Oscar nominations, however. During this most recent part of his career, Lemmon appeared in what might be his biggest fiasco to date, *Buddy, Buddy* (1981), and inexplicably has received some of his toughest and most downbeat reviews—inexplicable because they were in response to his finest work (in *Missing*, for example).

Then there was something called *A Sense of Humor*, a play by Ernest Thompson (*On Golden Pond*) in which Lemmon appeared opposite Estelle Parsons. It was the exact opposite of *Tribute*: It closed out-of-town.

The play dealt with a couple's struggle to comprehend their young daughter's suicide, and it was largely criticized for the author's use of inappropriate expletives to convey the parents' rage.

"We stuck with that sucker for five months," Lemmon notes, "but unfortunately Ernest Thompson, through various rewrites, was still unable to lick it and he finally called it quits. We felt that if we brought it into New York that the play would not make it critically. Ernest feels that he should leave it alone and come back to it some time in the future from a fresh point of view. Though flawed, it was an interesting play and I certainly have no regrets in doing it."

"Unfortunately, like the majority of plays, *A Sense of Humor* didn't work." Neither did his next two films, *Mass Appeal* and *Macaroni*.

Once *Macaroni* was completed, Lemmon segued almost immediately into Blake Edwards's highly independent and highly autobiographical film *Crisis*, which was retitled *That's Life* during production.

It was made with a small crew, causing some union problems, and just about everyone involved reportedly took deferred salaries, so that Edwards could bring it in for about $2,000,000. *That's Life* chronicles a long weekend during which all the members of a family experience personal crises.

A trip to Havana for the International Festival of New Latin American Cinema preceded the actor's return to Broadway in Jonathan Miller's controversial revival of Eugene O'Neill's epic drama of his disturbed family, *Long Day's Journey into Night*.

Lemmon spent his time in Havana playing celebrity and goodwill ambassador, visiting art and drama schools, attending screenings of his films *Missing* and *Some Like It Hot,* and dining with Fidel Castro at the home of Nobel Prize-winning novelist Gabriel Garcia Marques (*Erendira*).

The actor in Lemmon appreciated the actor in Castro.

"There is not a stand-up comic in the world who could hold the floor the way he did," Lemmon later commented. "The man is incredibly impressive. He has charisma down to his toenails."

Of the trip itself, Lemmon has confessed that he took it with the "hope that it will have a beneficial effect on our fellow countrymen and with the hopes that there will be further cultural exchange and an ease of whatever tensions exist."

Later, back in America, back on Broadway, Lemmon experienced one of his most exhilarating thrills in Miller's highly-publicized shortened version of the O'Neill play. Miller didn't exactly cut the four-hour play, but, rather, utilized the ideas of fast line-readings and bursts of overlapping dialogue, Robert Altman-style, thereby reducing the play's running time to a little less than three hours.

As expected, his revival—which opened Monday, April 28, 1986, at New York's Broadhurst Theater—elicited widely conflicting reviews, from pans to raves. Mostly, they were favorable, particularly to the cast.

In *The New York Times*, Frank Rich wrote: "There's a case to be made for Mr. Miller's experiment. The greatest play in our dramatic literature has become an icon that theatergoers can't always visit

Lemmon (center) In a drag chorus line of fellow Harvard Hasty Pudding Society alumni members during an evening in Sept., 1981, benefiting Harvard scholarships.

Lemmon with Cindy Ashley in a number from *Finian's Rainbow* from the PBS special *Musical Comedy Tonight—II*. The program aired on most Public Broadcasting stations on Feb. 11, 1982.

Lemmon on stage with Estelle Parsons in the play *A Sense of Humor.*

innocently anymore.

"This director wants us to see the work fresh, as if it and its autobiographical characters had no history and, to an extent, he succeeds. This is an engrossing evening for those who want to think about *Long Day's Journey into Night,* although not, I'm afraid, for those who want to feel it."

Rich noted that "Mr. Lemmon—his voice fading into a low rumble as his body sinks defeatedly into a couch—is affecting as he bitterly rues the financially lucrative role that sapped Tyrone's promise as an actor. He creates Tyrone the old ham, without being hammy himself. His mane of silver hair, whiskey voice and slightly stooped walk—not to mention his sense of humor—all serve the faded matinee idol well.

"But this star still can't quite bring himself to let an audience hate him, however transitory."

John Simon, writing for *New York* magazine, was a little less approving—well, a lot less. He said that the new production "is murder for the moods, meanings, and implications of O'Neill's masterwork. What should brood, bubbles; what should sing out, rattles on; what should groan or cry out in pain, motorcycles and machine-guns along."

For Simon, Lemmon represented "the greatest piece of miscasting."

"He plays Tyrone as if he were doing burlesque or, at best, a Billy Wilder movie with every lovable old trick and comic mannerism unleashed on O'Neill's tragedy.

"Not that the part, or the play, is without humor, but you cannot do James Tryone looking like the Kentucky Fried Chicken Colonel, and doing a cross between Alan King and Professor Irwin Corey, with cacklings and croonings and rubbery expressions reminiscent even of—of all people!—huggable old Jack Lemmon. Even his walk is absurd: a shuffling, shambling octogenarian's rather than that of a 65-year-old young for his age. O'Neill's Tyrone, the archetypal matinee idol, wasted his life touring in *The Count of Monte Cristo;* Lemmon's Tyrone must have been touring in *Abie's Irish Rose.*"

Nevertheless, the role won Lemmon another Tony nomination, and co-stars Bethel Leslie (as Mary Tyrone) and Peter Gallagher (as Edmund) also were cited. (Rich wrote that "Mr. Gallagher, as usual, is above reproach," while Simon applauded the talented young actor for managing "to convey the

illusion of a deliberate, spacious delivery while coerced to keep up with the pack.")

His recent dabbling in stage work notwithstanding (a dabble that followed an 18-year absence from it), movies remain Jack Lemmon's medium.

"Film is the greatest medium because it's practically limitless," says Jack, "but on stage you have only one shot. That's a challenge. And when the audience isn't good, you work hard as hell. It gets to be like a game. You try to get them. All of which is very good—it pulls and stretches you.

"Each time I give a performance—whether on stage or screen—I feel like I'm coming up to bat all over again. I'm riddled with professional insecurities, and it gets harder all the time.

"The big, big, *big* thing for an actor is to get over

Lemmon and Estelle Parsons with playwright Ernest Thompson, author of the ill-fated play, *A Sense of Humor.*

being afraid to expose himself. The day you can let yourself show through your screen character and not care whether somebody laughs or is shocked, you've got it made. For me, it's akin to analysis.

"You know what's a lot of baloney? This idea that artists have to be 'honest.' The fact is, you've got to be quite dishonest. Fabrication, make-believe, distortion—that's what we're all up to: living dreams.

"I guess there's more nonsense spoken and written about the acting profession than anything else. Take talent, for example. It's the last step in giving a good performance. It's all grind, grind, grind and adaptation and inner mobility. Talent is what packages all that.

"Without the drudgery, all the so-called talent in the world won't get you anywhere.

Lemmon as James Tyrone in *Long Day's Journey into Night.*

"You know what's awful to see? Actors using 'talent' or tricks or whatever to cover up their emptiness, their lack of connection with a part. They're cheating, plain and simple.

"The one supremely important thing is simplicity. One point at one time—not five different things to show off your 'great technique.' That's baloney. The best performances I've ever seen in my life have been terribly simple.

"Unselfishness," he concludes, "is another important commodity. It separates a first-rate actor from the others. He doesn't think of what he can do for himself, but what he can do for the scene."

Say no more.

To say that Jack Lemmon is immersed in his profession, or that he's dedicated to it or preoccupied with it—well, that would be an undeserving cliché.

Let's put it simply and say that his life has been a celebration of the acting profession.

Lemmon as James Tyrone, Kevin Spacey as Jamie Tyrone, Bethel Leslie as Mary Tyrone, and Peter Gallagher as Edmund Tyrone, in *Long Day's Journey into Night.*

When he isn't being driven towards acting by his nervous energy, Jack can be found playing around with one of his unpublished songs, what he calls "piano doodles," or fiddling with his ever-present cigar, or fishing. "It's my favorite thing in the world," he says of fishing. "I'm sure it's a need my body calls for. It's the only time I get to meditate."

Then there's his garden (even though he doesn't know the names of many things he's growing there), and his children—Chris, Courtney and Denise—and kids in general.

"I'm thrown in with young people all the time," smiles Jack, "and I love them. I get along with them and dig them. Kids today seem to have such an awful strain on them—too much to see and do.

"We spoil them because we know they're living with that big dark cloud hovering over them. And with their hectic activity, they're missing something I had.

"It was the excitement of looking forward to simple things, like a once-a-week movie. Now, everything is commonplace.

Besides, I'm a kid. All actors are, I guess. Kids playing at make believe."

"Jack really idolizes children," confides Felicia. "Show him a child in trouble and he cries. Show him a baby laughing, just laughing, and he cries. He blubbers all the time. It's disgusting!"

Then, of course, there's Felicia and Jack's relationship with her.

"She's so alive, so open to everything," says Jack.

"Before I met Felish, I never got angry. I was all bottled up, constricted emotionally. She opened me up. For the first time in my life, I could get *violently* mad . . . and I could feel an attraction that I never felt for any human being."

"Jack's the kind of man who wants to believe in everything, that everything is wonderful," Felicia explains, "and always will be. I taught him that there is no Santa Claus. Now he cares too much; he doesn't save himself."

Jack's one aim now is to stop worrying. "I always attach too much importance to everything that happens to me. My resolution is to worry less and enjoy life more."

Helping him to achieve this is his favorite relaxant—his piano.

As a fadeout, director Blake Edwards offers this story:

"On the set of *Days of Wine and Roses,* the piano was placed right next to my office. Between scenes, I wanted to rest or plan the next take.

"But Jack was constantly at the piano. One day, when he was playing, I couldn't stand it any longer. I called to the assistant director to move it to the other end of the set.

"While someone pushed the piano away and another grabbed the bench, Jack walked along, playing continuously.

"He didn't miss one note!"

Jack Lemmon rarely ever does.

It Should Happen to You !

A Columbia Picture (1954)

The Production Staff

Producer: Fred Kohlmar. *Director:* George Cukor. *Original Screenplay:* Garson Kanin. *Cinematographer:* Charles Lang. *Editor:* Charles Nelson. *Music:* Frederick Hollander. *Song "Let's Fall In Love":* Harold Arlen *(music)* and Ted Koehler *(lyrics). Sung by* Judy Holliday *and* Jack Lemmon. *Music Supervisor:* Morris Stoloff. *Orchestrations:* Arthur Morton. *Art Director:* John Meehan. *Set Decorator:* William Kiernan.

A Fred Kohlmar Production. A Columbia Pictures Release. Running Time: 87 minutes. In black-and-white.

The Cast

Gladys Glover: Judy Holliday. *Pete Sheppard:* Jack Lemmon. *Evan Adams III:* Peter Lawford. *Brod Clinton:* Michael O'Shea. *Mrs. Riker:* Con-

Quote-oriented advertisement for *It Should Happen To You!*

nie Gilchrist. *Entrikin:* Vaughn Taylor. *Sour Man in Central Park:* Heywood Hale Broun. *Con Cooley:* Rex Evans. *Don Toddman:* Arthur Gilmore. *Robert Grau:* Whit Bissell. *Bert Piazza:* Walter Klavun. *Panel Guest:* Melville Cooper. *Guest Stars:* Constance Bennett, Ilka Chase and Wendy Barrie.

The Movie

The ruthless "sink or swim" iffiness of making a full-fledged star debut in a major American comedy was practically negated in the case of Jack Lemmon—thanks largely to the knowledgeable and intelligent people surrounding him, the surefire material and the overall lack of pretension and ambition of both.

While certainly not a work of great cinematic power or grandeur, *It Should Happen To You!*—Jack's first film—emerged as (and has remained throughout the years) a lean, rich, impudent comedy sketch—studied, controlled, well-crafted and -timed, and modestly acted.

Since its unveiling early in 1954, the film—or more specifically, its material—has failed to age. Only the costumes, the landscape of old New York and director George Cukor's straightforward and relatively unimaginative staging betray the movie's age.

However, Garson Kanin's original script—about a "little person" and her quest for celebration—is as feisty, cynical and contemporary as ever, taking some well-deserved jabs at the media and advertising and at their dull-witted victims.

The film is a true original and has all the earmarks of a classic of the genre; it's always been rather surprising that *It Should Happen To You!* has never been numbered among the handful of truly revered screwball comedies (*Bringing Up Baby, The Palm Beach Story* and *It Happened One Night,* for example).

The basic triumphs of the film are Kanin's adept balancing of the ridiculous and the human, and the ingratiating low-keyed playing of Lemmon and Judy Holliday.

What's more, it boasts a tremendous (and tremendously funny) opening sequence which gets the film off with effortless grace: The setting is Central Park. It's a hot summer day. The place is crawling with people.

The camera picks up an attractive blonde (Holliday). Her name is Gladys Glover. She's the one we're interested in.

Gladys is deep in thought. That's why she's in the park; she thinks better in the park. She's walking barefoot; she thinks better when she's barefoot.

She's also feeding the pigeons. Not because they help her think better, however—she just likes them.

Meanwhile, a disagreeable man—annoyed by all the pigeons Gladys is attracting—accuses

With Judy Holliday, singing *Let's Fall in Love.*

her of using the birds as a cheap tactic for making a quick pickup.

"How'd ya like a slap in the face?" shouts Gladys. "Who's gonna try it?" the man snaps back. "Me, that's who!" says Gladys.

"And who are you?" asks the man. "Nobody, that's who!" Gladys admits.

Nobody. That's Gladys's problem. She's a nobody who wants to be somebody.

Gladys is an unemployed model from Binghamton, N. Y., who'll probably have to go home and work in the shoe factory. "Just like everybody else . . . and maybe marry the first guy who asks. Or the second."

Recording all this is Pete Sheppard (Lemmon), a would-be documentary filmmaker who offers Gladys the following advice: "Where there's a will, there's a way; and where there's a way, there's a will."

Spotting a giant billboard for rent on Columbus Circle—and remembering Pete's words—Gladys gets an idea. She uses her life savings to rent the billboard and have her name gloriously scrawled across it in bold-face type: G-L-A-D-Y-S G-L-O-V-E-R.

Her crazy plan works: All New York is buzzing about this Gladys Glover person, the mystery woman. Perhaps a relative of Kilroy?

With Judy Holliday.

Gladys's billboard, it turns out, is also coveted by a soap executive (Peter Lawford), who needs it for his late summer ad campaign. They make a deal; Gladys gets umpteen signs in return for that one.

With Judy Holliday.

With Judy Holliday.

Gladys is overjoyed; but Pete, now unofficially her boyfriend, is disgusted by the entire situation. His Gladys has become a joke, this year's freak act—the symbol of nothingness.

Fame at long last has reached out and embraced Gladys Glover. She's doing talk shows, ads and commercials now, but she's lost Pete. In one of his own documentary films, Pete says

goodbye (which, incidentally, makes for a charming movie moment).

The film ends on a happy note: Gladys and Pete marry—and what's more, he was the first guy to ask her.

"It's still a good film," says Jack of *It Should Happen To You!* "And Judy was the greatest actress I've ever worked with; absolutely sensa-

With Judy Holliday.

With wife Cynthia Stone on film's set.

tional. There isn't a superlative I can think of that doesn't befit her.

"She was one of the greats, and her early death was one of the great tragedies."

The Critics

The New Yorker:
It Should Happen To You! is the first Hollywood movie in a long time to employ satire to good advantage. The targets at which it aims—television, advertising and urban gullibility—are rather easily pinked, but the film works up a lot of pleasant comedy while cutting loose at them. Indeed, it has some of the flavor of *Nothing Sacred.*

Life:
Judy Holliday's *It Should Happen To You!,* an engaging fable about a girl from Binghamton, N. Y., who just couldn't stand not being famous, is one of the funniest films to come out of Hollywood.

Saturday Review:
It Should Happen To You!, Judy's latest, presents Garson Kanin at the top of his form. His script is smooth, consistently funny and generously barbed with satirical comment on the advertising business, real estate and TV.

Judy is utterly wonderful. It's her film all the way, despite close competition from a solid supporting cast headed by Peter Lawford, newcomer Jack Lemmon and Michael O'Shea.

And director George Cukor has polished every scene until it sparkles like a diamond. It almost doesn't matter that the diamonds aren't real.

Variety:
A generous helping of fun for the payee is projected in this very slick comedy toplining Judy Holliday. . . . The laugh range is from soft titters to loud guffaws as Cukor's smartly timed direction sends the players through hilarious situations. . . . Lemmon scores strongly in his first film appearance, farcing without forcing.

Phffft!

A Columbia Picture (1954)

The Production Staff

Producer: Fred Kohlmar. *Director:* Mark Robson. *Original Screenplay:* George Axelrod. *Cinematographer:* Charles Lang. *Editor:* Charles Nelson. *Music:* Frederick Hollander. *Scoring:* Morris Stoloff. *Orchestration:* Arthur Morton. *Art Director:* William Flannery. *Set Decorator:* William Kiernan.

A Fred Kohlmar Production. A Columbia Pictures Release. Running Time: 91 minutes. In black-and-white.

The Cast

Nina Tracy: Judy Holliday. *Robert Tracy:* Jack Lemmon. *Charlie Nelson:* Jack Carson. *Janis:* Kim Novak. *Mrs. Chapman:* Luella Gear. *Rick Vidal:* Donald Curtis. *Marcia:* Merry Anders. *Language Teacher:* Arny Freeman. *Dr. Van Kessel:* Donald Randolph. *Tommy:* Eddie Searles.

The Movie

How else can you treat marriage but as a comedy? Try being serious about it and it still comes out funny. A case in point is George Axelrod's

Original ad for *Phffft!*

With Jack Carson and Judy Holliday.

original screenplay for *Phffft!*, which is *very* funny—and not quite as cynical as it seems on the surface.

For his second screen appearance, Lemmon was reteamed with Judy Holliday in a lively tale about divorce—a tale that's unexpectedly promarriage. Come again? More or less, *Phffft!* is about an unsuccessful divorce.

Robert and Nina Tracy (Lemmon and Holliday) are stylish, affluent types, both with big careers in New York and a big home in the suburbs. Nina writes soap operas; Robert works as an attorney.

Their individual lives are a shambles because they're together. So there's a quick trip to Reno, a painless divorce and—phffft!

Instead of taking time to pick up the pieces and think things out, both run out and buy new wardrobes, take Mambo and language lessons and try rebirth via a few new "tricks."

With Kim Novak.

With Judy Holliday.

Nina gets tangled up with Robert's klutzy best friend (Jack Carson), an incredibly inept playboy-writer, while Robert discovers that sweet young things (Kim Novak) can be more of an annoyance than a passion.

Both are miserable now and soon come to realize that their occasional accidental meetings aren't so much of an embarrassment anymore.

So now their divorce is phffft! They pick up the pieces and start over again. (Besides, they were tired of filing separate tax returns.)

Phffft!, despite its sophistication (none of which has worn away), has remained pretty much of a nonentity film. Enjoyed by the public and dismissed by the critics as just another adequate comedy, the film was soon forgotten by both.

Director Mark Robson succeeded in giving the movie the feel of a drawing-room comedy, without having it seem too confined or stagey. (Axelrod based his script on one of his unproduced plays.)

With Judy Holliday.

The performances are smooth; the dialogue, witty and literate; and the highlight, a hilarious Mambo competition between Lemmon and Holliday.

"I always found *Phffft!* to be highly enjoyable," reminisces Jack. "I, of course, had immense respect for Judy Holliday, as you know, and I formed a lasting friendship with a gentleman I respect very much, Mark Robson, the director. And, also, George Axelrod who scripted it.

"I felt that the film was not entirely successful but that for the first half to two-thirds, it was fresh and extremely well done. I didn't think it sustained its promise—it just didn't sustain itself.

"But, in my opinion, it was definitely superior to the average light comedy of its time. It certainly was not as good as *It Should Happen to You!*

"Nevertheless, it had excellent performances by Judy (of course), Jack Carson, Luella Gear, and it started Kim Novak on her way to stardom.

"For whatever reasons, it seems to me that in recent years, Mark Robson has picked material that is far beneath his directorial talents."

The Critics

Newsweek:

Phffft! is a slickly mechanical comedy by George Axelrod, author of the Broadway hit, *The Seven Year Itch,* which is given infectious life by some subtle playing and Mark Robson's scherzo direction.

The divorced wife is acted by Judy Holliday, one of the sturdiest and most sardonic of troopers in the war between the sexes, and the divorced husband is Jack Lemmon, a young man who seems on the verge of a major Hollywood career and handles this stint with gentlemanly zip and charm.

Furthermore, there is Kim Novak as a beautiful young thing with eyes as wide as her morals, and Donald Curtis does a wonderful bit as an unctuous TV actor.

Axelrod's success here is drawn primarily from the casting job. Judy Holliday has had much better material in her time. And Lemmon deserves better.

Time:

Phffft! is the sound made by an expiring match—the kind that gutters out in gossip columns.

Jack Carson and Judy Holliday.

"Don't say it," runs the sales slogan for the picture, "see it!" The advice is sensible.

All three principals—Holliday, Lemmon and Carson—have spent so much of their acting careers in the straightjacket of formula farce that they wear it like high-fashion undies.

Holliday and Lemmon, after only two pictures together, must be acknowledged as the smoothest new comedy team in show business.

Saturday Review:

Jack Lemmon reaffirms the amiable impression he made in the last Judy Holliday picture, bringing a droll comic touch to the somewhat ungrateful role of Judy's adventure-seeking husband.

There is also some mild satirizing of radio and television soap opera in which, the script tells us, Judy specializes. All of this Mark Robson has directed, rather grimly, for laughs. Unfortunately, it adds up to, at best, moderate entertainment.

Three for the Show

A Columbia Picture (1955)

The Production Staff

Producer: Jonie Taps. *Director:* H. C. Potter. *Screenplay:* Edward Hope *and* Leonard Stern. *Based on a play by* W. Somerset Maugham. *Cinematographer:* Arthur Arling. *Editor:* Viola Lawrence. *Music:* George Duning. *Songs:* George *and* Ira Gershwin, Gene Austin, Roy Bergere, Harold Adamson, Hoagy Carmichael, Lester Lee, Ned Washington *and* Bob Russell. *Music Supervisors:* Morris Stoloff *and* Fred Karger. *Choreographer:* Jack Cole. *Art Director:* Walter Holscher. *Set Decorator:* William Kiernan.

A Jonie Taps Production. A Columbia Pictures Release. Running Time: 91 minutes. In color and CinemaScope.

Mercury Records soundtrack album MG 25204.

The Cast

Julie: Betty Grable. *Marty Stewart:* Jack Lemmon. *Vernon Lowndes:* Gower Champion. *Gwen Howard:* Marge Champion. *Mike Hudson:* Myron

Original ad for *Three for the Show*.

McCormick. *Colonel Wharton:* Paul Harvey.
Sergeant O'Hallihan: Robert Bice.

The Musical Numbers

Overture (Main Title)	Orchestra
"Which One?"	Marge Champion
"Down Boy!"	Betty Grable, Jack Lemmon,
Gower Champion	
"Someone to Watch Over Me"	
Marge Champion	
"Swan Lake Ballet"	Orchestra
"Three For the Show"	Orchestra
danced by Betty Grable,	
Gower Champion, Jack Lemmon	
"I've Been Kissed Before"	Betty Grable
"I've Got a Crush on You"	Jack Lemmon
and Betty Grable	
"The Homecoming"	Orchestra
danced by Jack Lemmon and	
Gower Champion	
"How Come You Do Me Like You Do?"	
Betty Grable	

With Betty Grable.

With Gower Champion.

"How Come You Do Me Like You Do?" (Reprise)
    Jack Lemmon and Betty Grable
Finale
    Marge and Gower Champion,
    Jack Lemmon and Betty Grable

The Movie

If it only had a quick flash of brilliance and some self-effacing humor, *Three for the Show* could have succeeded as a spoof of the kind of musicals its players, Betty Grable and Marge and Gower Champion, were churning out during the early Fifties.

CinemaScope had no sooner arrived than it was being wasted on veritable non-plots with big, splashy, TV-variety-show type production numbers. Such was the case with *Three for the Show*.

The "Enoch Arden" theme—already played to death in a slew of screen comedies and TV series—was resurrected and watered down, decorated with gaudy trappings and supplemented with nine or ten energetic, pointless and overproduced songs.

It's a mess all right and—for this very reason—it's also rather amusing. A truly witty mind might well have done some marvelous things with the dime-store ideas lurking throughout *Three for the Show*.

The plot casts Lemmon (in his first onscreen singing role) as a successful Broadway composer who's reported killed in action during the war (which one is never made clear). His wife, a musical comedy star (Grable), goes on to marry his best friend and former partner (G. Champion).

Meanwhile, as all good predictable plots would have it, Lemmon turns up, well and alive and longing for his wife.

So while Grable tries to decide between Lemmon and Champion, the three tentatively set up housekeeping together. On the sidelines throughout, watching this cozy set-up, is Grable's best friend (M. Champion), who's eagerly awaiting the leftover guy.

An earlier version of *Three for the Show* so disturbed the Roman Catholic Legion of Decency with its hanky-panky that it was awarded the Legion's "C" (condemned) rating.

It seems marriage and polygamy were treated a little too frivolously. Some judicious cuts subsequently raised the film's classification to a "B" (morally objectionable in part).

Despite the ligament-straining spirit of its production numbers, *Three for the Show* is nearly vapid and contains only one moment to cherish.

It's a rousing musical number in which Lemmon and Gower Champion, unaware of each other's presence, dance, run, jump, fly over tables and slam doors, in a harried attempt to make preparations for a romantic evening for "two."

Jack Cole did the choreography and he

deserves applause for a contribution which momentarily redeems the film.

The late Betty Grable was quite excited about Lemmon at the time and had been quoted as saying, "This Lemmon, if you will excuse the corn, is a peach. He's one terrific comedian."

Lemmon rates the film as one of his "major disappointments."

The Critics

Time:

"A good Hollywood musical," a director once remarked, "is like a fine glass. It only rings true when it's absolutely empty." By this standard, *Three for the Show* is a good musical—the best so far released in 1955. It has the inimitable zing of vacuity, and it has something more important: a fundamental lilt that travels from scene to scene and makes the picture musical even when the soundtrack is silent.

The best scenes in the picture are those in which the two men dance attendance on their mutual wife to some pretty, witty choreography by Jack Cole. All the dances, in fact, have just the right sort of scratch-pad casualness.

Betty Grable is still a fairly potent whiff of H_2O_2, and Jack Lemmon, who showed in *It Should Happen to You!* and *Phffft!* that he is an expert comedian, proves in this picture that he can sing and dance winningly too.

Newsweek:

This variation of the Tennyson Enoch Arden theme was a thin play when W. Somerset Maugham offered it as *Too Many Husbands* in 1919. It was just as thin, but passing good fun, when Jean Arthur played in a screen version under the same title in 1940. Now, by switching the story to a show-business background, Edward Hope and Leonard Stern get a springboard for a lively musical.

Betty Grable and the dancing Champions run high, wide and lissome in CinemaScope and Technicolor.

Lee Rogow in *Saturday Review:*

Three for the Show takes a tour through country that is familiar, if not necessarily dearly beloved. Surprisingly enough, however, producer Jonie Taps, director H. C. Potter, screenwriters Edward Hope and Leonard Stern and choreographer Jack Cole have supplied a pleasantly tinkling entertainment. Since the present trend in screen musi-

cals is frequently stupefying, this bright piece is welcome.

Variety:

The topsy-turvy world of show biz gets another lively going over in *Three for the Show*. A wacky comedy tailor-made to the talents of a good cast, it scores primarily in the song-and-dance department. Jack Lemmon, a comedian who knows how to punch across a line, is a big asset but unfortunately isn't given enough chance to do his stuff.

As Ensign Pulver.

Mister Roberts

A Warner Bros. Picture (1955)

The Production Staff

Producer: Leland Hayward. *Directors:* John Ford and Mervyn LeRoy. *Screenplay:* Frank Nugent and Joshua Logan. *Based on the play of the same title by* Thomas Heggen *and* Joshua Logan. *From the novel* Mister Roberts *by* Thomas Heggen. *Cinematographer:* Winton Hoch. *Editor:* Jack Murray. *Music:* Franz Waxman. *Orchestrations:* Leonid Raab. *Song* "If I Could Be With You One Hour Tonight." *Sung by* Jack Lemmon. *Art Director:* Art Loel. *Set Decorator:* William L. Kuehl.

An Orange Production. A Warner Bros. Release. Running Time: 123 minutes. In color, Cinema-Scope and Stereophonic Sound.

The Cast

Mister Roberts: Henry Fonda. *The Captain:* James Cagney. *Doc:* William Powell. *Ensign Pulver:* Jack Lemmon. *Lt. Ann Girard:* Betsy Palmer. *C.P.O. Dowdy:* Ward Bond. *Mannion:* Phil Carey. *Shore Patrol Officer:* Martin Milner. *Shore Patrolman:* Gregory Walcott. *Military Policeman:* James Fla-

Original ad for *Mister Roberts.*

60

With Henry Fonda.

vin. *Marine Sergeant:* Jack Pennick. *Dolan:* Ken Curtis. *Reber:* Nick Adams. *Stefanowski:* Harry Carey, Jr. *Bookser:* Pat Wayne. *Wiley:* Tiger Andrews. *Insigna:* Robert Roark. *Rodrigues:* Perry Lopez.

The Movie

It's always been rather difficult to pinpoint the quality of the John Ford–Mervyn LeRoy film version of *Mister Roberts*. There's a certain dramatic starkness about its story and setting, and its ending is essentially tragic.

But it's also brightened throughout by situations and dialogue that are rowdy, bawdy and wisecracking, and by its romantic view of heroism.

This dual quality of the piece is its hallmark—and its triumph is the single-minded integration of its ingredients, not by one director, but by *two* directors, both of whom worked independently of one another. (Ford started the film, was taken sick and replaced by LeRoy.)

While it enjoyed incredible success as a book and had a healthy 1,157-performance run on Broadway as a play, *Mister Roberts* is nevertheless remembered and cherished first and foremost as a movie.

It was one of the most eagerly awaited films of its day, one of the most well-received and popular and—as time has clearly proven—one of the most enduring.

Playing no small part in the film's success is

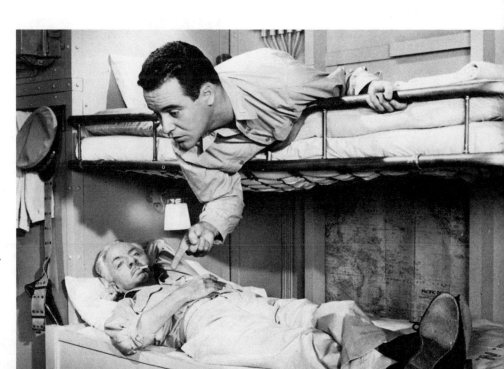

With William Powell.

With Betsy Palmer.

its cast: Henry Fonda, forever Mister Roberts; James Cagney and William Powell, two old, venerable Hollywood hands well-cast as the Captain and Doc, respectively; and fledgling Jack Lemmon, a standout as Ensign Pulver.

The four actors fit their roles perfectly, and the chemistry among them is candid and natural—the prime ingredient which cements the film's other ingredients together.

The plot is legend by now: While the war action rapidly passes him by, Lt. Doug Roberts (Fonda) peddles toilet paper and tooth paste as the indispensable cargo officer of the U.S.S. *Reluctant,* affectionately known as the Bucket.

Mister Roberts seems to divide his time equally between pep-talking his disorganized bunk-mate, Frank Pulver (Lemmon); being pep-talked himself by the ship's knowing doctor (Powell), and battling nonstop with the Captain (Cagney).

Roberts wants a transfer to another ship in the war zone, but the Captain—well aware of his value—continually refuses the requests.

Roberts isn't the only miserable and unhappy man aboard the Bucket; the crew in general is discontented and lonely and in need of a liberty.

The Captain refuses this, too—but changes

With Henry Fonda and William Powell.

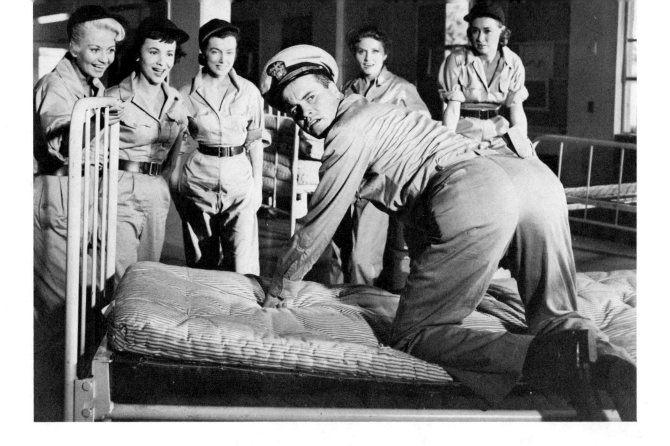

his mind when Roberts promises to discontinue his frequent requests for a transfer and also to abandon his rank insubordination.

Matters somehow worsen, with the Captain becoming more impossible and tyrannical. What's more, the crew is becoming quickly disillusioned by Roberts' new mealymounthed ways.

Then, suddenly, a crazy series of events takes place: The Captain's treasured potted palm tree is tossed overboard; there's a sudsy explosion in the ship's laundry and, best of all, Roberts receives orders to transfer to a destroyer.

Mister Roberts doesn't survive the war—at least, not physically. But spiritually, he carries on

With Betsy Palmer.

With Oscar for his portrayal of Ensign Pulver.

inside Frank and Doc and all the men aboard the Bucket.

"In my opinion," says Jack, "there has never been a director with a greater cinematic eye than John Ford. His shots are so often magnificent in their beauty, and the way he would stage his people within the shot often reminds me of a classic painting.

"And yet, the staging never is just for the sake of the shot. It is always totally legitimate.

"I was naturally quite apprehensive, as was the rest of the company, when Mervyn LeRoy replaced 'Pappy' Ford on the film.

"Mervyn, quite wisely, ran all of the existing footage that Ford had already shot and said that he would, to the best of his ability, try to complete the rest of the picture as close as possible to Ford's style and concept, that he would in no way attempt to alter any character conceptions that already existed.

"In other words, he was not going to try to make a Mervyn LeRoy film, his job would be to try and complete a John Ford film. Frankly, I think that is much more difficult to do than to create a film in your own style and manner.

"Considering that difficulty, I think Mervyn did an excellent job overall, especially with someone as unique and individual as John Ford.

"Incidentally, Josh Logan, who directed the original *Roberts* on Broadway, also had been ill during the filming, and when the picture was completed he then came to the coast and directed a couple of additional scenes in conjunction with Mervyn.

"So, we actually had three directors on the film. Which can be fascinating but can also give you a small stomach ache.

"All in all," he concludes, *"Mister Roberts* remains one of the great professional experiences of my life and certainly one of the most enjoyable. My initial respect for Hank Fonda, Jimmy Cagney and William Powell, only increased and we have all remained close friends ever since."

Lemmon won the Best Supporting Oscar of 1955 for his portrayal of Pulver in *Mister Roberts*, defeating Arthur Kennedy *(Trial)*, Sal Mineo *(Rebel Without a Cause)*, Arthur O'Connell *(Picnic)* and Joe Mantel *(Marty)*.

The Critics

Saturday Review:

In producing the film *Mister Roberts*, Leland Hayward has remained substantially faithful to the playscript . . . (and) has been particularly fortunate in obtaining the services of Henry Fonda in the title role, for this player enriches and illuminates the entire work by his performance.

The film moves in short spurts from highlight to highlight, the explosion in the laundry, the homemade Scotch whiskey, the riotous liberty, the epic discovery that bridge binoculars can be made to focus on the nurses' shower-room ashore.

Time:

The acting, direction and writing have all the high surface polish and potent inward efficiency of a 1955 car fresh from the assembly line.

Fonda, enlarging on his stage performance, has caught every nuance; William Powell, as the ship's doctor, is endlessly kind, beneficent and wise; Jack Lemmon proves once more that he is easily the most engaging of Hollywood's new comedians, and James Cagney makes his jack-in-the-box appearances with all the peppery rancor of a Mr. Punch.

The best evidence of the film's accomplishment is that *Mister Roberts* seldom drags during its more than two hours' running time.

Newsweek:

Mister Roberts is probably the most eagerly awaited movie of the year. It is also one of the best.

With Ward Bond.

With James Cagney, Henry Fonda and William Powell.

All the parts that were funny (in the book and the play) are still funny in this third go-round. Through his own special legerdemain, the doctor still makes Scotch out of grain alcohol, Coke, iodine and hair tonic.

A homemade firecracker still explodes in the laundry, cascading tons of soapsuds through the ship. Above all, the crew still hates the palm tree so dearly cherished by the captain.

Henry Fonda played Mister Roberts more than 1,000 times on Broadway, and he may well get his long overdue Oscar for his screen rendition of the role.

A. H. Weiler in *The New York Times*:

Now hear this! Another 21-gun salute is hereby accorded *Mister Roberts* and the raffish, rough and lovable World War II gobs who landed yesterday at the Music Hall.

Like its predecessors, this version of *Mister Roberts* is a strikingly superior entertainment.

Jack Lemmon's Ensign Pulver is a broad delineation of the amorous misfit, anxious to please his idol Roberts. He exhibits the explosive ebullience of a kid with a live frog in his britches.

Henry Fonda does not simply give his role a professional reading. He *is* Mr. Roberts. (His performance) evolves as a beautifully lean and sensitive characterization, full of dignity and power.

Describing the laundry explosion to Powell and Fonda.

Bob Fosse and Janet Leigh.

My Sister Eileen

A Columbia Picture (1955)

The Production Staff

Producer: Fred Kohlmar. *Director:* Richard Quine. *Screenplay:* Blake Edwards *and* Richard Quine. *Based on the play of the same title by* Joseph Fields *and* Jerome Chodorov. *From the New Yorker stories by* Ruth McKenney. *Cinematographer:* Charles Lawton, Jr. *Editor:* Charles Nelson. *Music:* George Duning. *Songs:* Jule Styne *(music)* and Leo Robin *(lyrics). Music Supervisors:* Morris Stoloff *and* Fred Karger. *Orchestrations:* Arthur Morton. *Choreographer:* Bob Fosse. *Art Director:* Walter Holscher. *Set Decorator:* William Kiernan.

A Fred Kohlmar Production. A Columbia Pictures Release. Running Time: 108 minutes. In color and CinemaScope.

The Cast

Ruth Sherwood: Betty Garrett. *Eileen Sherwood:* Janet Leigh. *Bob Baker:* Jack Lemmon. *Frank Lippencott:* Bob Fosse. *Wreck:* Richard York. *Helen:*

Original ad for *My Sister Eileen* as 1955 musical remake.

JACK LEMMON-106

With Betty Garrett (from top), Bob Fosse and Janet Leigh.

Lucy Marlow. *Chick Clark:* Tommy Rall. *Appopolous:* Kurt Kasznar. *Lonigan:* Horace McMahon. *Alice:* Queenie Smith.

The Musical Numbers

"Atmosphere" (Main Title)   Chorus
"As Soon As They See Eileen"   Betty Garrett
"I'm Great!"   Kurt Kasznar, Richard York,
        Betty Garrett, Janet Leigh
"I'm Great!" (reprise)
        Betty Garrett and Janet Leigh
"No Room for Mr. Gloom"   Orchestra
        danced by Bob Fosse and Tommy Rall
"There's Nothing Like Love"   Janet Leigh
        and Betty Garrett
"Give Me a Band and My Baby"   Janet Leigh,
        Betty Garrett, Bob Fosse, Tommy Rall
"It's Bigger Than You and Me"   Jack Lemmon
"There's Nothing Like Love" (reprise) Bob Fosse
"Conga!"   Orchestra
        danced by Betty Garrett, Janet Leigh
        and Male Ensemble
Finale ("Conga!" reprise)   Entire Cast

The Movie

On a much smaller scale than other film musicals produced at the time, but definitely superior to its peers, is Lemmon's fifth film, *My Sister Eileen*, a musicalized version of the Ruth McKenney *New Yorker* stories.

With Betty Garrett.

The movie is pleasingly modest and intimate and, for good measure, fairly drips with visual and vocal vitality and uninhibited choreographic zest.

None of the other big musicals of the day (*Oklahoma!, Guys and Dolls* and *Daddy Long Legs*, among others) is as proficient in blending song and dance and story in so diverting a way. What's more, the movie also succeeds in ladling out charm and sentiment in large yet palatable doses.

My Sister Eileen marks Lemmon's first union with director Richard Quine, who was to helm the actor in five subsequent films (*Operation Mad Ball, Bell, Book and Candle, It Happened to Jane, The Notorious Landlady* and *How to Murder Your Wife*).

"He's a very close friend of mine," says Jack of Quine, "and a very talented director. He knows the camera backward and forward and, in my opinion, uses it extremely well. He is absolutely marvelous with actors and I know of none

who have ever worked with him who didn't think that he was absolutely tops.

"If he can be faulted, it might be that he gets overly sentimental and romantic at times, rather than being objective."

The movie also marks Lemmon's first association with Blake Edwards—co-author of the screenplay with Quine—who went on to co-write *Operation Mad Ball* and *The Notorious Landlady* for the actor and to direct him in *Days of Wine and Roses* and *The Great Race*.

Quine intelligently peopled his film—both in front of the camera and behind: Jule Styne and Leo Robin collaborated on the movie's peppy score (unfortunately never recorded); Bob Fosse did the clever choreography and also plays the second male lead, and Betty Garrett and Janet Leigh complement each other perfectly as the two hopeful sisters from Ohio.

The plot has Leigh and Garrett—a would-be actress and a writer, respectively—arriving from Columbus and settling in colorful Greenwich Village. Their mutual aims are to (1) land employment and (2) avoid seduction.

That's pretty much the basis of the movie. The girls dance their way from job interview to audition to their tacky basement apartment, attracting an assortment of cads and girl-watchers along the way.

Lemmon plays a wolfish magazine editor interested in some of Garrett's stories and, in this role, he gets to excel in the film's most memorable moment—a musical seduction sequence titled *It's Bigger Than You and Me*.

Bob Fosse does a nice job as a soda-fountain clerk smitten with Leigh, and Kurt Kasznar and Dick York have their moments as the girls' conniving landlord and a fellow tenant, respectively.

All in all, *My Sister Eileen* is a very nice, uncomplicated little movie.

The Critics

Newsweek:

Catchy tunes, literate lyrics, excellent dancing and a pronounced lightness of spirit, all in the proper surroundings, make this version of a Broadway comedy hit one of the happier musicals that Hollywood has lately manufactured.

The makers of the movie have fitted their glimpses of Greenwich Village and a couple of other neighborhoods into a peppermint-colored world, which it would be very, very nice to inhabit. Their product is certain to make the young feel encouraged and the aging feel just a trifle lightheaded.

Betty Garrett and Janet Leigh play the sisters from Ohio. Jack Lemmon in the leading male romantic role is that rarity in movies, an engaging hero who is also a genuine comedian. Most of the dancing is done by Robert Fosse and Tommy Rall, and their dancing has a degree of excellence that is growing rare.

Lee Rogow in *Saturday Review:*

The major virtues of Columbia's charming musical mounting of *My Sister Eileen* are the cheerfully melodic score by Jule Styne and Leo Robin, dance numbers by Bob Fosse which are in the simple, impish, underproduced tradition of the in-between numbers of the early Astaire–Rogers films, a devastatingly humorous performance by the now-masterful Jack Lemmon, the offbeat but sparkling casting of dancers Bob Fosse and Tommy Rall, and Betty Garrett . . . who can sing and dance and deliver funny lines and do everything.

Another word about Jack Lemmon. Through some chance his past three or four pictures have required this busy actor to portray a seducer, and he has become a virtuoso of the man-and-woman-alone-in-the-bachelor-apartment scene.

In this one he sings "It's Bigger Than You and Me." As (Garrett) escapes into the elevator she delivers my favorite line in the picture: "Thanks for the floor show, but your prices here are ridiculous."

Don Miller in *Films in Review:*

Quine is a newish directorial talent whose style is based on simplicity and speed. The 109 minutes of *My Sister Eileen* do not seem too many.

Quine's continuity is smooth; the performers please; the musical numbers are well staged, especially a challenge dance between Bob Fosse and Tommy Rall. The former created the dances . . . (and) Quine's handling of them makes them seem cinematically fresh and creative.

There isn't enough for Jack Lemmon in *My Sister Eileen*, but what there is proves he is one of the few leading men who can be attractively funny.

Variety:

Even those well-acquainted with all of the material will find a freshness here that assures acceptance. Scripters Blake Edwards and Richard Quine have turned out a simplified filmusical, in that the tunes and dances come naturally to situations and are not overly staged.

With Kurt Kasznar (center).

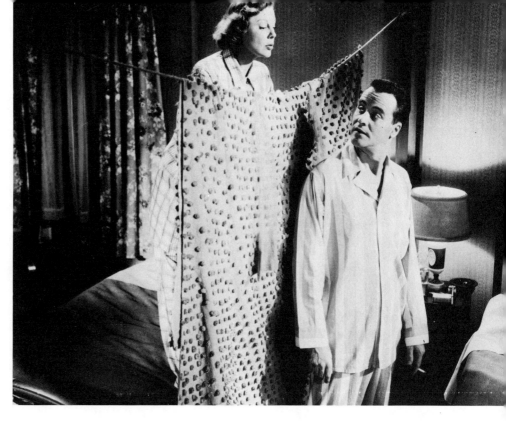

With June Allyson.

You Can't Run Away From It

A Columbia Picture (1956)

The Production Staff

Producer: Dick Powell. *Associate Producer:* Richard Sokolove. *Director:* Dick Powell. *Screenplay:* Claude Binyon *and* Robert Riskin. *Based on the screenplay* It Happened One Night *by Robert Riskin. From a short story by Samuel Hopkins Adams. Cinematographer:* Charles Lawton, Jr. *Editor:* Al Clark. *Music:* George Duning. *Songs:* Gene DePaul *(music) and* Johnny Mercer *(lyrics). Music Supervisor:* Morris Stoloff. *Orchestrations:* Arthur Morton. *Choreographer:* Robert Sidney. *Art Director:* Robert Peterson. *Set Decorators:* William Kiernan *and* Robert Priestly.

A Dick Powell Production. A Columbia Pictures Release. Running Time: 95 minutes. In color and CinemaScope.

Decca Records soundtrack album: DL 8396.

The Cast

Ellie Andrews: June Allyson. *Peter Warne:* Jack

Original ad for *You Can't Run Away From It.*

73

ith June Allyson.

With June Allyson.

Lemmon. *A. A. Andrews:* Charles Bickford. *George Shapely:* Paul Gilbert. *Fred Totten:* Stubby Kaye. *Danker:* Jim Backus. *Bus Driver:* Henny Youngman. *Gordon:* Allyn Joslyn. *Red:* Frank Sully. *Joe:* Dub Taylor. *Motel Proprietors:* Walter Baldwin, Howard McNear, Elvira Allman *and* Jack Albertson.

The Musical Numbers

"You Can't Run Away From It" (Main Title)
    The Four Aces
"Howdy, Friends and Neighbors!" Stubby Kaye,
    June Allyson, Jack Lemmon and ensemble
"Temporarily" Jack Lemmon and June Allyson
"Thumbin' a Ride"
    June Allyson and Jack Lemmon
"Scarecrow Ballet" June Allyson
"Old Reporters Never Die" Jack Lemmon
Finale Chorus

The Movie

Few films during the mid-Fifties were as eagerly awaited as this musical remake of Frank Capra's beloved *It Happened One Night.* Even fewer bit the dust as quickly.

What worked well in 1934 and was embraced by the public and critics alike seemed lackluster in 1956, thanks to unimaginative filmmaking and unnecessary updating.

It Happened One Night was never big on plot; that's part of its charm. What little plot it has simply cannot withstand tampering of any sort. It's delicate—and *You Can't Run Away From It* proves this.

The first mistake made by producer-director Dick Powell and his adapter Claude Binyon was to update the story from 1934 to 1956. This one change robbed the basic plotline of its essential "feel" and atmosphere.

Electing to use wide screen and color was another mistake. These innovations, while assisting other musicals at the time, worked against the tale's innate, two-character intimacy and also against the public's memory of *It Happened One Night* as a small, black-and-white story.

Luckily, the basic plot was retained, along with some of the breezy lines penned by Robert Riskin for the original film—but Powell's direction slowed down everything to the pace of a heavy drama. (Oddly enough, the original film runs 105 minutes, while the slower remake runs a mere 95 minutes.)

The casting, however, was—is—inspired, with Lemmon and June Allyson playing together as smoothly as Claudette Colbert and Clark Gable in the Capra version.

The addition of songs, surprisingly enough, also proved to be a nice touch, primarily because the songs themselves (by Johnny Mercer and Gene DePaul) are artless and unobtrusive and because Powell staged them in a casual, straightforward way. (In this case, his unimaginative staging works to good effect.)

Once again, the plot has to do with an

On location with June Allyson.

With director Dick Powell and June Allyson at on-set birthday party for Allyson.

heiress (Allyson) and her attempts to escape from her domineering father (Charles Bickford) to wed a fortune hunter.

She's front page headlines to most newspapermen—the biggest story of the year.

While en route to her fiance, she meets up with a reporter (Lemmon) who guarantees her delivery to her future husband if she'll promise him the exclusive story.

Chaos enters in the form of Cupid: The reporter falls in love with his exclusive story. But it's too late; tomorrow Allyson is to marry her fortune hunter.

Her father, who likes Lemmon's style, encourages his daughter to run away again—but this time from her own wedding.

She does; and she lives happily ever after with her reporter.

The Critics

Newsweek:

This purports to be a revival of the famous Gable-and-Colbert hit of 1934, *It Happened One Night*. It is more like a reburial of that droll film which started the screwball comedy cycle (and nearly ruined the undershirt business). The original . . . was a modest, history-making little picture.

Modest is not quite the word for the current version. . . . It frequently seems to be two versions of the same picture pasted together, one a musical and the other not, and neither one much of a comedy.

Lemmon has the light touch and the easy-going air, but Miss Allyson wears the determined look of a game little vaudeville entertainer rather than that of a romantic comedienne.

The Commonweal:

You Can't Run Away From It tries to re-do all the amusing incidents from the original, but somehow the jokes about the open road, motel, bus and jalopy don't seem as funny now as they did in the Depression Days, and the success of the film depends upon these jokes.

Although June Allyson and Jack Lemmon try very hard to get an occasional assist in a song with Stubby Kaye or in a laugh-provoking episode with Paul Gilbert, they do not get much help from director Dick Powell, who is pretty heavy-handed about the whole thing. Neither does the music come to the aid of the story, which certainly needs a lift.

Time:

The new version has lost the social point of the old, along with other things. Dick Powell is at the megaphone, rather than (Frank) Capra, and he uses the instrument less as a director should than he did when he was a baby-faced crooner—to make things loud and corny.

Further, Claude Binyon has thumbsily rewritten the script, and many of the sly little scenes have been converted into thwacking big musical numbers, set to some remarkably unmusical music.

Both of the big names have been replaced by other big names (June Allyson and Jack Lemmon) and the new people give it all they've got.

The fact that, despite these drawbacks, *You Can't Run Away From It* is a slightly better-than-average movie is a striking tribute to the lasting human interest of the basic situation: Boy meets girl, boy loses girl, boy gets girl.

Variety:

Miss Allyson and Lemmon are an affable combo in the leads, she looking chic and playing it straight as the rich chick and he handling bits of business with provocative brazenness.

Fire Down Below

A Columbia Picture (1957)

The Production Staff

Producers: Irving Allen *and* Albert Broccoli. *Director:* Robert Parrish. *Screenplay:* Irwin Shaw. *Based on the novel* Fire Down Below *by* Max Catto. *Cinematographer:* Desmond Dickinson. *Editor:* Jack Slade. *Music:* Arthur Benjamin, Kenneth V. Jones *and* Douglas Gambley. *Conducted by* Muir Mathieson. "Harmonica Theme": Jack Lemmon. *Song* "Fire Down Below": Lester Lee *and* Ned Washington. *Sung by* Jeri Southern. *Choreographer:* Tutte Lemkow. *Set Designer:* John Box.

A Warwick Production. A Columbia Pictures Release. Running Time: 116 minutes. In color and CinemaScope.

Decca Records soundtrack album: DL 8597.

The Cast

Irena: Rita Hayworth. *Felix:* Robert Mitchum. *Tony:* Jack Lemmon. *Harbor Master:* Herbert

Original ad for *Fire Down Below.*

RITA **HAYWORTH** is the man-burnt woman of it...

ROBERT **MITCHUM** is the woman-scorched man of it...

JACK **LEMMON** is the wild spark that sets it off...

Flaming out of the Caribbean...the big excitement, the burning excitement!

FIRE DOWN BELOW

CINEMASCOPE TECHNICOLOR®

Screenplay by IRWIN SHAW · Directed by ROBERT PARRISH · IRVING ALLEN and ALBERT R. BROCCOLI · A WARWICK PRODUCTION · A COLUMBIA PICTURE

Lom. *Doctor Sam:* Bernard Lee. *Miguel:* Anthony Newley. *Jimmy Jean:* Edric Connor.

The Movie

In *Fire Down Below,* Lemmon got a chance to display his dramatic side on screen for the first time and, despite the overall feebleness of the film that contains it, his performance comes as a pleasant surprise to anyone familiar only with his light comedic talents.

He also got a chance to show off his musical ability, not on screen as he did in some of his earlier musicals, but off screen as composer of one of the film's themes.

Lemmon penned the "Harmonica Theme," which like the film, has been spectacular in its lack of success and recognition. "To date," says Jack, "I've made something like seventeen dollars in royalties from it."

Fire Down Below, with its exotic background of tropical calypso-land and its assortment of overheated characters, was adapted by Irwin Shaw from a Max Catto novel about a love triangle amidst adventure.

Lemmon and Robert Mitchum play two small-time smugglers who will run anything—guns, cargo, women—for a price.

Enter Rita Hayworth as a woman with a past. She wants clandestine transport to a distant island where, she hopes, she can forget the past and start a new life.

Lemmon—as an easygoing, boyish type—finds the woman sad and affecting and promptly falls in love with her. The more cynical Mitchum also desires her but for baser reasons.

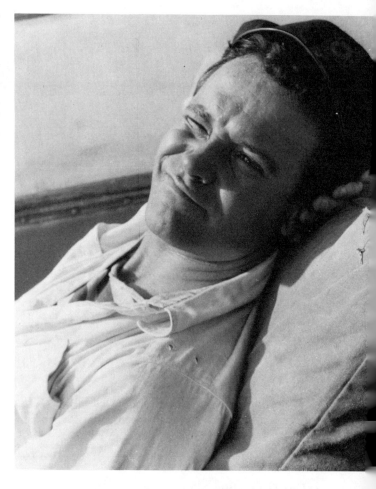

Upon arrival, Lemmon and Hayworth depart together, leaving Mitchum behind to operate the boat alone. Lemmon's plans to marry Hayworth are thwarted when Mitchum pulls a double-cross

With Rita Hayworth.

78

With Robert Mitchum and Rita Hayworth.

Studio shot publicizing Lemmon's authorship of the film's *Harmonica* Theme.

that has Lemmon eventually being pursued by the police.

Lemmon flees to another island, leaving Mitchum to get cozy with Hayworth, proving that they're two of a kind.

Returning for revenge, Lemmon becomes trapped in the bow of a collision-smashed ship. He's rescued by Mitchum and, by fadeout time, the three agree that Mitchum and Hayworth are indeed two of a kind and deserve each other.

The Critics

Time:

Fire Down Below rises high and could have soared higher but for a curious fact: Its proper beginning seems uncomfortably wedged in its middle. Two of the three principals disappear in the midst of the story for half an hour of screen time. The curious result is a fast-paced adventure yarn laced around a taut interlude of high drama.

The ending is unexpected, satisfying and far from standard. Sleepy-eyed Robert Mitchum never will wake up, but here his somnolence is quite effective. Rita Hayworth and Jack Lemmon are both wide awake and turn in solidly realistic performances.

Despite some purple dialogue ("You're driving me mad, authentically mad!") and its involuted continuity, *Fire Down Below* is a triangle story with unusual tensile strength.

Newsweek:

It is doubtful that the makers of *Fire Down Below* set out to create a new art form, but that is what they wound up with—something which might be called the one-picture double bill. In the present instance, one watches a steaming tropical love triangle for about an hour, and then, without warning, the picture abruptly becomes a suspense thriller which quickly drives that other movie completely out of mind.

Jack Lemmon, an engaging young actor who has heretofore been a comedian, does exceedingly well with the virtually motionless, cold-sweat role of a man imprisoned in a thicket of twisted steel.

The picture was expensively filmed in and around Trinidad, in color, and might be said to make squalor look just about as lush as it can get.

Operation Mad Ball

A Columbia Picture (1957)

The Production Staff

Producer: Jed Harris. *Director:* Richard Quine. *Screenplay:* Jed Harris, Blake Edwards *and* Arthur Carter. *Based on the play of the same title by* Arthur Carter. *Cinematographer:* Charles Lawton, Jr. *Editor:* Charles Nelson. *Music:* George Duning. *Scoring:* Morris Stoloff. *Song* "Mad Ball": Fred Karger *(music) and* Richard Quine *(lyrics). Sung by* Sammy Davis, Jr. *Art Director:* Robert Boyle. *Set Decorators:* William Kiernan *and* Bill Calvert. A Jed Harris Production. A Columbia Pictures Release. Running Time: 105 minutes. In black-and-white.

Original ad for Operation Mad Ball.

With Kathryn (Grant) Crosby.

The Cast

Pvt. Hogan: Jack Lemmon. *Lieut. Betty Bixby:* Kathryn (Grant) Crosby. *Capt. Paul Lock:* Ernie Kovacs. *Colonel Rousch:* Arthur O'Connell. *Yancey Skibo:* Mickey Rooney. *Cpl. Bohun:* Dick York. *Pvt. Widowskas:* James Darren. *Cpl. Berryman:* Roger Smith. *Pvt. Grimes:* William Leslie. *Pvt. Bullerd:* Paul Picerni. *Madame LaFour:* Jeanne Manet.

The Movie

"At first," points out Richard Quine, who directed Jack in this, his first full-fledged starring role, "Jack was doing all the roles Glenn Ford turned down. But after *Operation Mad Ball,* the cry went out. 'This is perfect for Jack Lemmon!' Every guy who ever wrote a line of comedy dialogue wanted him."

Operation Mad Ball—Jack's eighth film—is a military comedy, a genre which has always seemed slightly contradictory: An Army post is about as unlikely a place (and subject) for comedy as you're likely to find. Which probably explains why most military comedies are of the black variety.

This G.I. frolic is no exception. Its enlisted men are work-boggled, regulation-dominated and woman-starved, and forever at war with their seemingly sadistic superiors, with the war prisoners, the native civilians and the whole bloody system itself.

A party is in order. So thinks Private Hogan (Lemmon). Not just a party, but "the maddest mad ball in the history of the Army."

The film that follows is a sort of Fifties version of Robert Altman's *M*A*S*H,* boasting the same amount and quality of irreverent and black humor but a lot less blood.

Making arrangements for an off-limits Mad Ball seems to invite immediate complications, in the form of super-nasty Captain Paul Lock (the late Ernie Kovacs): a conniving French opportunist named Madame LaFour (Jeanne Manet), who's

With Arthur O'Connell (left), Kathryn (Grant) Crosby and Ernie Kovacs.

With Dick York.

supplying the quarters; and Hogan's sweetie, nurse Betty Bixby (Kathryn Grant Crosby), who's sweet but strictly Regular Army (shades of M*A*S*H's Hot Lips here).

There's a lot of running, jumping, double crosses and double takes throughout, as Hogan desperately irons out every wrinkle and foul-up. Effectively abetting him is the Army's foremost wheeler-dealer, M/Sgt. Yancey Skibo (Mickey Rooney).

The performances in *Operation Mad Ball* are unbeatable. Jack is especially savvy here and seems to be having a field day in his hilarious in-and-out, French-English battles with the unreasonable Jeanne Manet.

Kovacs made his film debut here, and an auspicious and very funny one it is. He's matched —and sometimes surpassed—by Rooney, who's rarely been better. All are aided by the nonstop clever (and adult for its time) dialogue by playwright Arthur Carter, his co-adapter Blake Edwards and producer Jed Harris.

"Although *Operation Mad Ball* is a 'little' picture compared to many that I have appeared in," opines Jack, "it remains one of the most memorable to me personally.

"First, I think it was an outstanding comedy— one of the best I have ever been in. It was fresh material, it had an excellent cast, and it was directed with complete understanding, style and verve by Quine.

"It was an extremely happy company, and we all loved what we were doing. This helped create an energy that I think enhanced the film greatly.

"It also, of course, marks the debut of a man of immense talent, Ernie Kovacs. My relationship with Ernie, personally and professionally, will always remain very dear to me.

"Incidentally, *Mad Ball* was one of Billy Wilder's favorite movies at the time, and was extremely instrumental in his wanting me to do *Some Like It Hot*.

The Critics

Saturday Review:

Those reliable targets for humorous assault, our Army and Navy, have been set up again in *Don't Go Near the Water* and *Operation Mad Ball*. Both are in the tradition of wacky comedy, but of the two, *Operation Mad Ball* is clearly the more expert, perhaps because it keeps building remorselessly for laughs instead of taking substantial time-outs for romance, as the other does.

Jed Harris has put together a nice package. Ernie Kovacs was a first-rate choice, and an offbeat one, for the role of an embittered martinet and officer scourge of the medics. Arthur Carter's screenplay offers Kovacs the best opportunity he has had so far to display his talents.

The movie also has the easygoing skills of Jack Lemmon to recommend it, and the two of

83

them make a fine team. (It's) the funniest Hollywood job of the year.

Paul Ludwig in *Films in Review:*
An unusually good comedy cast enables this film's none too original script to engender a few laughs. For the most part, *Operation Mad Ball*'s comedy is zany, and even German prisoners of war are given "businesss" that is laugh-getting.

Jack Lemmon, TV comic Ernie Kovacs, Mickey Rooney, Kathryn Grant and the always reliable Arthur O'Connell, all help to give pace to the macabre humor of this comedy about GIs eager for a ball. George Duning's score contributes to the film's general verve.

America:
The significant thing about *Operation Mad Ball* is not so much that it is irreverent as that it is terribly funny. Generally speaking, the picture belongs in the honorable but almost extinct tradition of really inventive screwball farce.

Ernie Kovacs makes a most auspicious screen debut.

Mark Nichols in *Coronet:*
In this hilarious movie, Lemmon is at his nervous best as the conniving GI. TV comedian Kovacs makes a fine "heavy" and Mickey Rooney hammers home his antic part. Kathryn Grant is around for love interest.

Time:
Operation Mad Ball is a routine regimental farce, but fast and snafurious. In his first movie role, comic Kovacs is approximately terrific, the funniest new funnyface that has been seen on screen in years. His sneeringly ingratiating personality has all the morbid fascination of a mentholated cigar.

John McCarten in *The New Yorker:*
Operation Mad Ball whirls along, neatly and quickly developing some funny ideas. As the hero of the piece, Jack Lemmon shows a nice gift for portraying the ingenious low man on the military totem pole.

Watching Mr. Lemmon and Mr. Kovacs run through a few reels together, I reflected fleetingly on the likes of Edmund Lowe and Victor McLaglen and Karl Dane and George K. Arthur, who played Marine and Army braves after the First World War, and reached the conclusion that movies have made a couple strides in the right direction.

With Kort Falkenberg (left), William Leslie and Roger Smith.

Cowboy

A Columbia Picture (1958)

The Production Staff

Producer: Julian Blaustein. *Director:* Delmer Daves. *Screenplay:* Edmund H. North. *Based on the Novel* My Reminiscences as a Cowboy *by* Frank Harris. *Cinematographer:* Charles Lawton, Jr. *Editor:* Al Clark. *Music:* George Duning. *Scoring:* Morris Stoloff. *Orchestrations:* Arthur Morton. *Titles:* Saul Bass. *Art Director:* Cary Odell. *Set Decorators:* William Kiernan *and* James M. Crowe.

A Phoenix Production. A Columbia Pictures Release. Running Time: 92 minutes. In color.

Decca Records soundtrack album: DL 8684.

The Cast

Tom Reece: Glenn Ford. *Frank Harris:* Jack Lemmon. *Maria Vidal:* Anna Kashfi. *Doc Bender:* Brian Donlevy. *Charlie:* Dick York. *Paul Curtis:* Richard Jaeckel. *Mike Adams:* James Westerfield.

Original ad for *Cowboy.*

With Anna Kashfi.

Joe Capper: King Donovan. *Mr. Fowler:* Vaughn Taylor.

The Movie

Cowboy—Lemmon's second dramatic screen appearance and his one and only western—stands as a model saddle-soap saga and a refreshing refurbishment of the genre.

It's a western with no villains, no bandits, no rustlers and no mortgage-bound heroines. Its title tells all: It's a no-nonsense look at the American cowboy.

"It's also the first cowboy picture to be called *Cowboy*," reports Jack. "Which is funny when you think of all the thousands of westerns that have been made."

With *Cowboy*, director Delmer Daves has turned out a work of rugged honesty, visual beauty and stubborn individuality. The film works on every level and in every department; its ingredients jell so well that the finished product is like an artless ballad that might be shared around a campfire.

Authenticity fairly oozes from Edmund H. North's adaptation of Frank Harris's autobiographical series of pulp-like sketches, *My Reminiscences as a Cowboy*, with the first third of the script being devoted to careful character exposition and development and the remaining two-thirds to a depiction of life on the trail.

Lemmon plays author Harris in the film—a young Chicago hotel clerk and a tenderfoot yearning to be a cowboy. He befriends a successful cattleman (Glenn Ford, in a strong characterization), lending Ford money for a poker game with the promise of partnership coming in return.

Ford, essentially a private person and a loner, doesn't cotton to the idea of a partnership and is bent on making life on the already-rugged trail more miserable than usual for Lemmon.

Life on the trail teaches Lemmon that only the cattle count, not the men who die along the way. It also teaches patience and understanding—to both men.

In the end, the two men roar back to Chicago—a little trailworn, a lot wiser and eager for their next partnership.

"You don't know what suffering is," says Jack, "if you're not used to a saddle and have to stay on one all day. I bled.

"We shot the script in sequence, which means that I was on a horse six or seven hours a day for over a month. I had to learn to ride for the film and, eventually, learned during the course of the filming.

With Glenn Ford (left), Brian Donlevy and Richard Jaeckel.

"This worked out okay because, in the story, I play a guy who's misguided and trying to be tough. The character has never been on a horse before and has to bluff his way.

"So throughout the filming, I progressed along with the character. By the time we finished, I was thinking of buying a horse!"

Even Lemmon's inexperience as a horseman provided the film with authentitcity, somehow working in smoothly with George Duning's wonderful score of vital frontier ballads and Charles Lawton, Jr.'s exquisite photography.

Cowboy stands as one of the most interesting and important westerns ever made. It should be revived every year.

The Critics

Arthur Knight in *Saturday Review:*
Jack Lemmon and Glenn Ford work splendidly together as the novice and his trail-wise mentor, George Duning has created a beautiful score out of frontier ballads, and Charles Lawton, Jr.'s color cameras capture the spirit of the film in images that are strong, dynamic, vigorously handsome, never simply picturesque.

Above all, it is a film that shows cowboys at their proper job, neither romancing the ranchowner's daughter nor shooting it out at the O.K. Corral.

Variety:
Jack Lemmon gives a performance that broadens his range greatly, completely convincing as he matures from comical young tenderfoot into a man and a trail boss.

Philip T. Hartung in *The Commonweal:*
It isn't every day that a western is made specially for adults. Such a film is *Cowboy*, which is as stark as its title. Edmund H. North based his script on Frank Harris's *My Reminiscences as a Cowboy* and made no attempt to prettify the plot or themes.

With Glenn Ford.

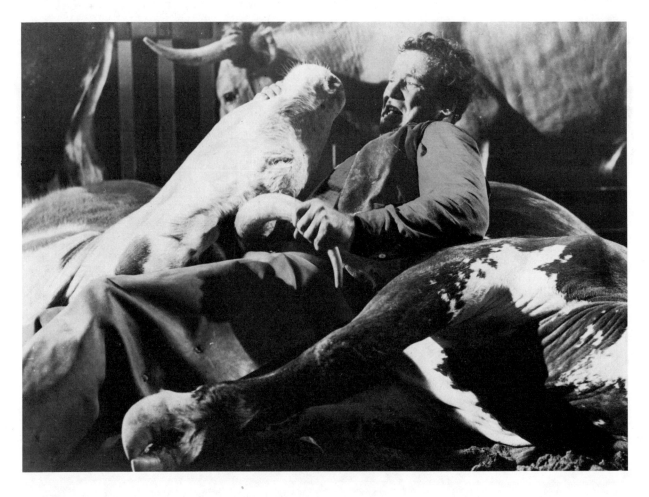

All of *Cowboy* is determined to take the poetic and bookish quality out of life on the range. While producer Julie Blaustein has given (the film) a handsome production in Technicolor and director Delmer Daves has spared no effort to show that men can be crueller than animals, the picture manages to have many poetic passages in spite of its theme.

Newsweek:
Once or twice in a decade, a motion picture comes along which is destined to be hailed as a moviemaking milestone. The label, "milestone," is a little too impressive for the present film, but it could certainly be called, say, a furlong post.

Cowboy—totally villainless and as uncontrived as its title—shuns the beaten paths of movie westerns simply by staying on the beaten paths of the real West.

Time:
(The movie) describes with an engaging mixture of saddlesore truth and reach-for-leather fiction what a cowboy's life was like in the Old West, and how an Easterner learned to live it.

Albert Turner in *Films in Review:*
Cowboy has a few artificial plot gimmicks and practically all of its action arises naturally out of the habits and customs which constituted life on the trail.

An unusually good cast is well directed by Delmer Daves. Glenn Ford actually comes to life in some of his scenes as the cattleman who pays, by taking on a partner, for his gambling losses in Chicago. Jack Lemmon will surprise you as the tenderfoot partner who learns how brutalizing life on the trail can be.

Moira Walsh in *America:*
I rather think the film's self-consciously different portrait of a cowboy is as naively romantic and remote from actuality as the conventional stereotype. But the picture itself, decked out elaborately and tastefully in Technicolor, is off the beaten cowpaths and is great fun to watch.

With Kim Novak.

Bell, Book and Candle

A Columbia Picture (1958)

The Production Staff

Producer: Julian Blaustein. *Director:* Richard Quine. *Screenplay:* Daniel Taradash. *Based on the play of the same title by* John Van Druten. *Cinematographer:* James Wong Howe. *Editor:* Charles Nelson. *Music:* George Duning. *Art Director:* Cary Odell. *Set Decorator:* Louis Diage. *Color Effects:* Eliot Elisofon.

A Phoenix Production. A Columbia Pictures Release. Running Time: 103 minutes. In color.

Colpix Records soundtrack album: CP 502.

The Cast

Sheperd Henderson: James Stewart. *Gillian Holroyd:* Kim Novak. *Nicky Holroyd:* Jack Lemmon. *Sidney Redlitch:* Ernie Kovacs. *Mrs. DePass:* Hermione Gingold. *Queenie:* Elsa Lanchester. *Merle Kittridge:* Janice Rule. *Henderson's Partner:* Howard McNear.

The Movie

Lemmon is most discreet about those movies of his which he dislikes "because there's more than one person that goes into the making of a motion picture."

Original ad for *Bell, Book and Candle.*

With Elsa Lanchester (left) and Kim Novak.

But he is willing to admit that Richard Quine's film version of John Van Druten's play, *Bell, Book and Candle,* is one movie from which he "never derived much pleasure."

It's easy to understand why. His role in the film is the smallest, the least important and the least challenging part he's ever played and especially seems pale after the meaty bits he did in the immediately preceding *Operation Mad Ball* and *Cowboy.*

Also, it's the only time in his career that Lemmon has been relegated to "co-starring" status.

And there's also the tough scene-stealing competition with which he had to contend—Ernie Kovacs, Elsa Lanchester and Hermione Gingold.

Of Lanchester and Gingold, who are marvelous in the movie, Jack says: "With those two old girls, you have to watch your step. They're great scene stealers, and both are hysterically funny."

The film itself is only so-so, despite its physical beauty (James Wong Howe's photography is an absolute ripper), technical competence and grand cast. Or perhaps it's all these things which accentuate the overall weakness of the plot.

It's a fragile, whifty to-do—never serious, never very funny—which likens love to witchcraft.

Director Quine's execution of it, at least till half-way, is able to overcome the slightness of it all. Quine establishes his style from the very first shot, stressing super-cinematics (Howe's camerawork and George Duning's lilting but obtrusive score), overplotting and characterization.

It's a bewitching style which serves the material well for a while and then becomes as thin as the storyline itself.

In this go-round, Lemmon plays a member of a family of New York witches, which includes Kim Novak (his sister) and Elsa Lanchester (his aunt). Plus a cat named Pyewacket.

Novak meets James Stewart on the eve of his marriage to Janice Rule, her former college rival, and immediately proceeds to break up the relationship. Via her powers, Novak makes Stewart fall in love with her.

She becomes nervous when brother Lemmon teams up with witch specialist Ernie Kovacs to work on a book for publisher Stewart, and ultimately tells Stewart about her kinship to witchcraft.

They break up but, because of the spell, Stewart is still smitten with her. So he seeks out Hermione Gingold, as another witch, to break Novak's spell on him.

Pyewacket and Lanchester, however, also get into the act, working their special voodoo which leaves Novak free of her witch's powers and unites her again with Stewart.

The Critics

Arthur Knight in *Saturday Review:*

In adapting it, Daniel Taradash has managed to retain both the polish and the comedy, even though its edges are often blunted by his stars, James Stewart and Kim Novak.

Nevertheless, the film's gay and captivating supporting cast—Jack Lemmon, Ernie Kovacs,

Hermione Gingold, Elsa Lanchester—amply convey the supernatural humors that Mr. Van Druten had envisioned.

Henry Hart in *Films in Review:*
Rarely has so much cinematic talent been expended so successfully on so little. Indeed, *Bell, Book and Candle* is so entertaining the superior filmmaking that went into it could be easily overlooked.

The fragility of the play has survived translation to the screen. In fact, the play has been enhanced—by some of the best practitioners of the cinematic magic art that producer Julian Blaustein could hire.

Scriptwriter Daniel Taradash has preserved John Van Druten's wit as well as his cynicism. Art director Cary Odell and set decorator Louis Diage have greatly abetted plausibility. All of which is effectively photographed by James Wong Howe with special colors effects by Eliot Elisofon.

Miss Novak's usual lifelessness is an asset in this film, and director Richard Quine got an effective performance out of her. Only Jack Lemmon, as a warlock (male witch), is inadequately used.

Time:
John Van Druten's comedy about contemporary witches cast enough of a spell on theatergoers to give it a six-month run on Broadway. But somewhere between Broadway and Hollywood, the broomstick broke down.

The part is almost perfectly written for Kim Novak. The script quickly announces that as a witch she is not supposed to blush, cry or indeed have very much of an expression at all. James Stewart stumbles around most of the time with a vaguely blissful expression—rather like a comic-strip character who has just been socked by Popeye. Fortunately, the supporting cast is unusually strong.

Newsweek:
Hollywood has done it again. If there is one thing the movie industry will always be famous for, it's tampering with preconceived notions.

Now, in *Bell, Book and Candle*, Hollywood has glamorized the witch. What Broadway started, Hollywood has polished off with the most blinding polish imaginable.

The exorcise receives an extra fillip in the appearances of a manic trio of comic characters named Ernie Kovacs, Elsa Lanchester and Hermione Gingold.

Jack Lemmon is also on hand as a wise-cracking warlock, but he is outclassed by the scene-stealing competition.

As for the stars of the piece, Miss Novak, for all her bewitching powers, plays her usual unearthly self; and Jimmy Stewart, of course, *always* plays Jimmy Stewart.

With Elsa Lanchester (left), Kim Novak, Ernie Kovacs and James Stewart.

With Joe E. Brown.

Some Like It Hot

A United Artists Picture (1959)

The Production Staff

Producer: Billy Wilder. *Director:* Billy Wilder. *Screenplay:* Billy Wilder *and* I. A. L. Diamond. *Suggested by a story by* R. Thorton *and* M. Logan. *Cinematographer:* Charles Lang, Jr. *Editor:* Arthur Schmidt. *Music:* Adolph Deutsch. *Song Supervisor:* Matty Malneck. *Art Director:* Ted Haworth. *Set Decorator:* Edward G. Boyle. *Choreographer:* Wally Green.

An Ashton Production. A Mirsch Company Presentation. A United Artists Release. Running Time: 120 minutes. In black-and-white.

United Artists Records soundtrack album: UAS 5030.

The Cast

Sugar Kowalczyk: Marilyn Monroe. *Joe/Josephine:* Tony Curtis. *Jerry/Daphne:* Jack Lemmon. *Spats:* George Raft. *Osgood Fielding III:* Joe E. Brown. *Mulligan:* Pat O'Brien. *Sweet Sue:* Joan Shawlee. *Little Bonaparte:* Nehemiah Persoff.

Original ad for *Some Like It Hot.*

Toothpick Charlie: George Stone. *Beinstock:* Dave Barry. *Poliakoff:* Billy Gray.

The Musical Numbers

"Runnin' Wild"   Marilyn Monroe
"Down Among the Sheltering Palms"
    Sweet Sue's Society Syncopators
"By the Beautiful Sea"
    Sweet Sue's Society Syncopators
"I Wanna Be Loved by You"   Marilyn Monroe
"I'm Through With Love"   Marilyn Monroe

The Movie

Billy Wilder's *Some Like It Hot* seems like such a perfect screen comedy that it's nearly impossible to envision it in any other way, shape or form. It's that situation where the right script, the right director and the right cast came together at the right time.

It defies duplication. And yet, *Some Like It Hot* came close to being a different movie. For one thing, it came close to being made without Jack Lemmon.

Wilder, having seen and enjoyed Lemmon

With Tony Curtis.

in Quine's *Operation Mad Ball,* sat down with his writing buddy, I. A. L. Diamond, and penned the Jerry/Daphne role especially for Lemmon.

Tony Curtis was already set for the other musician role in the film.

Mitzi Gaynor was being pursued for the Sugar role when it occurred to Wilder and Diamond that their cast would lack one really strong marquee name. So they decided to rewrite Jerry/Daphne for Frank Sinatra, certainly a superstar.

The situation was reversed, however, when Marilyn Monroe expressed a desire to play Sugar. With their superstar lead signed up, Wilder and Diamond served Lemmon his meaty, raw-slab-

With Marilyn Monroe and director Billy Wilder.

of-a-part which the actor immediately tore into, making it his very own and clearly illustrating what bravado is all about.

Set in 1929 Chicago, *Some Like It Hot* comically chronicles the adventures of a couple of musicians (Lemmon and Curtis) who witness a gangland killing on St. Valentine's Day and, in an attempt to save their own skin, join an all-girl orchestra, Sweet Sue's Society Syncopators.

The troupe, luckily, is heading to Miami Beach for an engagement at the swank Seminole Ritz, where trouble strikes all over the place.

It seems Curtis is smitten with the band's lovelorn singer (Monroe), while Lemmon is being pursued by a rich, decaying playboy (Joe E. Brown). What's worse, the gang and its leader (George Raft) are attending a convention (Friends of the Italian Opera) at the Ritz. Amen.

Everything turns out fine, however: Curtis gets Monroe, Brown gets Lemmon, and the movie drives home the message that "nobody's perfect."

"You know what the highest scene is in the picture?" asks Jack. "The engagement scene. When I first read those two pages of dialogue, I told myself, 'This is it!'

"And Billy is so great at giving you bits of business to help with your staging. When that scene was written, I couldn't think of anything to do while delivering my lines.

"Billy suggested that since I had just been dancing the fandango with Joe E. Brown, it would be natural for me to come home playing maracas. The idea pumped energy into my action and gave the entire scene flavor.

"Actually, *Some Like It Hot* is one long series of clichés, older than putting a lampshade on your head and pretending you're a guy dressed as a dame.

"Billy made two hours unforgettable by inventing stuff, all of which had been done; only he made you forget obviousness after obviousness.

"And he did it on a plane that, while it's a naughty picture, it isn't a dirty or vulgar picture.

"As for Marilyn, she was a good light comedienne, unique. She wasn't that enormously talented, but her gift was knowing how to use the special kind of talent she possessed to great advantage.

With Billy Gray (left) and Tony Curtis.

With Sweet Sue's Society Syncopators.

97

Rehearsing with director Billy Wilder.

"I found that I couldn't really get to know what was inside her, despite a good working relationship. She would put up a glass window, and never let anyone in.

"Anyone looking at her in retrospect could see that she was never really happy, never really fulfilled, never able to live with being M-A-R-I-L-Y-N M-O-N-R-O-E."

The Academy of Motion Picture Arts and Sciences nominated Lemmon for his first Best Actor award in 1959 but ultimately awarded the prize to Charlton Heston for *Ben Hur*.

The other nominees were James Stewart *(Anatomy of a Murder)*, Laurence Harvey *(Room at the Top)* and Paul Muni *(The Last Angry Man)*.

For his role of Daphne in *Some Like It Hot*, Lemmon imitated some of the Auntie Mame-type behavior of his mother, using her sense of humor, madcap ways and unexpected eccentricities to good advantage.

The Critics

The New Yorker:

Some Like It Hot is a jolly, carefree enterprise in which some old phrenetic nonsense of Mack Sennett is restored to the screen.

The result of a scriptural collaboration between Billy Wilder and I. A. L. Diamond, the picture brings back the madcap days of the Twenties, depending for the most part on the sort of transvestite comedy that has made such a durable commodity of *Charley's Aunt*.

The actors assembled for the project are an

With Tony Curtis.

98

With Tony Curtis (left) and set visitor Maurice Chevalier.

estimable lot, and among them none is more effective than Jack Lemmon, portraying the frightened bass player.

Newsweek:

It is a joy to see that old pro, producer-director Billy Wilder, putting low comedy back in the movies where it belongs. *Some Like It Hot* is a wacky sex farce which is also a satire on old gangster movies and Mack Sennett comedies.

Female impersonation, a risky business, is handled here to good effect because it is treated with taste. Lemmon, an accomplished comedian, gets more laughs than Curtis, although Curtis has more to do (he wins Marilyn). As for Miss Monroe, she is, as usual, an extremely effective female impersonator herself.

Time:

Marilyn Monroe's first picture in nearly two years is a double-barreled period piece: It not only parodies the freewheeling, gangster-ridden

Twenties, but it recalls the pie-throwing farce of cinema's infant days.

Lipsticked, mascaraed and tilting at a precarious angle, actor Lemmon digs out most of the laughs in the script. As for Marilyn, she's been trimmer, slimmer and sexier in earlier pictures.

A. H. Weiler in *The New York Times:*
Mr. Wilder, abetted by such proficient operatives

With Marilyn Monroe (center) and
Beverly Wills.

as Marilyn Monroe, Tony Curtis and Jack Lemmon, surprisingly has developed a completely unbelievable plot into a broad farce in which authentically comic action vies with snappy and sophisticated dialogue.

Ellen Fitzpatrick in *Films in Review*:
I suppose Billy Wilder is entitled to a farce now and then but I personally wish he'd stick to ironical and satiric comedy. He's not at home in a burlesque show, which is all *Some Like It Hot* is.

(It's) a spoof of the 1920s, but much of the spoofing is heavy-handed and much of it is in poor taste.

Tony Curtis and Jack Lemmon are quite good as the impecunious musicians who dress up as girls and join an all-girl band to escape the gangsters who know they witnessed a gangland massacre. In fact, *Some Like It Hot* works largely because of Curtis and Lemmon. And (because of) Billy Wilder's filmmaking know-how. Which should be put to better use.

100

With Doris Day and Sam the Lobster.

It Happened to Jane

(also known as **Twinkle and Shine**)

A Columbia Picture (1959)

The Production Staff

Producer: Richard Quine. *Executive Producer:* Martin Melcher. *Director:* Richard Quine. *Screenplay:* Norman Katkov. *From a story by* Max Wilk *and* Norman Katkov. *Cinematographer:* Charles Lawton, Jr. *Editor:* Charles Nelson. *Music:* George Duning. *Scoring:* Morris Stoloff. *Orchestrations:* Arthur Morton. *Song "It Happened to Jane":* Joe Lubin *and* I. J. Roth. *Sung by* Doris Day. *Song "Twinkle and Shine":* Dunham. *Sung by* Doris Day. *Song "Be Prepared":* Fred Karger *(music) and* Richard Quine *(lyrics). Sung by* Doris Day *and* Jack Lemmon. *Art Director:* Cary Odell. *Set Decorator:* Louis Diage.

An Arwin Production. A Columbia Pictures Release. Running Time: 98 minutes. Edited Version: 90 minutes. In color.

The Cast

Jane Osgood: Doris Day. *George Denham:* Jack Lemmon. *Harry Foster Malone:* Ernie Kovacs. *Larry Hall:* Steve Forrest. *Billy Osgood:* Teddy Rooney. *Uncle Otis:* Russ Brown. *Betty Osgood:*

Original ad for *It Happened to Jane.*

a warm, wonderful movie that's stacked with joy for the whole family!

It's even bigger than its wonderful cast! Its small-town warmth has a big-city bounce. Its story has a special bigness of its own. In fact—it's bigger than all of us!

COLUMBIA PICTURES presents

DORIS DAY · **JACK LEMMON** · **ERNIE KOVACS**

IT COULD HAVE HAPPENED TO YOU— OR YOU—OR YOU... but—

IT HAPPENED TO JANE

co-starring STEVE FORREST · Screenplay by NORMAN KATKOV · From a story by MAX WILK and NORMAN KATKOV
Produced and Directed by RICHARD QUINE · Executive Producer—MARTIN MELCHER · AN ARWIN PRODUCTION

━━━ GUEST STARS ━━━
BILL CULLEN · DAVE GARROWAY · STEVE McCORMICK · JAYNE MEADOWS · GARRY MOORE · HENRY MORGAN
BOB PAIGE · BETSY PALMER

EASTMAN COLOR

Gina Gillespie. *Crawford Sloan:* Walter Greaza. *Homer Bean:* Parker Fennelly. *Matilda Runyon:* Mary Wickes. *Selwyn Harris:* Casey Adams. *Aaron Caldwell:* John Cecil Holm.

The Movie

From the same mold as some of Frank Capra's brighter and more cynical comedies, *It Happened to Jane* employs the standard ingredient of Americana to charming effect.

Its cast is attractive and comically alert, its New England settings beautiful and soothing, and its story concurrently improbable and possible. All have been molded by director Richard Quine into an entirely pleasing entertainment.

Among its chief treats is its storyline. Doris Day plays an attractive widow who lives with her two children in small-town Cape Ann, Maine, and raises lobsters for a living. Her beau here is Lemmon, playing an energetic young attorney.

Anyway, one fine day, a trainload of dead lobsters is returned to Day on Old 97. It seems that railroad neglect is responsible for the damage—both to the lobsters and to Day's reputation as a reliable businesswoman.

So Day and Lemmon decide to take railroad magnate Harry Foster Malone (the late Ernie Kovacs, doing an impersonation of Columbia's Harry Cohn) to court.

Malone fights back, however, and before too long, the entire country is witnessing and cheering an outright battle.

But everything ends happily. Day gets her

With Doris Day.

lobster business back intact. Lemmon gets Day (his proposal to her makes for the film's most enchanting scene). And the evil railroad magnate gets his comeuppance.

It Happened to Jane should have succeeded.

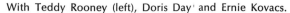

With Teddy Rooney (left), Doris Day and Ernie Kovacs.

With Doris Day, singing *Be Prepared*.

But it didn't—neither critically nor financially. A year later, Columbia tried circulating an edited version of the movie, under the title *Twinkle and Shine*, but that was equally unsuccessful.

Still, Lemmon has some affection for the movie.

"It could have been a good light comedy," he says, "but it somehow got screwed up in the editing. The footage Dick Quine shot wasn't bad, but the finished film didn't measure up."

The Critics

Time:

Comic (Ernie) Kovacs turns a fairly unfunny script into a funny farce—the success story of a self-made monster.

"Why," asks a small boy, gazing up into the homely face of Kovacs, "are you so mean?" Smugly lipping his expensive Havana, Kovacs

simpers like a contented cigaroyle at one of the nicest things anybody has ever said to "the meanest man in the world."

Philip T. Hartung in *The Commonweal:*

It Happened to Jane sees life as a comedy. Very funny it is, thanks mainly to producer-director Richard Quine, who has put together a nice slice of modern Americana that belongs to the school of *Mr. Deeds Goes to Town* and *Mr. Smith Goes to Washington*.

Although the picture is a little too long, it is a delight from beginning to end. Norman Katkov's pleasant script, the nice-color photography of New England and environs, and the good-humored cast, contribute to the fun.

Without preaching, Richard Quine uses Doris Day's bubbling enthusiasm and Ernie Kovacs' growling meanness to great effect. *It Happened to Jane* should happen more often.

104

With Doris Day and Steve Forrest.

Variety:

Up to a point, this is a funny comedy. The point is reached about three-quarters of the way through when the film abruptly changes form and loses momentum, never to regain it. Jack Lemmon plays with a broad style that's effective, retaining just a remote connection with enough reality so his romantic attachment to Miss Day is acceptable.

Effinham Fownes in *Films in Review:*

It Happened to Jane could be much more than an exceptionally well-directed vehicle for Doris Day, Jack Lemmon and Ernie Kovacs. It could be the harbinger of a return to the Capra-like comedy-cum-Americana of the Thirties.

It Happened to Jane is set in a small Maine town—how little non-Western U.S. scenery has been in U.S. movies lately; it is light-hearted, well-intentioned and for most of 100 minutes, amusing. In short, it's entertainment.

From (his) talented comedians, and able supporting players, director Richard Quine has gotten performances that make this picture a really exceptional comedy. He knows how to make people laugh.

This is the best comedy, and the best picture, he has directed to date. It is funnier, and much pleasanter, than his *Operation Mad Ball.*

With Doris Day (left), Teddy Rooney and Gina Gillespie.

With Shirley MacLaine.

The Apartment

A United Artists Picture (1960)

The Production Staff

Producer: Billy Wilder. *Director:* Billy Wilder. *Original Screenplay:* Billy Wilder *and* I. A. L. Diamond. *Cinematographer:* Joseph LaShelle. *Editor:* Daniel Mandell. *Music:* Adolph Deutsch. *Art Director:* Alexander Trauner. *Set Decorator:* Edward G. Boyle. *Associate Producers:* Doane Harrison *and* I. A. L. Diamond.

A Mirisch Company Presentation. A United Artists Release. Running Time: 125 minutes. In black-and-white and Panavision.

United Artists Records soundtrack album: UAS 6105.

The Cast

C. C. "Bud" Baxter: Jack Lemmon. *Fran Kubelik:* Shirley MacLaine. *J. D. Sheldrake:* Fred MacMurray. *Dr. Dreyfuss:* Jack Kruschen. *Mr. Dobisch:*

Original ad for *The Apartment.*

With Shirley MacLaine.

With Shirley MacLaine (left) and Edie Adams.

Ray Walston. *Miss Olsen:* Edie Adams. *Margie MacDougall:* Hope Holiday. *Sylvia:* Joan Shawlee. *Mr. Kirkeby:* David Lewis. *Karl Matuschka:* Johnny Seven. *Mrs. Dreyfuss:* Naomi Stevens.

The Movie

So impressed with Lemmon's walloping performance in his *Some Like It Hot,* producer-writer-director Billy Wilder made himself (and Lemmon) a verbal promise: "Someday I'm going to write a role expressly for you."

The Apartment—a gem that grows and glows in retrospect—is Billy Wilder's "tribute to Jack Lemmon," a performer whom Wilder considers "the most consummate and appealing actor since the early Charlie Chaplin."

Lemmon returned the favor with an ingratiating, totally naturalistic performance as an ambitious office worker who mixes sex with success by lending out his apartment to various superiors. "Getting Ahead" is the name of the game.

Not the most savory role admittedly; however, there's a school of thought which holds that Lemmon could make even a slimy sort like Sammy Glick likeable and affecting. *The Apartment* proves it.

Lemmon's warmth for the Wilder classic hasn't subsided over the years.

"I always felt," says Jack, "that Billy Wilder grew a rose in a garbage pail with this one. He was throwing cold water right in our faces about the terribly false premises with which most of our society lives.

"He challenged our priorities and the way we rationalize our behavior on the grounds of getting ahead in America—at a time when it wasn't fashionable to challenge these things. He gave us a pretty good jolt, and it hasn't been done a hell of a lot better since then."

A commentary on the buttoned-down mind and the aspirin age, the bittersweet plot of *The Apartment* casts Lemmon as an IBM operator

actor will bring. Like the nose-spray bit. That was my idea.

"I was working out the cold scene in my dressing room without props, when suddenly I saw my hand clench on the line: 'But I *won't!*' I thought: *'This is it!'*

"I went to the prop department, because there's no point talking to the director; you have to try it first. I experimented with all kinds of sprays, punching different size holes in them, and finally used skim milk so the spray would show.

"The first time I tried it on the set, the spray went low and splurted all over the script girl. Everybody broke up. MacMurray played it exactly the way he did in the picture—just glanced at the spray, and then went on. Billy liked it, so we kept it in.

With Shirley MacLaine and Fred MacMurray.

determined to better himself—employment-wise —by lending his apartment to his bosses for their romances.

Meanwhile, he harbors a love for one of the building's elevator operators (Shirley MacLaine), a sweet-but-downtrodden thing who's the current romance of the company's biggest boss (Fred MacMurray).

The telling film walked away with five Academy Awards, including Best Picture of 1960. For their candid observations of life, both Lemmon and MacLaine received nominations in the Best Actor and Best Actress categories.

Lemmon lost out to Burt Lancaster for the latter's performance in *Elmer Gantry*. The year's other nominees were Trevor Howard *(Sons and Lovers)*, Laurence Olivier *(The Entertainer)* and Spencer Tracy *(Inherit the Wind)*.

"Billy's scripts," offers Jack "are amazing. They take a year and a half to write and everything's in them; but everything. He *sees* scripts. A script is to be played, not read. So if something doesn't look right in action, he'll change it.

"That's the great thing about Billy; he doesn't impose himself before he sees what the

"Do you remember the scene where I come home and just start cleaning up the place, like I'd done it every night for years before? The average director would be afraid to play it like Billy did. They'd say, 'Let's get on to more action.'

"But Billy let the scene run two or three minutes. And he invented ideas as he went along. Like when I was cooking, having me straining the spaghetti through a tennis racquet. When he told me that, I knew it was just the right touch.

"In Billy's scripts, I can't remember a single word that would have made me feel uncomfort-

109

With Shirley MacLaine.

able. With a good script, you get impressed with what they *didn't* write.

"When Billy told me the story of *The Apartment,* I signed before it was even written. I'd have signed if he'd said he was going to do the phone book."

The Critics

Time:

The Apartment is the funniest movie made in Hollywood since *Some Like It Hot.* What's more, it was made by the same two men, producer-director Billy Wilder and writer I. A. L. Diamond, and features the same deft comedian, Jack Lemmon. There the similarities end.

The Apartment is a comedy of men's-room humors and water-cooler politics that now and then among the belly laughs says something serious and sad about the struggle for success, about what it often does to a man, and about the horribly small world of big business.

Director Wilder handles his players superbly. He holds an amazingly tight rein on actress Mac-Laine, which gives her performance a solidity she seldom achieves. Yet it is actor Lemmon, surely the most sensitive and tasteful young comedian now at work in Hollywood, who really cuts the mustard and carries the show.

Newsweek:

Not to beat around the bush, *The Apartment* is a very funny movie that can take a place among the finest comedies Hollywood has turned out.

With director Billy Wilder.

Lemmon, who is required to be on camera most of the time, manages to stay funny throughout, and his timing is superb. In spite of a Best Supporting Actor award, Lemmon has been "arriving" for about six years. He can now be pronounced definitely here.

Bosley Crowther in *The New York Times:*
A gleeful and sentimental film . . . kept on the side of taste and humor by the grand performance of Jack Lemmon, who takes precedence as our top comedian by virtue of this film.

And there's a splendid performance by Shirley MacLaine. Mr. Wilder's direction is ingenious and sure, tumbling with wit.

Saturday Review:
In Hollywood there is no one more expert at putting a movie together than Billy Wilder. Last year, with *Some Like It Hot,* he knew exactly what he was doing, and he made the funniest picture of the year, meanwhile showing Jack Lemmon how to be a first-rate clown.

He used Jack Lemmon again in *The Apartment,* but Mr. Lemmon isn't so successful this time around, and the trouble may be due to some odd story confusions.

Mr. Wilder demonstrates his accustomed skill, Miss MacLaine and Mr. Lemmon work their heads off to achieve "sincere" portrayals, and Edie Adams and Fred MacMurray give accomplished performances in subordinate roles. Too bad the story isn't up to them.

John McCarten in *The New Yorker:*
Let's take a look at *The Apartment.* The hero of the thing is a youthful organization man, and a difficult one to sympathize with as he goes about turning his home into a kind of brothel for his bosses, and Mr. Wilder and Mr. Diamond, in putting together their script, seem never to have decided whether his conduct is prankish or deplorable.

Jack Lemmon plays the lead, and he is supported by Shirley MacLaine and Fred MacMurray. Miss MacLaine and Mr. MacMurray use Mr. Lemmon's place as a pad until our hero decides he's in love with Miss MacLaine. These are gray-flannel beatniks, all right. If you want them, take them.

With Cantinflas.

Pepe

A Columbia Picture (1960)

The Production Staff

Producer: George Sidney. *Associate Producer:* Jacques Gelman. *Director:* George Sidney. *Screenplay:* Claude Binyon *and* Dorothy Kingsley. *Adaptation:* Leonard Spigelgass *and* Sonya Levien. *Based on a play by* L. Bush-Fekete. *Cinematographer:* Joe MacDonald. *Editors:* Viola Lawrence *and* Al Clark. *Art Director:* Ted Haworth. *Set Decorator:* William Kiernan. *Choreographers:* Eugene Loring *and* Alex Romero. *Music:* Johnny Green. *Songs:* André Previn, Hans Wittstatt, Dory Previn, Augustin Lara *and* Maria Lara.

A George Sidney Production. A Columbia Pictures Release. Original Running Time: 195 minutes (plus intermission). Edited down to varying lengths during its initial theatrical engagements. In color and CinemaScope.

Colpix Records soundtrack album: SCP 507.

The Cast

Pepe: Cantinflas. *Suzie Murphy:* Shirley Jones. *Ted Holt:* Dan Dailey. *Auctioneer:* Carlos Mon-

Original ad for *Pepe.*

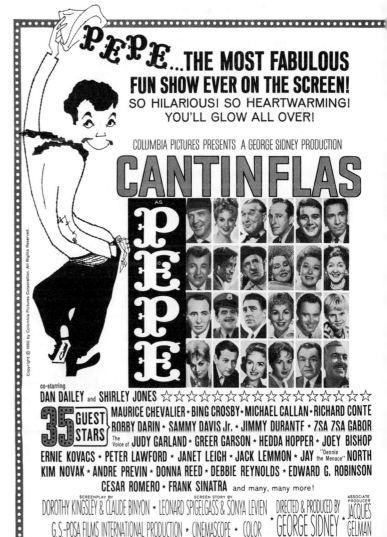

Kroll caricature shows *Pepe* star Cantinflas surrounded by the film's guest stars: (foreground) Greer Garson, Edward G. Robinson, Debbie Reynolds, Sammy Davis, Jr., Ernie Kovacs, Kim Novak, Bing Crosby, Shirley Jones, Dan Daily and (background) Caesar Romero, Jack Lemmon, Jimmy Durante, Hedda Hopper and Maurice Chevalier.

talban. *Guest Stars:* Jack Lemmon, Kim Novak,, Janet Leigh, Frank Sinatra, Dean Martin, Edward G. Robinson and others.

The Musical Numbers

"That's How It Went, All Right"	Bobby Darin
"The Rumble"	André Previn
danced by Michael Callan, Matt Mattox and Shirley Jones	
"The Far Away Part of Town"	Judy Garland
danced by Dan Dailey and Shirley Jones	
"Hooray for Hollywood"	Sammy Davis, Jr.
Fantasy Dance	danced by Cantinflas
and Debbie Reynolds	
"Mimi" and "September Song"	
	Maurice Chevalier
"Mimi" (reprise)	Maurice Chevalier,
Cantinflas, Dan Dailey	
"Pepe"	Shirley Jones
"Lovely Day"	Shirley Jones

The Movie

George Sidney's *Pepe* is what you might call an assembly-line blockbuster—a three-hour variety show wherein another movie star pops up every five minutes, does his specialty and then disappears.

Thirty-five guest stars appear here, all somehow related to Columbia—either as contract player (e.g., Kim Novak) or TV series star (Donna Reed) or headliner in a recent Columbia effort (Frank Sinatra, who had just worked on *The Devil at Four O'Clock).*

In the case of Jack Lemmon, he was a contract player and, as such, was recruited for a day-or-two's worth of work. For his bit here, Lemmon wisely elected to hide behind the Daphne make-up he wore in *Some Like It Hot.*

Actually, everything considered, *Pepe* isn't all that bad; in fact, it has built-in appeal for film freaks. Its plot has to do with a little Mexican (Cantinflas) who, while in search of his pet horse in Hollywood, elbows with Chevalier, Durante, Novak and, of course, Lemmon.

The sequence involving Jack is a fairly amusing "mistaken identity" to-do, with Lemmon changing in and out of his Daphne costume and confusing the daylights out of little Cantinflas.

The most memorable portion of the film, however, is devoted to a dance (a la *West Side Story)* called "The Rumble," played on-screen by its composer, André Previn, and danced by Shirley Jones, Michael Callan and Matt Mattox. It's highly sensual and almost out-of-place in this family film.

Another nice added touch is Shirley Jones's sprightly rendition of the obligatory title song—which, in this case, is wonderful and works out fine.

The Critics

Life:

As bright and happy a bauble as Hollywood has ever packaged, *Pepe* is full of fun and frolic. The movie, done by George Sidney, has dancing,

Jack Lemmon recreating "Daphne," his character from *Some Like It Hot*.

singing, teasing tricks, stormy love between men and women, deep understanding love between a man and a white horse.

Above all it has Cantinflas, the world-famous pantomimist and Latin America's greatest movie star. He plays Pepe, a poetic peon who travels to Hollywood to be near Don Juan, his beloved horse who had been sold into Yanqui captivity.

He has many amazing adventures, plays a genie in a tequila jug and meets film stars. Some, like Dan Dailey and Shirley Jones, play roles in the movie. Others, like Debbie Reynolds, Frank Sinatra, Dean Martin, Jack Lemmon, Kim Novak, Jimmy Durante, Maurice Chevalier, Tony Curtis and Janet Leigh play their own amusing selves.

New York *Daily News:*

A joyous production crammed with delightful entertainment . . . studded with many of the most glittering names in filmland and adorned with beauty, exquisite color, popular vocalizing and expert dancing.

Los Angeles Herald Express:

A cornucopia of entertainment. Warm, clean, one of the most enjoyable pictures of the year. An Academy Award calibre performance by Cantinflas. Rich in imagination, sentiment, beauty and laughter.

The Wackiest Ship in the Army

A Columbia Picture (1961)

The Production Staff

Producer: Fred Kohlmar. *Director:* Richard Murphy. *Screenplay:* Richard Murphy. *Adaptation:* Herbert Margolis *and* William Raynor. *Based on a story by* Herbert Carlson. *Cinematographer:* Charles Lawton, Jr. *Editor:* Charles Nelson. *Music:* George Duning.

A Fred Kohlmar Production. A Columbia Pictures Release. Running Time: 99 minutes. In color and CinemaScope.

The Cast

Lt. Rip Crandall: Jack Lemmon. *Ensign Tommy Hanson:* Ricky Nelson. *Commander Vandewater:* John Lund. *Patterson:* Chips Rafferty. *Capt. McClung:* Tom Tully. *Maggie:* Patricia Driscoll. *Josh:* Joby Baker. *Sparks:* Warren Berlinger. *Chief Mate MacCarthy:* Mike Kellin. *Lt. Foster:* Richard Anderson. *Johnson:* Alvy Moore.

The Movie

For his starring role in this uneventful little military comedy-drama, Lemmon resurrected the Navy cap he wore to good advantage in *Mister Roberts*. Both the hat and the role fit perfectly.
The film itself, however, was out of place at

Original ad for *The Wackiest Ship in the Army.*

this point in his career. A long-delayed property, which had been on Lemmon's agenda since 1959, *The Wackiest Ship in the Army* came on the heels of a comparatively more sophisticated *The Apartment.*

The comparison was jarring; *The Wackiest Ship in the Army* came as a distinct disappointment and, in a sense, as a step downward.

The movie isn't necessarily *bad*, although it is rather lopsided, falling uncertainly somewhere between comedy and drama. It's simply depressingly minor and might have been better placed a bit earlier in Lemmon's career.

The role Lemmon plays in the movie was made for him; it's the movie itself and the timing of its release that were off.

As Lieutenant Rip Crandall, a peacetime sailing expert, Lemmon is tricked by his superior (John Lund) into accepting command of an aged sailing vessel called the *Echo* and transporting a coast watcher to an enemy-held Pacific island.

Trouble is, the *Echo*'s crew—except for the second in command (Ricky Nelson)—is in worse shape than the vessel. So Lemmon is forced to teach the men fundamentals, resorting to the most elementary instructing techniques.

With Ricky Nelson.

With Ricky Nelson.

117

With Patricia Driscoll.

The ship sets out on its mission, successfully delivers the scout and ultimately is overtaken by the Japanese.

At this point, the film abruptly abandons comedy for suspense, with the crew suddenly and triumphantly counterattacking the Japanese and returning from its mission with information that eventually leads to the defeat of the enemy in the Bismarck Sea battle.

The film's most memorable scene has Lemmon and Nelson teaming up in a candid song-and-piano duet.

The Critics

Bosley Crowther in *The New York Times:*
What could be more outrageous, more offensive to naval dignity, more inviting to the conventions of what is known as service farce? Nothing.

At least, that's the spirit in which Richard Murphy has assumed the responsibility of writing and directing this gaudy color film.

We've got to hand it to him and to his rambunctious crew: They do all the things that are expected to provoke recognitional guffaws—bump their heads, make wry faces at the coffee and get knocked overboard by the boom. Let's say it comes out a zany and occasionally amusing farce. Yachtsmen should find it good fun.

Stanley Kauffmann in *The New Republic:*
But the film has Jack Lemmon in the leading role; and for myself, I would go to see anything of his just to watch him in motion. He plays here with his usual neat, precisely timed Airedale energy, with a nervous intelligent concentration

With Ricky Nelson and Patricia Driscoll.

Ricky Nelson (singing).

behind even the prattiest of his falls that lifts the part out of comic mechanics into mild virtuosity.

Lemmon's material differs widely in quality from film to film, but he has so far prevented anything he has done from sinking into tedium.

We can hope that his next film will be more than the rescue operation that this is.

Saturday Review:
Despite the genial script, taut direction and some rousing action for a finale, however, the picture rests its major weight upon the constantly shrug-

ging shoulders of Jack Lemmon. Nor is this confidence misplaced.

Lemmon has become the perfect personification of all harassed mankind, the outranked, outnumbered, outmanipulated little fellow with sound instinct and bad judgment. Whether in gray flannels or khaki, he is one who is always taken advantage of. And if in the end he emerges triumphant, it is because of a basic decency rather than superior cunning or sudden inspiration.

It is a character equally valid for farce or

With John Lund (left) and Ricky Nelson (saluting).

119

drama—and in *The Wackiest Ship in the Army*, Mr. Lemmon suggests that he has sure instincts for both. Thanks largely to his work, the film is more than just another service comedy.

The Commonweal:

Much less pretentious and much more funny is *The Wackiest Ship in the Army*, one of those zany service comedies that make audiences laugh and laugh without making them realize that the subject matter is often quite serious. Jack Lemman plays (his role) with just the right combination of spit-and-polish, surprise, and determination not always to be the underdog.

Time:

Comedian Jack Lemmon is a thirty-five-year-old graduate of Andover and Harvard who somehow manages to look like The Eternal Milkman. He has nice average features, stands a nice average height, speaks average American.

His comedy is the comedy of the hopelessly normal, mass-produced Joe in the hopelessly insane, mass-produced situation. In six years and fourteen pictures, he has become a master of the vacant take, the eloquent huh, the rare, precise grimace, the sudden, desperate, Lemmoniacal burst of energy.

With Lemmon on deck, *The Wackiest Ship in the Army* will surely enjoy favorable gales of laughter; without him it would undoubtedly have sunk without a glug in the neighborhood "tanks". . . . Writer-director Richard Murphy keeps his *Ship* scudding along as though it had somewhere to go, and he keeps the screen jumping with excitement.

Above all, he keeps his camera trained on funnyman Lemmon, who saves scene after scene with a pert piece of mugging, and hits the jackpot on any payoff line. Recipe for Hollywood producers: Tee-hee is better with Lemmon.

With John Lund (center) and Ricky Nelson.

Andre Gille (left) and Pascal Lamorisse.

Stowaway in the Sky (Le Voyage en Ballon)

A Lopert Picture (1962)

The Production Staff

Producers: Filmsonor S.A. *and* Films Montsouris. *Director:* Albert Lamorisse. *Original Screenplay:* Albert Lamorisse. *English Narration:* S. N. Behrman. *Cinematographers:* Maurice Fellous *and* Guy Tabary. *Aerial Cinematographer:* Albert Lamorisse. *Music:* Jean Prodomides.

Produced by Filmsonor S.A. and Films Montsouris. A Jalem Production Presentation. Distributed by Lopert Pictures Corporation. Running Time: 82 minutes. In color and Helivision.

Philips soundtrack album: PHS 600-029.

The Cast

Narrator: Jack Lemmon. *Tou-Tou:* Maurice Baquet. *Grandfather:* André Gille. *Pascal:* Pascal Lamorisse.

The Movie

Recipe for *Stowaway in the Sky* (follow carefully): First, take *Around the World in 80 Days.* Subtract the Jules Verne derring-do. Next, reduce the all-star cast to three players. Confine location photography. Finally, add a delightfully Gallic score, rich with concertinas.

Original ad for *Stowaway in the Sky.*

ALBERT LAMORISSE the creator of the prize winning film THE RED BALLOON brings you a film of breathless adventure and matchless beauty...to delight the young at heart

STOWAWAY IN THE SKY

with MAURICE BAQUET ANDRE GILLE and PASCAL LAMORISSE
narrated by
JACK LEMMON
narration written by
S. N. BEHRMAN
written and directed by
ALBERT LAMORISSE filmed in HELIVISION
prints by TECHNICOLOR.
PRODUCED BY FILMSONOR S.A. AND FILMS MONSOURIS
A JALEM PRODUCTIONS PRESENTATION
DISTRIBUTED BY LOPERT PICTURES CORPORATION

Pascal Lamorisse (left) and Andre Gille.

If you crave a decidedly American flavor, add some narration by Jack Lemmon, for good measure.

The result is a fancy-free little caprice which uses the faintest of storylines as an excuse for traveling around sunny, picturesque France. Not the most exciting of films, but certainly charming, harmless and diverting.

Lemmon himself imported this little French bon-bon, under the auspices of his Jalem company, and rather than have the film subtitled or dubbed, he had S. N. Behrman write voice-over narration which Lemmon speaks off-screen.

Released in France under the title *Le Voyage en Ballon* (roughly, "The Balloon Voyage"), the movie was concocted by Albert Lamorisse, who scored in the mid-Fifties with *The Red Balloon*, now consideed a classic of sorts.

Set around the turn of the century, *Stowaway in the Sky* has to do with an old man (André Gille) who invents a sixty-foot balloon and goes aloft in it to tour France.

As it turns out, the man's grandson, Pascal (Pascal Lamorisse), stowed away in the basket, and together they leisurely float through the air, enjoying breathtaking views of the Arc de Triomphe, Eiffel Tower, Etoile, Place de la Concorde and Notre Dame. All this is accompanied by a marvelous score by Jean Prodomides.

The Behrman narration—and there's plenty of it—was written from the point of view of the little boy and is read by Lemmon with wide-eyed, boyish enthusiasm, full of underlined words and exclamation points.

Très gentil!—as the boy in the film would say.

The Critics

Louis Corbin in *Films in Review:*
To photograph this pleasant eighty-minute aerial travelogue over Paris and other parts of France, Albert Lamorisse, who made *The Red Balloon* five years ago, took a camera up in a helicopter. He photographed not only the world below, but also a real balloon in actual flight.

In the balloon, for story purposes, a grandfather and his little grandson are capering through the atmosphere.

Some of the individual shots—Paris, Strasbourg Cathedral, Koenigsberg Castle, a stag hunt, the Loire Valley, Chateau Chenonceaux, storks in flight—have visual beauty and interest, but Lamorisse's storyline is fatuous.

A narration spoken by Jack Lemmon, who financed this Lamorisse effort, was partially written by S. N. Behrman, and it's so bad Behrman should refund whatever he was paid.

Instead of having enabled Lamorisse to photograph a real balloon, rather than a toy one as before, Lemmon would have been better advised to have induced Lamorisse to go down to the Camargue again. There are quite a few good stories for filmmakers in that little-known section of France, where Lamorisse made an excellent film in 1954 called *White Mane*.

New York Post:
Absolutely fascinating. There's adventure, excitement, emotion, comic invention and the very beauty of it all overwhelms you.

New York Herald Tribune:
Oh, by all means, this is a movie to see. One with sensuous beauty, cunningly timed excitements, suspense and comedy. One of those beauties that come along maybe once in a decade, if we're lucky.

123

With Kim Novak.

The Notorious Landlady

A Columbia Picture (1962)

The Production Staff

Producer: Fred Kohlmar. *Director:* Richard Quine. *Screenplay:* Blake Edwards *and* Larry Gelbart. *Based on the story* The Notorious Tenant *by* Margery Sharp. *Cinematographer:* Arthur Arling. *Editor:* Charles Nelson. *Music:* George Duning. *Chase Music:* Gilbert and Sullivan. *Song* "A Foggy Day in London Town": George Gershwin *(music) and* Ira Gershwin *(lyrics). Orchestrations:* Arthur Morton. *Art Director:* Cary Odell. *Set Decorator:* Louis Diage. *Gowns:* Kim Novak. Executed by Elizabeth Courtney.

A Fred Kohlmar–Richard Quine Production. A Columbia Pictures Release. Running Time: 127 minutes. In black-and-white.

The Cast

Carlye Hardwicke: Kim Novak. *William Gridley:* Jack Lemmon. *Franklyn Ambruster:* Fred Astaire. *Inspector Oliphant:* Lionel Jeffries. *Mrs. Dunhill:* Estelle Winwood. *Mrs. Brown:* Philippa Bevans. *Miles Hardwicke:* Maxwell Reed. *Dillings:* Rich-

Original ad for *The Notorious Landlady.*

Columbia Pictures presents A Fred Kohlmar-Richard Quine Production

kim NOVAK ♡ JACK LEMMON ♡ fRED ASTAIRE

DiD SHE... OR DiD SHE? The Police think she murder her husband!!... the roomer thinks it's just a rumor!!!! Don't **you** miss the uproarious goings-on!!!

THE **Notorious Landlady**

with LIONEL JEFFRIES ESTELLE WINWOOD

Screenplay by LARRY GELBART and BLAKE EDWARDS • BASED ON A STORY BY MARG

PRODUCED by fred KOHLMAR • DiRECTED BY RICHARD

ard Peel. *Little Boy:* Scott Davey. *Stranger:* Henry Daniell. *Old Man in Wheelchair Wearing a Derby:* John Uhler Lemmon II.

The Movie

The incredibly well-thought-out, suspenseful and witty screenplay for Richard Quine's *The Notorious Landlady*—penned by Larry Gelbart and Blake Edwads—qualifies the 1962 movie for the short list of gems in the comedy-mystery genre.

Using foggy London as its backdrop (actually the movie was made in Hollywod, U.S.A.) and a short story by Britisher Margery Sharp as its inspiration, the Gelbart–Edwards script takes devilish pride in mixing a silky blonde murder suspect and a lovesick American diplomat with dark alleys, poison kidney pies, lethal matrons and, naturally, a desperate chase along the rocky cliffs of Penzance.

It's a marvelous bit of storytelling—full of smart dialogue and some sly tingles-with-a-wink —as well as a successful combination of comedy and suspense, thanks largely to director Quine's knowledge of the camera and timing and his way with the ingratiating star players.

The film marks Lemmon's fifth (and best)

With John Uhler Lemmon II.

125

With Kim Novak

cinematic association with Quine, his third (and last) with Kim Novak and his first (and only) with Fred Astaire.

He plays William Gridley, an American diplomat newly arrived from Saudi Arabia to serve at our embassy in London.

The deft suspense and literate humor start cascading when Gridley happens to rent a flat from beautiful but mysterious Carlye Hardwicke (Novak), also an American and the chief suspect of Scotland Yard in the murder of her missing British husband.

Gridley is persuaded by his boss, Franklyn Ambruster (Astaire), and Inspector Oliphant (Lionel Jeffries) of the Scotland Yard to do some inside detecting. Grudgingly, he agrees.

Chaos strikes when the "dead" husband (Maxwell Reed) suddenly turns up one night and is promptly murdered by Carlye. With the long-missing body now in tow as evidence, the authorities arrest Carlye and place her on trial.

The tragic situation—a mere matter of self-defense—is cleared up unexpectedly by Mrs. Brown (Philippa Bevans), the paid companion of Carlye's elderly neighbor, Mrs. Dunhill (Estelle Winwood). Mrs. Brown tells the court that she witnessed the shooting herself through an adjacent window.

She's lying, of course; Mrs. Dunhill really witnessed it all, including a heated conversation between Carlye and her husband about a certain pawn ticket. She told everything to Mrs. Brown.

The valuable pawn ticket, never mentioned during the trial, is Mrs. Brown's assurance of a life of luxury. She wants it, even if it means blackmail and murder—the blackmail of Carlye and the murder of Mrs. Dunhill.

With Fred Astaire.

126

With Kim Novak.

The film ends with everyone—Mrs. Brown, Carlye, Gridley, Ambruster and Oliphant—making a mad dash to Penzance where Mrs. Dunhill is holed up now in a rest home. A hilariously choreographed chase follows, good prevails and the mystery is solved.

Lemmon, who has a personal reservation or two about *The Notorious Landlady* because "it becomes bogged down in rapid plot changes that are difficult to follow," is nevertheless in fine comedic form here. Perhaps at his peak.

About the time of the release of *The Notorious Landlady*, author-critic Richard Schickel wrote in his book, *The Stars*, that Lemmon would one day be looked upon as "the comic quintessence of his age."

This "quintessence" is evident throughout *The Notorious Landlady*.

The Critics

Bosley Crowther in *The New York Times:*
Credit a clever little story by Britain's nutmeggy Margery Sharp and a comic performance by Jack Lemmon that twinkles like a mischief-maker's eyes for the unexpected good humor that generally crackles and pops in Columbia's *The Notorious Landlady*, which came to the Criterion and the Beekman yesterday.

With Kim Novak.

With Kim Novak.

From the moment he pokes the doorbell of Kim Novak's London house and starts sparkling brightly on the instant she guardedly answers it, he is full of delightful little gurgles, witty sayings, appreciative looks and all the amusing indications of a healthy fellow falling—well, in love. Well worth the viewing.

Edith Oliver in *The New Yorker*:
I don't see how anyone could help but have a good time watching Jack Lemmon, Fred Astaire and a British actor named Lionel Jeffries, all of them expert comedians, in a comedy of murder called *The Notorious Landlady*.

(The film) gives Mr. Lemmon many chances to go scampering up and down stairs and in and out of hiding, and to look alternately innocent and desperate. His clowning, while it is not quite vintage Lemmon, being a bit too broad and obvious, is awfully good clowning all the same.

Together with its makers, (the actors) have fashioned a picture that is entertaining and exciting, often simultaneously, and that ends with a wildly funny chase ... along the cliffs of Penzance ... while a uniformed band on a bandstand plays gems from Gilbert and Sullivan, hitting "Come, Friends, Who Plough the Sea" at just the right moment. The background music, by the way, is delightful all the way through.

Ernest Schier in the *Philadelphia Bulletin*:
Taking a tip from British comedy, *The Notorious Landlady* slides from sophistication to farce, with only a silky bump between the two styles, to tell a fresh and merry tale of a young diplomat who falls in love with a damsel suspected of murder.

Giving every indication that he has payed respectful attention to the British method of making comedies, director Richard Quine puts his stars through their paces with as much appreciation of the dialogue as for the visual laughs.

Lemmon and Astaire are bonny fellows for this stylish sort of romp—call it a romantic suspense comedy—and even Miss Novak, usually such a glum girl, positively shines with cheerfulness.

Relaxing on the set with director Richard Quine.

With Lee Remick.

Days of Wine and Roses

A Warner Bros. Picture (1962)

The Production Staff

Producer: Martin Manulis. *Director:* Blake Edwards. *Screenplay:* J. P. Miller. *Based on the TV play of the same title by J. P. Miller. Cinematographer:* Phil Lathrop. *Editor:* Patrick McCormack. *Music:* Henry Mancini. *Song* "Days of Wine and Roses": Henry Mancini *(music)* and Johnny Mercer *(lyrics). Art Director:* Joseph Wright. *Set Decorator:* George James Hopkins.

A Martin Manulis Production. A Warner Bros. Release. Running Time: 117 minutes. In black-and-white.

The Cast

Joe Clay: Jack Lemmon, *Kirsten Arneson:* Lee Remick. *Jim Hungerford:* Jack Klugman. *Arneson:* Charles Bickford. *Debbie:* Debbie Megowan. *"Red" Leland:* Alan Hewitt. *Trayner:* Jack Albertson. *Dottie:* Maxine Stuart. *Liquor Store Proprietor:* Ken Lynch.

Original ad for *Days of Wine and Roses.*

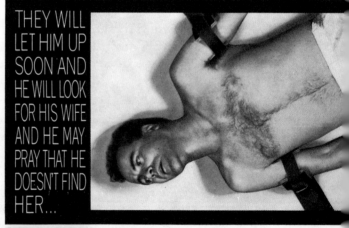

THEY WILL LET HIM UP SOON AND HE WILL LOOK FOR HIS WIFE AND HE MAY PRAY THAT HE DOESN'T FIND HER...

JACK Lemmon and **Lee Remic**

"DaYS OF WIne anD ROSES" IT IS DIFFERENT. IT IS D MOST OF ALL, IN ITS OWN FYING WAY, IT IS A LOVE

Co-Starring CHARLES BICKFORD JACK KLUGMAN · A MARTIN MANULIS Production · Music by HENRY MANCINI · Written by JP MILLER · Produced by MARTIN MANULIS · Directed by BLAKE EDWARDS · WARNE

130

The Movie

> "They are not long,
> the days of wine and roses:
> Out of a misty dream
> Our path emerges for a while,
> then closes,
> Within a dream."
>
> —*Ernest Dowson*

With Lee Remick.

This thought is echoed—handsomely and hauntingly—in Blake Edwards' *Days of Wine and Roses,* a razor-sharp observation of good times and alcoholism, bad times and alcoholism and the lingering memories of both.

Essentially, J. P. Miller's incisive screenplay is about the eternal triangle—man, woman and booze; a close study of a couple brought together by social drinking and ultimately separated and destroyed by it.

Miller based his script on his successful teleplay which was produced during the late Fifties with Cliff Robertson and Piper Laurie in the leading roles. (Robertson, incidentally, was the second husband of Cynthia Stone, Lemmon's first wife.)

The script's traditional narrative—directed by Edwards unobtrusively as a character study—details the meeting of Joe Clay (Lemmon), an ambitious public relations man, and Kirsten Arneson (Lee Remick), a sweet young secretary with a passion for chocolate.

Joe is both hard-working and hard-drinking—two qualities which neither impress nor amuse Kirsten. With charm going for him, however, he wins her over, courts her, eventually introduces her to social drinking (via chocolate-y Brandy Alexanders) and marries her.

Life is fine—at first—until Joe's drunkenness ruins his professional life, and Kirsten's private drinking damages their personal lives.

Joe, always aware of his drinking problem, seeks out help as an alcoholic; Kirsten refuses to accept the word "alcoholic," passing her drinking off instead as a lack of discipline.

Joe manages to cure himself and start afresh. Kirsten, however, confesses to her dependence on booze, adding that she loves it, can't bear the idea of going without it and, what's more, that she resents Joe's soberness.

Their marriage—their relationship—is over now. As Kirsten walks away, in the direction of a neon sign blinking the word, B-A-R, Joe sees his path closing within a dream.

"Few films have ever been closer to me," says Jack of *Days of Wine and Roses*. "There wasn't any of this 'I saw your last picture and liked it' which is what I get with my comedies. People *really* cared.

"You can now definitely-probably understand what I mean when I say that a movie that sells tickets and is successful by somebody else's standards can upset you after you've done a picture like this one. People in this business can't understand that, for some reason."

Jack's performance under Blake Edwards' direction brought him another Academy Award nomination as Best Actor. Lee Remick was also nominated as Best Actress.

Gregory Peck, however, walked off with the award for his role in *To Kill a Mockingbird*. Also nominated were Burt Lancaster (*Birdman of Alcatraz*), Marcello Mastroianni (*Divorce, Italian Style*) and Peter O'Toole (*Lawrence of Arabia*).

The Critics

The New Yorker:

My admiration for Mr. Lemmon, in particular, is so unbounded that I not only recommend the picture to others, no matter what their status as drinkers may be, but intend to see it again myself, hoping against hope that it won't encourage me to renounce the evils of alcohol forever.

. . . in the course of this sorry journey Mr. Lemmon is dazzling, funny, anguished, indignant, rueful, affectionate, cruel, or what you will—we share, watching his performance, the actor's joy in having reached the point in his career where he feels, and is right to feel, that there's nothing he can't bring off.

Saturday Review:

Lemmon has said that it took more than two years to get the production off the ground. It was worth waiting for—for Lemmon, and the film's potential audience as well. *Days of Wine and Roses* forces recognition of the fact that Lemmon is not only one of our ablest young

With Lee Remic

With Jack Klugman.

comedians, but actually one of the screen's finest all-around performers.

His naturalistic style of acting is so highly developed (here) that when at one point he walks blindly into a pane of glass, the entire audience winces with him. His scene in the greenhouse, careening crazily from table to table, smashing flowerpots with hands that have become animal claws, writhing on the ground in an agony of feral frustration—this is something beyond performance.

But the main thing is his eyes—bright and snapping in the early sequences, dark and dead at the film's finale.

There is one astonishing moment when, in huge close-up, we can actually see the light of consciousness flicker out of them.

Newsweek:

The film fails. The fault is not an upbeat ending, but the mere fact that there is any ending at all. The ending, here, denatures the alcoholism, turning it from grim reality to dramatic device, and escaping from the battle of the bottle into a more manageable battle of the sexes.

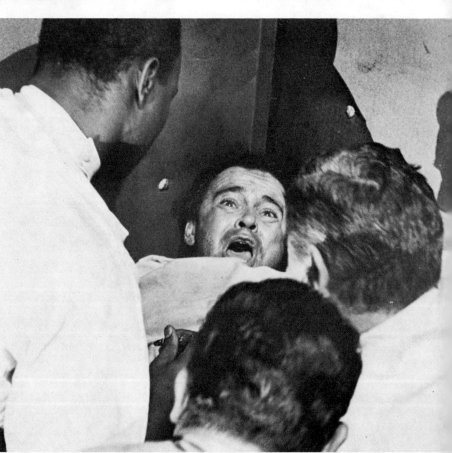

Jack Lemmon.

What makes the film especially regrettable is that, until the strategic error at the end, it is an entirely honest effort, credibly written, intelligently directed and brilliantly acted. Neither Lemmon nor Remick has ever been this good before.

Time:

Strong stuff, and director Blake Edwards does not dilute it. The liquor flows hard and fast, and the scenes in the alcoholic ward are guaranteed to take the lining off a sober spectator's complacency.

Then and always, Lemmon's portrayal is easily the most intelligent, intense and complex performance so far accomplished by an actor who started out as a light comedian but apparently can do darn near anything he pleases in front of a camera and most of the time do it better than any American cinemactor of his generation.

In this picture Lemmon starts out as a gay and gloriously funny falling-down drunk; as his disease progresses he regresses with a ferocity few players could express and fewer still control; at the climax he is simply a maniacal infant screaming for his bottle.

With Shirley MacLaine.

Irma La Douce

A United Artists Picture (1963)

The Production Staff

Producer: Billy Wilder. *Director:* Billy Wilder. *Screenplay:* Billy Wilder *and* I. A. L. Diamond. *Based on the musical play of the same title by* Marguerite Monnot, Alexander Breffort, Julian More, David Heneker *and* Monty Norman. *Cinematographer:* Joseph LaShelle. *Editor:* Daniel Mandell. *Music:* André Previn *and* Marguerite Monnot. *Choreographer:* Wally Green. *Art Director:* Alexander Trauner. *Set Decorator:* Edward Boyle.

A Phalanx Production. A Mirisch Company–Edward L. Alperson Presentation. A United Artists Release. Running Time: 146 minutes. In color and Panavision.

United Artists Records soundtrack album: UAS 5109.

The Cast

Nestor: Jack Lemmon. *Irma La Douce:* Shirley MacLaine. *Moustache:* Lou Jacobi. *Lefevre:* Herschel Bernardi. *Hippolyte:* Bruce Yarnell. *Lolita:* Hope Holiday. *Amazon Annie:* Joan Shawlee.

Original ad for *Irma La Douce.*

a story of passion, bloodshed, desire and death ...everything in fact, that makes life worth living

THE MIRISCH COMPANY AND EDWARD L. ALPERSON PRESENT

JACK LEMMON **SHIRLEY MacLAIN**

BILLY WILDER'S

IRMA LA DOUCE

PRODUCED AND DIRECTED BY BILLY WILDER SCREENPLAY BY BILLY WILDER AND I. A. L. DIAMOND ART DIRECTOR ALEXANDER TRAUNER

MUSIC SCORE BY ANDRE PREVIN

TECHNICOLOR® PANAVISION® PRESENTED IN ASSOCIATION WITH PHALANX PRODUCTIONS, INC. RELEASED THRU UNITED ARTISTS

Kiki: Grace Lee Whitney. *Suzette Wong:* Tura Santana. *Mimi the Mau Mau:* Harriet Young.

Narrator: Louis Jourdan.

The Movie

If a study were taken, it would probably be found that few stories in the literary and entertainment worlds have not been indebted to the zippy, jazzy, hard-boiled and sentimental world of the prostitute.

Billy Wilder's sprawling, colorful film version of the international stage hit, *Irma La Douce*, is not so much a tribute to that world as it is an overall tribute to the prostitute's place in the history of the arts.

Irma La Douce, while admittedly not a total artistic success, looms as the queen of the prostitute genre, by simple virtue of its size and scope, its opulence and color, its spirit and eye-winking fun and its immense popularity (it's grossed over twelve millions dollars to date).

With Lou Jacobi.

With Shirley MacLaine.

In adapting the original play with I. A. L. Diamond, Wilder shed his usual cynicism, taking the bright, breezy route to the story, rather than the this-is-a-rotten-but-funny-world approach.

Wilder's *Irma La Douce* is French in its setting, plot and moral atmosphere but intensely American in its style and feel and distinctly Hollywood in its look.

Romping against art director Alexander Trauner's color-laden recreation of Les Halles, a veritable Gallic Disneyland, are the very American Jack Lemmon and Shirley MacLaine, boyish and girlish, respectively, and therefore perfect contrasts to the storyline's essentially sordid goings-on.

With other, less wide-eyed players in the leading roles, it's doubtful that mass, general audiences would have readily accepted *Irma La Douce* in its day. But Lemmon and MacLaine are innocents—amoral not immoral, naughty but nice. Playful.

For the film, Wilder and Diamond relegated some of the play's original stage songs to the background as mood music, but nevertheless retained the speed and lilt of the musical. In fact, in retrospect, Wilder's songless version of *Irma* is so bouncy and feisty that it plays more like a musical than the original musical did.

The film opens with a clever pre-title introduction to "poule" (i.e., prostitute) Irma the Sweet (MacLaine), showing her various devious ways of conning "le grisbi" (extra money) out of her customers.

Enter Nestor Patou (Lemmon), a "flic" (cop) whose only other assignment was guarding a school playground, for which he was awarded a

medal of honor. Now, he's patrolling Les Halles, specifically Rue Casanova, MacLaine's turf.

Being a gung-ho sort, Lemmon raids the hotel out of which MacLaine and her colleagues work. Which is unfortunate because one of the girls' customers is his chief of police (Herschel Bernardi).

He's kicked off the police force but is taken in by MacLaine who wants him as her new "mec" (pimp). He agrees and, for a while, everything is fun and games and more fun.

It's inevitable that Lemmon, now in love with MacLaine, becomes hopelessly jealous of her customers. So with the help of bistro-owner Moustache (Lou Jacobi), he invents Lord X.

The idea is for Lord X to pay MacLaine 500 francs a week. In that way, she won't have to spend time with any other men. It's also Lemmon's plan to play Lord X himself. Which means MacLaine would be spending all her nights with him exclusively.

To finance this scheme, Lemmon borrows money from Jacobi and is forced to work days (while MacLaine's asleep) in the nearby vegetable market.

Between Lord X's gentle, generous ways and Lemmon's constant weariness, MacLaine becomes disillusioned and suspicious. She's certain that Lemmon is spending all his free time with other women, spending *her* money. So she convinces Lord X to take her back to England with him.

Now, Lemmon is jealous of Lord X and is forced to carry out a "crime passionel." He murders Lord X by tossing his clothes and umbrella into the Seine. He's promptly arrested.

Convinced by Jacobi that no one would ever believe his incredible story of multiple identity, Lemmon pleads guilty and is sentenced to fifteen years of hard labor.

When he hears that MacLaine is pregnant, Lemmon escapes from prison, "resurrects" Lord X to prove his innocence and marries the little mother-to-be.

At the wedding ceremony, an unexpected guest appears: Lord X! But, as Jacobi points out, "that's another story."

"The prostitute," says I. A. L. Diamond, "is one of the most pervasive figures in literature and has always held a peculiar fascination for writers and audiences.

"On screen, she is usually portrayed as a hard-boiled 'hostess,' or a tragic figure leaning against a lamppost. But the *poules* around Les Halles, whatever their personal problems, are a raucous bunch. And this is the spirit we have tried to capture on film."

The Critics

Bosley Crowther in *The New York Times:*
Who would have dreamed that Billy Wilder could make a bright and yet acceptable film out of the Gallic naughtiness and mischief of the stage show *Irma La Douce?*

Not I, for one, with all due deference to the eminent director's comic skill and his ability to handle raw material with deceptively silken gloves.

Well, surprise, surprise! He's gone and done it. He's made a brisk and bubbly film.

Whether acting the naive policeman or slyly impersonating a buck-toothed and one-eyed English peer, Mr. Lemmon is little short of brilliant—vigorous, incisive and deft. His magnificently keen and agile clowning is what really carries this film.

And he also contributes to the character a little genuine sentiment. A good bit of that is delivered by Shirley MacLaine. (She) too has a wondrously casual and candid air that sweeps indignation before it and leaves one sweetly enamored of her. Though the film is less hers than Mr. Lemmon's, she is cheerful, impudent and droll.

The New Yorker:
If anything attractive and amusing happens in the picture, it is because Jack Lemmon and Shirley MacLaine take over the proceedings and almost

With Shirley MacLaine and Bruce Yarnell.

With Shirley MacLaine.

With Shirley MacLaine.

With Shirley MacLaine.

quite comfortably in their costumes. Miss MacLaine is nice, but too wise to be innocent, which Irma must be to make her seamy story funny and convincing.

Lemmon, however, even without an accent, has never been better. He saves the Wilder reputation—and the picture with it. He is hilarious whether battling feebly with a hulking mec, being jammed into a girl-filled paddy wagon, or preparing to bed down with Irma.

He shyly clips newspapers over the blindless windows, then fumbles with his buttons, finally rips his shirt off, and gingerly edges into bed, looking about as cool and casual as a grounded flounder.

Hollis Alpert in *Saturday Review:*
Now and then the gags work, but often they don't, especially when the characters make feeble references to current Hollywood movies. Where the (stage) musical left much to the imagination, the movie makes everything heavily clear.

It should be said, by the way, that since both Lemmon and Miss MacLaine are skillful, amusing performers they bring considerable life to the movie.

But the script is another matter—too often unfunny, a laborious recapitulation of the original plot when it should have been deft and nonchalant, and spelled out to the point of boredom and, I fear, a certain vulgarity.

succeed in purging them of squalor. Their American faces and American voices betray Mr. Wilder's worst intentions; a couple of vivid and gifted comics, in a vehicle totally unsuited to them, manage to justify themselves and it by failing to embody their assigned characters.

Newsweek:
As the stars, Shirley MacLaine and Jack Lemmon are absurdly un-French, but both of them fit

142

With Carol Lynley.

Under the Yum-Yum Tree

A Columbia Picture (1963)

The Production Staff

Producer: Frederick Brisson. *Director:* David Swift. *Screenplay:* Lawrence Roman *and* David Swift. *Based on the play of the same title by* Lawrence Roman. *Cinematographer:* Joseph Biroc. *Editor:* Charles Nelson. *Music:* Frank DeVol. *Song* "Under the Yum-Yum Tree": Sammy Cahn *and* James Van Heusen. *Sung by* James Darren. *Choreographer:* Robert Tucker. *Production Designer:* Dale Hennesy. *Set Decorator:* William Kiernan.

A Sonnis-Swift Company Production. A Columbia Pictures Release. Running Time: 110 minutes. In color.

The Cast

Hogan: Jack Lemmon. *Robin:* Carol Lynley. *David:* Dean Jones. *Irene:* Edie Adams. *Dorkus:* Imogene Coca. *Murphy:* Paul Lynde. *Charles:*

Original ad for *Under the Yum-Yum Tree.*

Robert Lansing. *Tenants:* Asa Maynor, Pamela Curran *and* Jane Wald.

The Movie

David Swift's production of *Under the Yum-Yum Tree* was pretty much a victim of its time. By 1963, audiences (particularly critics) were starting to sour towards the Doris Day–Rock Hudson romps and towards sex comedies in general.

There were simply too many of them, with each one becoming bolder, more suggestive and increasingly vulgar. But they were *fun* and, for adults, harmless. Nevertheless, they came under attack and were, in actuality, criticized out of existence.

In its day, *Under the Yum-Yum Tree* was one of the boldest sex comedies, oozing with a smarmy smirkiness that bordered on irresponsible self-indulgence on the part of its makers.

A few years earlier, it probably would have been considered a trail blazer among slick sex comedies, but in 1963, in the midst of *Hud* and *Tom Jones* and *Lilies of the Field,* it was immediately written off as a foul horror and a low point in serious American filmmaking.

Coming on the heels of sexy *Irma La Douce,* the Swift comedy proved to be especially injurious to Lemmon's reputation among critics and blemished him in their eyes (a reaction which had sad, harmful effects on the critical reception of his next movie, the innocent and charming *Good Neighbor Sam).*

With Dean Jones and Carol Lynley.

Lemmon's old chum, Richard Quine, refused to direct the film and had to sacrifice a reported $100,000 to get out of the commitment.

"I just couldn't say, 'Jack, be a Peeping Tom,' " says Quine. "I couldn't say, Jack, be salacious.' "

And Lemmon himself isn't exactly enamored of the film, even though it is one of the prime reasons he made Top Male Box Office Star of 1964. He's called it, "a real crock."

Prejudices aside, however, *Under the Yum-Yum Tree* remains an entertainingly funny, com-

With Edie Adams (left), Carol Lynley, Paul Lynde, Imogene Coca and Dean Jones.

145

petently made and enthusiastically acted sex comedy and is worth seeing for its excellent cast alone. (Edie Adams, for example, excels in a barber shop bout with Lemmon and hasn't been as good since.)

Based on the Lawrence Roman stage success (which, incidentally, was written with Lemmon in mind but ultimately essayed by Gig Young), the plot deals with a premarital experiment between a college couple (Carol Lynley and Dean Jones).

They plan to live together platonically to test their "character compatibility." Lynley finds a charming apartment whose lecherous landlord (Lemmon) rents to young, attractive females only.

Since Lynley is young, attractive and female, Lemmon rents her the apartment, unaware that Jones will be on hand, too, constantly fouling up his planned seductions.

The remainder of the film has Lemmon rushing around with dizzying glee, desperately trying to dispose of Jones and have his way with Lynley.

Observing throughout on the sideline are his nosey housekeeper and envious custodian (Imogene Coca and Paul Lynde) and his former girlfriend (Adams), who happens to be Lynley's aunt.

The Critics

Brendan Gill in *The New Yorker:*

I can't tell you how *Under the Yum-Yum Tree* ends, because I didn't stay long enough to find out. Nevertheless, I stayed too long for my own good.

It's a disgusting comedy, in which we're supposed first to be titillated to hear young people speak of sleeping together and then to be reassured when they carry on and on and on about not quite doing so.

I admire Mr. Lemmon and I beg him to turn over a new leaf before it's too late.

With Edie Adams.

Time:

The only thing that matters is Jack Lemmon. Lemmon's lecher is hilarious—partly because Lemmon is a marvelously skillful comedian, partly because he looks like a boy scout playing Bluebeard. And in his satyr is a satire: A Pan in deadpan, a caricature of every young goat who can't say naaaaa.

Ellen Fitzpatrick in *Films in Review:*

I'm such a wholehearted admirer of Jack Lemmon that I suffered throughout this farce. Lemmon's forte is projecting the comic aspects of innocence amid the corrupt, not in mugging the farcical aspects of a corrupt man in the midst of innocence.

Coming on the heels of *Days of Wine and Roses* and *Irma La Douce,* the present film can do Lemmon's career real damage.

Lawrence Roman's stage play has been so grossly exaggerated that Lemmon's efforts to portray a lecherous landlord are doubly unbelievable.

Arthur Knight in *Saturday Review:*

Despite his indubitable proficiency, despite his ineffable charm, however, Jack Lemmon is unable to conceal completely the true scurrility of the character he plays—punching up each scene for forced farcical values is hardly a help.

Nevertheless, there is no question but that

Publicity shenanigans with Carol Lynley.

Lemmon carries the film, and carries it precisely in the direction that its authors, (Lawrence) Roman and David Swift, intended—as close to the border separating the risque from the downright lewd as they could possibly get without risking the Legion of Decency's "C" rating.

The fact that "nothing happened" makes it all the more unsavory.

With Dean Jones.

With Romy Schneider.

Good Neighbor Sam

A Columbia Picture (1964)

The Production Staff

Producer: David Swift. *Associate Producer:* Marvin Miller. *Director:* David Swift. *Screenplay:* James Fritzell, Everett Greenbaum *and* David Swift. *Based on the novel* Good Neighbor Sam *by* Jack Finney. *Cinematographer:* Burnett Guffey. *Editor:* Charles Nelson. *Music:* Frank DeVol. *Production Designer:* Dale Hennesy. *Set Decorator:* Ray Moyer.

A David Swift Production. A Columbia Pictures Release. Running Time: 130 minutes. In color.

The Cast

Sam Bissell: Jack Lemmon. *Janet Lagerlof:* Romy Schneider. *Minerva Bissell:* Dorothy Provine. *Howard Ebbets:* Michael Connors. *Simon Nurdlinger:* Edward G. Robinson. *Edna:* Linda Watkins. *Earl:* Robert Q. Lewis. *Reinhold Shiffner:* Louis Nye. *Prostitute:* Joyce Jameson. *Irene Krump:* Anne Seymour. *Jack Bailey:* Charles

Quote-oriented ad for *Good Neighbor Sam*.

148

With Junkmobile.

Lane. *Larry Boling:* Neil Hamilton. *Commercial Singers:* The Hi-Lo's.

The Movie

David Swift's *Good Neighbor Sam* revolves about two affably trivial little stories—(1) the efforts of an advertising man to retain his image as "a good, clean-living family man" in the eyes of his agency, and (2) his beautiful neighbor's attempts to claim her fifteen-million dollar inheritance.

When the two situations merge, the complications are hilariously involved, very Lubitsch-like in tone and merriment. Throughout, Lemmon is delightful, alternately befuddled and frantic—not unlike early Cary Grant (in *Mr. Blandings Builds His Dream House,* for example).

As the titular Sam Bissell, Lemmon works for Burke and Hare, an ad agency which elects to put him in charge of its most important account,

Nurdlinger's Dairy Company. Old Mr. Nurdlinger (Edward G. Robinson), it seems, has this hang-up about fidelity in marriage—and, well, Lemmon is the straightest, most happily married man in the company.

Meanwhile, back at home, Lemmon's wife (Dorothy Provine) is celebrating a reunion with her old college chum (Romy Schneider) who's back in town to claim her inheritance.

There's a snag in her grandfather's will, however: She gets the money only if she's living happily with her husband (Michael Connors). Unfortunately, Schneider and Connors are now separated and, what's more, deadly enemies.

Two cousins are out to get the money and have hired a private investigator (Louis Nye) to snoop around and prove Schneider's marriage dead.

For the time being, while everything is up in

149

With Romy Schneider (left) and
Dorothy Provine.

the air and uncertain, Schneider rents the house
next door to Lemmon and Provine and asks Lemmon to pose as her husband until she gets the
money. She offers her good neighbor Lemmon a
million dollars to carry out the masquerade. He
agrees.

With the snoopy private eye on hand constantly, Lemmon is forced to bed down nightly
in Schneider's house. Meanwhile, Connors pops
up and, in turn, is obliged to move in temporarily with Provine.

Making matters worse is Robinson, who has
come to believe that Schneider is Lemmon's
"little lady." He also feels that they're the perfect
couple to splash across billboards to sell his milk
products.

The agency carries out the assignment behind Lemmon's back, so as to surprise him. Soon,
Lemmon and Schneider—identified as "Mr. and
Mrs. Sam Bissell"—are posted on billboards
everywhere.

Schneider panics. What if her cousins should
see them? She's not supposed to be Mrs. Sam
Bissell. Desperately and hectically, Lemmon and
Schneider spend the night defacing every last
poster.

By daybreak, Lemmon is back with Provine,

150

Schneider is back with Connors and all are richer from the ordeal.

The Critics

Jack Thompson in the
New York Journal-American:

A hilarious farce—the kind that Irene Dunne and Katharine Hepburn used to do with Cary Grant—is back in the sparkling *Good Neighbor Sam*, at the Victoria, Fine Arts and Baronet Theaters.

This fast-moving, laugh-provoking film has the benefit of the presence of Jack Lemmon, the most expert farceur of our time, who is perfectly seconded by the luscious Romy Schneider. She is as skilled in comedy as Lemmon is and they make an exceptionally attractive team.

In spite of the length, the pace rarely slackens and director David Swift shows great flair for comic invention. It is nice to have a suave, zany comedy back again.

Cue:

Jack Lemmon, as clean-living Sam Bissell, is indeed a good neighbor. He comes bearing the gifts of laughter, enough to enable any theater showing this film to put up a "laughs guaranteed" sign.

Lemmon is at his comic best portraying a man happily married, but unhappily wedded to a dull advertising job and daily routine.

The screenplay is sharp, the direction by David Swift fast, although this is another case of not knowing when to quit. With tightening, it could have been so much better. But as is, this

comedy in color is a very welcome summer arrival.

Edith Oliver in *The New Yorker:*
That most fastidious actor and comedian Jack Lemmon makes his way through a clutter of gags and capers, some of them bright and amusing, some tiresome, in *Good Neighbor Sam.*

Through all of these shenanigans, Mr. Lemmon's clowning is, as usual, splendid. There are, heavens knows, dead stretches in the picture, which goes on for over two hours, but none when he is around. He can make any material seem fresh.

A. H. Weiler in *The New York Times:*
Lemmon does not let his fans down in giving a spirited performance full of proper mugging and candid delivery of a dialogue that draws laughs and sympathy. He is as natural as a man deeply in love with his wife, confused and hypnotized by the comely lass who has been thrust into his suddenly mixed-up life and shocked by the changes in his once-boring job.

With Dorothy Provine (left), Vicki Cos and Kym Karath.

Lemmon and company breathlessly toss gags from bedrooms to advertising offices with verve and vigor.

Dorothy Masters in the New York *Daily News:*
Whimsy and slapstick are ingeniously invested in laughing stock. The casting is astute, the players are in empathy and the musical theme is the best in years.

Moira Walsh in *America:*
I must admit I found this film a considerable improvement over most of its kind. Much of it was genuinely funny in a spontaneous creative way.

Besides, though this sounds like a contradiction of something already said, its values are frequently quite sound. For example, the film's indictment, both serious and satiric, of unprincipled advertising practices, comes through.

Also, the movie picks its way through the risque complications with care and precision, directing the audience's laughter toward the right things for the right reasons.

With Romy Schneider.

With Virna Lisi.

How to Murder Your Wife

A United Artists Picture (1965)

The Production Staff

Producer: George Axelrod. *Executive Producer:*
Gordon Carroll. *Director:* Richard Quine. *Original Screenplay:* George Axelrod. *Cinematographer:* Harry Stradling. *Editor:* David Wages. *Music:* Neal Hefti. *Production Designer:* Richard
Sylbert. *Choreographer:* Robert Sidney.

A Jalem Production. A United Artists Release.
Running Time: 108 minutes. In color.

United Artists Records film-score album: UAS
5119.

The Cast

Stanley Ford: Jack Lemmon. *Mrs. Ford:* Virna Lisi.
Charles: Terry-Thomas. *Harold Lampson:* Eddie
Mayehoff. *Edna Lampson:* Claire Trevor. *Judge
Blackstone:* Sidney Blackmer. *Tobey Rawlins:*
Max Showalter. *Dr. Bentley:* Jack Albertson. *District Attorney:* Alan Hewitt. *Harold's Secretary:*
Mary Wickes.

Original ad for *How To Murder Your
Wife.*

The Movie

Lemmon has referred to Richard Quine's *How to Murder Your Wife* as "an almost perfect comedy."

"Until the trial sequence, the film is brilliant," says Jack. "Then it seems to fall off a bit. It's one of my favorites, though, and the best film I did with Quine.

"He's a good friend of mine and could have become a major directorial force, but severe personal problems hindered his career. I'll explain that a bit: Some directors can have a barrage of problems at home, but once they're behind those cameras, the blinders are on.

"They have the self-discipline to block out any problems that might interfere with their work. Billy Wilder can do this, for instance.

"But with Dick, it's difficult. His problems intrude upon him. He can't seem to keep his private life out of his work. Maybe he's just too gentle to be a director."

How to Murder Your Wife to date stands as Lemmon's last film with Quine and it serves as a beautiful finale. Although not as funny as *Opera-*

With Terry-Thomas and Virna Lisi.

tion Mad Ball or as creative as *The Notorious Landlady*, two of their previous efforts together, the movie is a stylish stab at Thirties-style comedy, with Lemmon again doing the Cary Grant bit.

The plot, dreamed up by George Axelrod, is extremely original and diverting.

Historically, men hate marriage and the hero (Lemmon) of *How to Murder Your Wife*—predictably—is no exception. He's a cartoonist, creator of the noted "Bash Brannigan, Secret Agent" strip, who has a reputation for acting out all of his character's antics before committing them to paper.

He's also a bachelor—that is, until he awakens one morning after a wild party only to discover that he married the girl (Virna Lisi) who popped out of the cake.

Now, how to get rid of her?

It's impossible. Lisi is Italian, barely speaks English and, what's more, doesn't believe in divorce. So the marriage continues onward.

Meanwhile, Lemmon's comic strip has evolved into "The Brannigans," a humorous to-do modeled after his real-life marriage. But his fans want the secret agent stuff back again.

155

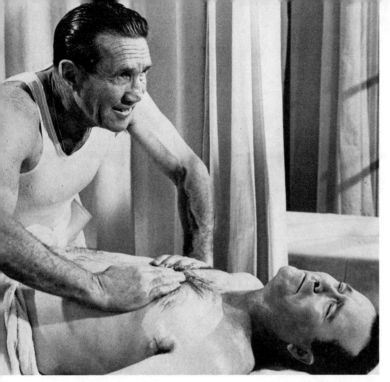

Lemmon obliges them by mapping out a scheme for Bash to kill off Mrs. Brannigan. Lisi discovers it, assumes Lemmon intends to "practice" it on her and immediately heads homeward to Italy without explanation.

When the Brannigan murder strip hits the newsstands, there's an uproar. Everyone assumes Lemmon really murdered Lisi. She's not on hand to prove them wrong—and the Brannigan strip nearly serves as a signed confession.

A wickedly funny trial follows, one that somehow finds Lemmon innocent. When Lisi re-appears, Lemmon realizes that he really does love her—and marriage, as well.

The Critics

Judith Crist in the *New York Herald Tribune:*
Well now. Here we have a great big slick Technicolor comedy starring Jack Lemmon, written and produced by George Axelrod and directed by Richard Quine—all of whom have indeed been involved with great big slick Technicolor comedies. But what's new is that this one, labeled *How to Murder Your Wife,* is funny—funny enough to make you realize what a long time it's been between laughs.

Mr. Axelrod has returned to his original style of writing deft satire and broad comedy for people who can read and write and Mr. Quine keeps pace with the screenplay.

And in the second place—or should it be first—Mr. Lemmon is leerless and he and his able colleagues in the cast prove that they are funny people.

The New Yorker:
The movie is both extremely funny and—what is rare in a comedy, and especially in a comedy full of chases, pratfalls, goofballs and spilled soup—very pleasant to look at, and I suspect that we have Axelrod to thank for this, he having acted as the producer of the picture as well as the author of its screenplay.

With Eddie Mayehoff.

With Terry-Thomas.

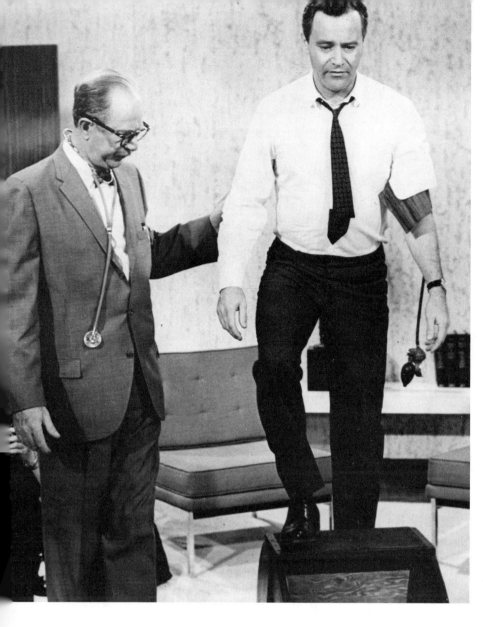

With Jack Albertson.

(The lead character) is played with cunningly calculated abandon by Jack Lemmon, released in the nick of time from the sophomoric salacities of *Irma La Douce* and *Under the Yum-Yum Tree*.

Bosley Crowther in *The New York Times*:

It's a good thing nobody is likely to take *How to Murder Your Wife* seriously, or the public impulse it could kindle might be headed *How to Murder George Axelrod*.

Never have I seen a movie, serious, comic or otherwise, that so frankly, deliberately and grossly belittled and ridiculed wives.

Woman as a domestic fixture is practically vilified in Mr. Axelrod's little preachment on the joys and advantages of bachelorhood.

Indeed, so completely anti-marriage is Mr. Axelrod's fanfaronade, which he has diabolically compounded by producing it handsomely with those two comic fellows, Jack Lemmon and Terry-Thomas, as his top advocates, that women might be expected to charge it with their slivering fingernails, if it weren't such an obvious lot of nonsense and didn't contain its own built-in riposte.

Time:

How to Murder Your Wife is a nimble comedy that doesn't make much sense because it makes nonsense, most of it screechingly funny and played by knockabouts who know that the slapstick was invented for keeping an idea aloft, not for beating it into the ground.

Jack Lemmon, too often compelled to flail around in boudoirs as the All-American lecher, demonstrates that he can wipe the leer off his face and make homicidal impulses more hilarious than hard breathing.

With Peter Falk.

The Great Race

A Warner Bros. Picture (1965)

The Production Staff

Producer: Martin Jurow. *Director:* Blake Edwards. *Original Screenplay:* Blake Edwards *and* Arthur Ross. *Cinematographer:* Russell Harlan. *Editor:* Ralph E. Winters. *Music:* Henry Mancini. *Song* "The Sweetheart Tree": Henry Mancini *(music)* and Johnny Mercer *(lyrics). Sung by* Natalie Wood. *Song* "He Shouldn't-a Swang On Me!": Henry Mancini *(music) and* Johnny Mercer *(lyrics). Sung by* Dorothy Provine. *Choreographer:* Hermes Pan. *Production Designer:* Fernando Carrere. *Set Decorator:* George James Hopkins.

A Patricia-Jalem-Reynard Production. A Warner Bros. Release. Running Time: 153 minutes. In color and Panavision.

RCA film-score album: LSP 3402.

The Cast

The Evil Professor Fate: Jack Lemmon. *The Great Leslie:* Tony Curtis. *Maggie DuBois:* Natalie Wood. *Max:* Peter Falk. *Hezekiah:* Keenan Wynn.

Original ad for *The Great Race*.

Jack Lemmon as Professor Fate.

With Tony Curtis.

Lily Olay: Dorothy Provine. *Henry Goodbody:* Arthur O'Connell. *Hester Goodbody:* Vivian Vance. *Rolfe Von Stuppe:* Ross Martin. *Texas Jack:* Larry Storch. *Prince Hapnik:* Jack Lemmon.

The Movie

The two big "physical gag" super-comedies released in 1965—*Those Magnificent Men In Their Flying Machines* and *The Great Race*—don't hold a candle to any of the old slapstick flicks they're supposed to be emulating.

Blake Edwards' *The Great Race,* for example, is dedicated to "Mr. Laurel and Mr. Hardy," but is nothing like that duo's celebrated antics at all.

While Laurel and Hardy's modest, black-and-white shenanigans always seemed akin to an intimate, one-to-one joke-swapping session with the audience, Edwards sacrifices the small stuff for cheap, protracted, strident bits done up to accommodate Panavision.

After an amusing set of titles, *The Great Race* proceeds without much wit or charm, remaining largely laggard in pace throughout its unreasonable and unnecessary 153 minutes.

With Tony Curtis and Natalie Wood.

Set around the turn of the century, the comedy details the comic rivalry between a daredevil hero (Tony Curtis) and a daredevil villain (Lemmon).

An auto race from New York to Paris is announced: Curtis promptly enters his new car (of gleaming white, of course) and Lemmon, always the rival, swears to beat him with his malevolent black horror-on-wheels.

Also entered in the race is Natalie Wood as an emancipated woman covering the event for the New York *Sentinel.*

And they're off!

Early in the 22,000-mile race, Wood's roadster breaks down and she is forced to alternate between the vehicles of snarling Lemmon and chauvinistic Curtis—and with each zam, pow, thump, she makes an effective costume change.

The race, which goes just about everywhere, is fierce and frantic, with Lemmon playing dirty all the way with his deadly car equipped with cannon, smoke screen and snow-melting prow.

Along the way, the trio stops off in Carpania for a vest-pocket edition of *The Prisoner of Zenda,* with Lemmon standing in for the kingdom's endangered royal Prince, who happens to be his lookalike. At this juncture, there's time out for a wild cream pie fight.

Jack Lemmon as Prince Hapnik.

The race is on again soon after the Carpania stopover and the entrants are now nearing the finish line. Curtis is about to win but stops long enough to kiss Wood, making it possible for Lemmon to streak by and win the race.

Feeling cheated, nevertheless, Lemmon demands a rematch. Curtis agrees. And again, they're off!

In his one and only villainous role to date, Lemmon is delightfully dirty and double-dealing throughout and is at his most gleeful when he's at his worst. Curtis nicely contrasts by underplaying it every step of the way.

There's little doubt that Lemmon and Curtis make a smooth screen team, but *The Great Race* has too much ho-hum and not enough ha-ha to show the wondrous effectiveness of their chemistry.

The Critics

Time:

The Great Race is the most expensive comedy ever filmed; but there the superlatives end: It is not exactly the worst.

The movie's main problem is that director Blake Edwards has put it together like a hobbyist assembling a model kit into an authentic reproduction of a 1908 Hupmobile.

Jack Lemmon, reading his lines at a steady 130 decibels, is the spoof villain.

Newsweek:

The most shocking waste is that of Jack Lemmon, a comedian of proven competence. The dim-witted script gives him nothing to do but cackle maniacally through a succession of predictable

161

Hirschfeld caricature of Natalie Wood, Jack Lemmon and Tony Curtis in *The Great Race.*

With Peter Falk.

gags that would eventually pall in a Tom and Jerry cartoon.

The Great Race may be all right for children who have never seen truly vigorous and unself-conscious comedy on the screen, but adults should be admitted at kiddie prices.

The New Yorker:
As it stands, it's . . . charm that the long, ungainly operation lacks, though many of the individual scenes are ravishing to behold, and the action is ideally frantic.

Jack Lemmon plays the role of the villainous, black-garbed Professor Fate and tears a comic passion to tatters with his usual grace.

Cue:
Trying oh-so-hard to be a scream, *The Great Race* seldoms succeeds in being more than just noisy, busy and heavy-handed.

Wilfrid Mifflin in *Films in Review:*
Except for the clever credit titles designed by Depatie–Freleng, and ingenious effects by Danny Lee, *The Great Race* is a great bore. Lemmon and (Keenan) Wynn are licked by the banal script.

Ernest Schier in the *Philadelphia Bulletin:*
The Great Race has motor trouble and practically none of it is under the hood. . . . Most of the gags prove to be duds and even an all-out custard pie battle, with literally thousands of pies, cannot lighten the forced tone of an overwrought effort to recapture the carefree days of silent screen.

The Pie Fight.

With Walter Matthau.

The Fortune Cookie

A United Artists Picture (1966)

The Production Staff

Producer: Billy Wilder. *Director:* Billy Wilder. *Original Screenplay:* Billy Wilder *and* I. A. L. Diamond. *Cinematographer:* Joseph LaShelle. *Editor:* Daniel Mandell. *Music:* André Previn. *Song* "You'd Be So Nice To Come Home To": Cole Porter. *Sung by* Judi West. *Art Director:* Robert Luthardt. *Set Decorator:* Edward G. Boyle.

A Phalanx–Jalem Production. A Mirisch Corporation Presentation. A United Artists Release. Running Time: 125 minutes. In black-and-white and Panavision.

United Artists Records soundtrack album: UAS 5145.

The Cast

Harry Hinkle: Jack Lemmon. *Willie Gingrich:* Walter Matthau. *Sandy Hinkle:* Judi West. *Luther "Boom-Boom" Jackson:* Ron Rich. *Mrs. Gingrich:*

Original ad for *The Fortune Cookie.*

With Judi West and Walter Matthau.

Marge Redmond. *Mother Hinkle:* Lurene Tuttle. *Mr. Purkey:* Cliff Osmond. *Max:* Noam Pitlik. *O'Brien:* Harry Holcombe. *Thompson:* Les Tremayne. *Mr. Jackson:* Archie Moore.

The Movie

"Hurrying down the sideline," reads an early descriptive segment in the Billy Wilder–I. A. L. Diamond screenplay for *The Fortune Cookie*, "is the operator of Camera Four—this is the guy we're really interested in.

"His name is Harry Hinkle, and he will be thirty-six next September. That makes him a Virgo—and if he had read his horoscope, he would've stayed in bed today.

"He wears a duffel coat, knitted cap, gloves and a headphone, and his face is blue with cold. His camera is a portable job, and he schleps it on his shoulder."

Harry Hinkle (Lemmon) is spending a gloomy, bone-chilling Sunday afternoon covering the Cleveland Browns–Minnesota Vikings game for CBS. It's an assignment which leaves him unconscious.

During the game, Lemmon is accidentally hurled across the sideline by a 220-pound black halfback named Luther "Boom Boom" Jackson (Ron Rich).

The incident leaves Lemmon steamrolled, a bit dizzy but little else. Nevertheless, Lemmon's brother-in-law, a shyster lawyer named Willie Gingrich (Walter Matthau), sees a solid court case in the affair and makes immediate plans to sue the team, the stadium and the broadcasting company for an aggregate of one million dollars.

All Lemmon has to do is pretend he's in pain; an old spinal injury will take care of the X-Rays. It's a fraud—but so what?

"They've got so much money," points out Matthau, "they don't know what to do with it. They've run out of storage space. They have to microfilm it."

Lemmon eventually goes along because Matthau has him convinced that the money will entice back his runaway wife (Judi West), whom he still loves.

For the next few days, Lemmon is worked over by the insurance investigators' doctors with complicated equipment, while hired detectives spy on him day and night.

With Judi West.

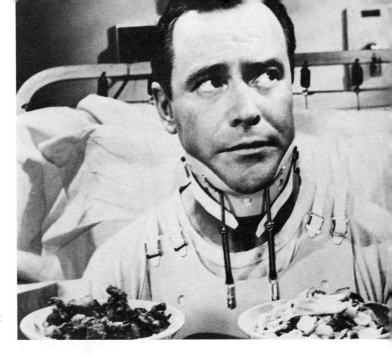

Meanwhile, back at Cleveland Stadium, Rich is finding it increasingly difficult to play ball, ridden with guilt over Lemmon's accident and convinced that he crippled a man.

Lemmon inevitably starts to crumble from all the pressure: West and Matthau have become overly gleeful about the anticipated loot and Rich's career seems to be going down the drain.

Then there's the advice offered to Lemmon on a note inside a fortune cookie: "You can fool all of the people some of the time, and some of the people all of the time—but you can't fool all of the people all of the time."

At this point, Lemmon announces his fakery, walks out on Matthau and West and seeks out Rich to apologize.

And that's the way it crumbles—cookie-wise.

It's a fairly well-known fact that Wilder got his idea for *The Fortune Cookie* while watching a TV football game.

"Billy," says Jack, "saw a huge fullback make an end sweep, gallop out of bounds and fall right on top of a spectator.

"He saw this thing, and said to himself, 'That's a movie and the guy underneath is Lemmon!' And that's how *The Fortune Cookie* happened."

The Critics

Judith Crist in the *World Journal Tribune:*
The old Billy Wilder is back with *The Fortune Cookie* and a case of grand and glorious larceny committed by Walter Matthau, who walks away with everything in sight and sound.

By the "old" Mr. Wilder we mean that shrewd observer of Americana whose cynicism was tempered by a keen and subtle sense of humor. (Here) the producer-director has come up with a wild bit of nonsense about insurance fraud that has a field day with the morality of modern average men and of legal beagles.

Beyond the superlative Mr. Matthau, (Wilder) has Jack Lemmon, turned straight-man by virtue of Matthau's brilliance in the juicier role, but doing very nicely as the schnook caught between the neckbrace and honesty and his love for an ungood woman.

Vincent Canby in *The New York Times:*
Billy Wilder is a cranky, perhaps even dangerous,

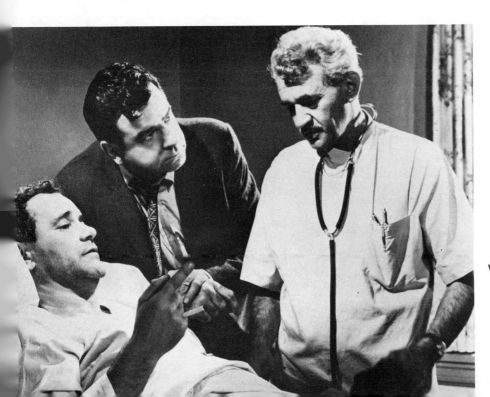

With Walter Matthau and Harry Davis.

167

man. That is, he is an unregenerate moralist whose latest vision of the American Dream, titled *The Fortune Cookie*, is a fine, dark, gag-filled hallucination, peopled by dropouts from the Great Society.

It is an explosively funny live-action cartoon about petty chiselers who regard the economic system as a giant pinball machine.

Mr. Lemmon is the perfect knucklehead, a guy with a wet noodle for a spine, who can't help being sentimental about a girl even while she's picking his pockets.

Richard Schickel in *Life:*

Technically, Lemmon does a superb job in the main role, but he just naturally exudes too much intelligence to be totally believable as the easily led TV cameraman. The picture really belongs to Matthau, who is rapidly becoming the W. C. Fields of the Sixties.

Time:

Director Billy Wilder has taken the very rash risk in this film of spiking his big gun. He keeps Jack Lemmon, a funnyman-in-motion who lacks the

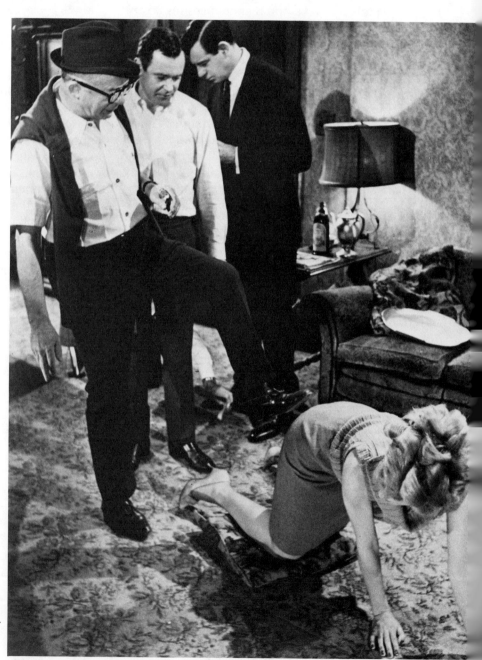

With director Billy Wilder, Walter Matthau and Judi West.

With Ron Rich.

instincts of a sit-down comedian, sitting in a wheelchair that makes him seem foolish but never funny. With Lemmon immobilized, only a miracle could save the show from being as sedative as Wilder's last picture, *Kiss Me, Stupid.*

Fortunately, something like a miracle is at hand: Walter Matthau.

The New Yorker:
What gives a saving humanity to *The Fortune Cookie* is the delightful performances by Mr. Lemmon and Mr. Matthau.

Joseph Morgenstern in *Newsweek:*
Lemmon shows how funny and touching a skilled comedian can be within the physical confines of a neck brace and an electric wheelchair.

He also shows how generous an actor can be, for he must have known that the script gave the best of everything to Matthau, whose performance is a wonder.

He is big and bold and less afraid of a close-up camera than any actor alive. His hands are always in motion, as if searching for something to finagle, and he never lets go of a scene until it is finished.

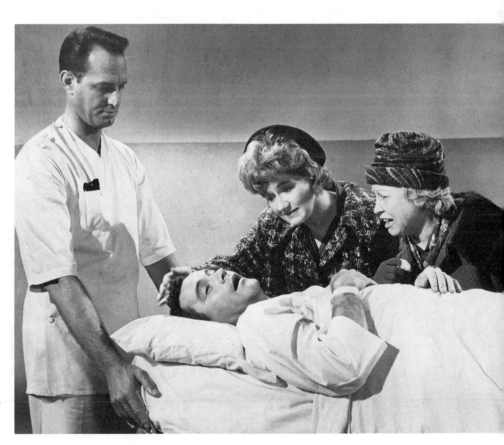

With Bill Christopher, Marge Redmond (center) and Lurena Tuttle.

With Elaine May and Peter Falk.

Luv

A Columbia Picture (1967)

The Production Staff

Producer: Martin Manulis. *Executive Producer:* Gordon Carroll. *Director:* Clive Donner. *Screenplay:* Elliott Baker. *Based on the play of the same title by* Murray Schisgal. *Cinematographer:* Ernest Laszlo. *Editor:* Harold F. Kress. *Music:* Gerry Mulligan. *Song "Love Casts Its Shadow Over My Heart":* Irving Joseph *(music),* Murray Schisgal *(lyrics). Sung by* Elaine May, Jack Lemmon *and* Peter Falk. *Production Designer:* Al Brenner. *Set Decorator:* Frank Tuttle.

A Martin Manulis Production. A Columbia Pictures Release. Running Time: 95 minutes. In color and Panavision.

The Cast

Harry Berlin: Jack Lemmon. *Milt Manville:* Peter

Original ad for *Luv*.

170

Hirschfeld caricature of the cast of *Luv*: Elaine May, Peter Falk, Nina Wayne and Jack Lemmon.

Falk. *Ellen Manville Berlin:* Elaine May. *Linda Manville:* Nina Wayne. *Attorney Goodhart:* Eddie Mayehoff. *Junkmen:* Paul Hartman *and* Severn Darden.

The Movie

"Some plays should never be filmed." You've heard it before, perhaps too hastily about the wrong play. In the case of Murray Schisgal's *Luv*, however, it's accurate.

The material's whifty ways and cartoonlike characters—charming and acceptable in the make-believe world of the theater—emerged as grotesqueries in Clive Donner's too-literal film translation of 1967.

On screen (and in wide-screen Panavision, no less), the piece plays like a piece of draff—looking amateurish, excessive and, somehow, unoriginal and illiterate—with a plot that becomes tedious early on.

Lemmon (who foolishly went down to 136 pounds for the role) plays a total failure, a full-time hobo ready for the river. His troubles started on graduation day from college when a pooch upped and urinated all over his new trousers. Ever since, he's been unlucky.

Lemmon is about to end it all and jump off the Manhattan Bridge when he's stopped by

With Elaine May.

Peter Falk, an old college chum who's a success: two cars, a motorcycle, a house in the suburbs, an intellectual wife, the whole schmeer.

Falk has his reasons for befriending Lemmon, however. He's in love with another woman (Nina Wayne) and would like to dump his wife (Elaine May) on Lemmon. He hates intellectuals, see?

When Lemmon and May meet, it's nearly love at first sight. Falk and May divorce and go their separate ways with their respective new mates.

Wayne turns out to be a slob—a personality type which Falk hates more than intellectuals. May, meanwhile, is fed up with her platonic marriage to Lemmon.

Realizing they still love each other, Falk and May plan to dump Wayne on Lemmon. But the trick fails. In this case, it's hate at first sight. The only thing left is murder.

May lures Lemmon back to the Manhattan Bridge with the hope he'll decide to jump. When she hastily pushes him in, she falls in herself. Falk, hiding in the shadows of the bridge, dives in to save her.

With Peter Falk.

Meanwhile, Lemmon is drowning. But not for long. Wayne happens by (she's an ardent jogger, see?) and dives to his rescue. They make body contact and decide they really do love one another.

And the four losers live happily ever after.

The Critics

Cue:

Consider the difference between Alan Arkin and Jack Lemmon as performers and that's the tip-off to what you'll find in the screen version of the play *Luv.*

Lemmon handles the movie chores with his customary competence and milks everything dry in the laughter department.

Lemmon's style, plus the manner in which the film has been directed by Clive Donner, turns the property into a picture of very general comic appeal.

Kathleen Carroll in the New York *Daily News:*

Luv, that is, the movie version of Murray Schisgal's Broadway bonanza, has no heart. Not that the film at the DeMille and Coronet Theatres isn't a near-faithful extraction of Schisgal's play.

Jack Lemmon wasn't meant to be Harry. He may *look* like a loser—Bowery thin with rheumy eyes. But looking isn't enough; and trying so hard to be funny in the part is too much.

With Elaine May.

With Elaine May.

Bosley Crowther in *The New York Times*:

It has Jack Lemmon staggering dumbly through the surrealistic role of a consistently frustrated loser who is kept from jumping off the Manhattan Bridge by the chance intervention of an old schoolmate, played moronically by Peter Falk.

And it has Elaine May prissing haughtily as the latter's know-it-all wife, who is fobbed off on Lemmon to clear the way for Falk to another "luv."

The three of them clomp and clown broadly . . . (and) tend to become monotonous, especially the blowsy Mr. Lemmon and the starchily dead-panned Miss May.

Wilfrid Sheed in *Esquire*:

Luv is technically a New York movie, but by the simple insertion of Jack Lemmon it has given itself that Bel Air look. The original play, safe in the hands of Alan Arkin, included a batch of kitsch intellectualism, alienation and whatnot. It was probably kinder not to tell Lemmon about this. (He is one of Hollywood's most intelligent actors, but don't expect miracles.)

Anyhow, the whole sense of Western thought, misunderstood and in bad decay, that makes New York living what it is has gone from the movie, save for the brooding features of Elaine May which tell it all.

Time:

Of the three principals, only Elaine May, as the wife, is well cast, but she is pitching in a game with no catchers. Peter Falk is too simian and heavy for the popinjay part of her wayward husband, and as a Jewish urban type, Jack Lemmon is frantic without being funny.

Luv is too good a comedy to die this way: people who have never seen it will do better to find a road company of the play.

The New Yorker:

Murray Schisgal's *Luv*, now filmed by Clive Donner, is a funny and very American suppressed howl about . . . too many words chasing too little feeling, too much dulled general speech for personal things best expressed by shutting up. Jack Lemmon (performs) in a high tragic mood less funny than ordinariness would be.

With Elaine May.

173

With Walter Matthau.

The Odd Couple

A Paramount Picture (1968)

The Production Staff

Producer: Howard W. Koch. *Director:* Gene Saks. *Screenplay:* Neil Simon. *Based on his play of the same title. Cinematographer:* Robert B. Hauser. *Editor:* Frank Bracht. *Music:* Neal Hefti. *Art Directors:* Hal Pereira *and* Walter Tyler. *Set Decorators:* Robert Benton *and* Ray Moyer.

A Howard W. Koch Production. A Paramount Release. Running Time: 105 minutes. In color and Panavision.

Dot Records soundtrack album: DLP 25862.

The Cast

Felix Unger: Jack Lemmon. *Oscar Madison:* Walter Matthau. *Cecily Pigeon:* Monica Evans. *Gwendolyn Pigeon:* Carole Shelley. *Roy:* David Sheiner. *Speed:* A. Larry Haines. *Vinnie:* John Fiedler. *Murray:* Herbert Edelman.

The Movie

"Jack Lemmon and Walter Matthau are *The Odd Couple.*

Original ad for *The Odd Couple.*

With Walter Matthau.

Note the "are." That's what was used in the ads for the film. It could have been just plain "in." But "are" makes it seem permanent.

The men deserve the distinction because they alone (with a little help from Neil Simon's very funny dialogue, of course) make the film snap, crackle and pop, causing it to succeed in spite of Gene Saks's very humdrum direction of the material.

With Saks behind the camera, making all the decisions and giving all the orders, the movie looks and plays uncannily like an elongated TV situation comedy (not all that much unlike the series that was ultimately spawned from the play and the movie).

Billy Wilder wanted very much to direct the movie and, with him in charge, the finished product might have been a more durable and tougher movie, perhaps one even approaching classic stature.

Paramount, however, favored Saks who had just successfully helmed *Barefoot in the Park* for

With A. Larry Haines (left), Herb Edelman, David Sheiner, John Fielder and Walter Matthau.

With Carole Shelley (left), Monica Evans and Walter Matthau.

the company and who was less expensive than Wilder.

Lemmon had the right in his contract to disapprove of the director and, when he didn't disapprove of Saks, gossip columnists suggested that the incident ended the Wilder–Lemmon friendship.

"It was a case of Paramount opting for the more economical choice," explains Richard Carter, Lemmon's long-time friend and press agent. "It was also a case of Lemmon being helpless to prevent that choice without 'disapproving' Saks.

"You might say that Jack was in the middle. But he did *not* select Gene Saks over Billy. Time, fortunately, has mellowed the situation."

"It would have been very interesting to see what Billy would have done with the material," reflects Jack. "His concept would have been completely different."

The role of Felix Unger in *The Odd Couple* was a choice but dangerous one for Lemmon. It could be played any number of ways, with a broad interpretation the most obvious way.

Lemmon's broad overplaying in *The Great Race* and *Luv*, both topheavy with mugging, brought him much criticism. On the other hand, his effective and affecting low-keyed performance in *The Fortune Cookie* practically went by unrecognized.

"Underplaying vs. overplaying," says Jack, "is a controversial point. I would tend to under rather than over play. I, of course, might not be able to judge my results accurately, and that goes for *The Odd Couple*, too, but I can only hope that I did not broaden the character too much."

With Carole Shelley (left), Walte Matthau and Monica Evans.

Hirschfeld caricature of Matthau and Lemmon as Oscar and Felix.

The finished product shows Lemmon playing his character virtually dead straight, not only turning in a naturalistic performance but also keeping the character, despite his prissiness thoroughly masculine throughout.

Lemmon plays an about-to-be-divorced man who tries to adjust to his newly-restored freedom by moving in with his best friend (Matthau) who's divorced—and very, very sloppy.

This causes complications because Lemmon has a fetish for cleanliness and order. Before long, the boys are bickering back and forth about such trivialities as footprints on the kitchen floor,

a deflated soufflé, cigarette smoke and whatnot.

A series of riotous domestic quarrels and threats follows—and in the end, this "marriage," too, alas, ends in a divorce.

Throughout, Lemmon conveys the subtle idiosyncrasies of a fault-finding hypochondriac with a mania for order, while Matthau, the perfect foil, epitomizes tackiness with mud-covered sneaks, beer-stained sweatsuit and incredible bad habits and facial expressions.

The Critics

Renata Adler in *The New York Times:*
Jack Lemmon plays the weepy, hypochondriacal one in the apron. Since the part is less broadly comic than he is used to—it teeters between being soulful and unendurable—Mr. Lemmon sometimes overacts.

Joseph Morgenstern in *Newsweek:*
Lemmon, as a definitive hypochondriac, makes a marvelous moment out of clearing his Eustachian tubes, and his compulsive dusting is consistently funny.

Matthau, who moves like an arthritic heel-and-toe walker on a sticky treadmill, is beautifully, unyieldingly malevolent in his attitude toward order and his fear that Lemmon, once banished, may yet return as a ghost, "haunting and cleaning, haunting and cleaning."

Judith Crist in New York magazine:
A funny thing happened at Radio City Music Hall this week and more I can't wish but that it should happen to you. *The Odd Couple,* one of the very best comedies to have emanated from Broadway

With Herb Edelman, Walter Matthau and David Sheiner.

in recent years, arrived on screen not only intact but actually enhanced by the transition.

As to enhancement, above all there's Jack Lemmon to make Felix a revolting mass of tics and twitches and fussbudgetry, to hit that fine high of comedic performance that we have long expected from Lemmon but rarely received. The essence of the Felix character is that with all the priggishness and domesticity it be a thoroughly male one—and the slightest hint of camp or flick of wrist could destroy the entire point of the play. Lemmon is pure platinum at long last.

Harriet Gibbs in *Films in Review:*

Jack Lemmon is one of our best comedians, a gifted actor and a fine human being, but he should stop accepting the kind of scripts he does. In this one he merely stooges for Walter Matthau, an actor of incomparably smaller range.

And the script! It really isn't funny. The characterizations are uninteresting; the dialogue is middle-middle class Riverside Drive; and the denouement settles nothing.

Time:

Although he is one of Hollywood's most polished performers, Lemmon often strains to achieve the lines of tension that characterized Art Carney's high-strung stage interpretation of the role.

With Walter Matthau.

The film owes its comic force to two stars—one visible, the other unseen. Walter Matthau, with his loping, sloping style, mangled grin and laugh-perfect timing, may well be America's finest comic actor. And playwright Neil Simon occasionally takes off his clowns' masks to show the humans beneath.

Stanley Kauffmann in *The New Republic:*

In *(The Odd Couple)* Matthau co-stars with Jack Lemmon, who is one of the hybrid star-types—Joe Average but a bit too good-looking and adroit to be only Joe Average and latterly too obtrusive a performer to let his Joe Average personality work.

With Walter Matthau.

With Sally Kellerman.

The April Fools

A Cinema Center–National General Picture (1969)

The Production Staff

Producer: Gordon Carroll. *Director:* Stuart Rosenberg. *Original Screenplay:* Hal Dresner. *Cinematographer:* Michel Hugo. *Editor:* Bob Wyman. *Music:* Marvin Hamlisch. *Song* "The April Fools": Burt Bacharach *(music) and* Hal David *(lyrics). Sung by* Dionne Warwicke. *Song* "I Say a Little Prayer": Burt Bacharach *(music) and* Hal David *(lyrics). Sung by* Susan Barrett. *Art Director:* Robert Luthardt. *Production Designer:* Richard Sylbert. *Set Decorator:* William Kiernan. *Choreographer:* Marc Wilder.

A Cinema Center Films Presentation. A Jalem Production. Released by National General Pictures. MPAA Rating: M. Running Time: 95 minutes. In color and Panavision.

Columbia soundtrack album: OS 3340.

The Cast

Howard Brubaker: Jack Lemmon. *Catherine Gunther:* Catherine Deneuve. *Ted Gunther:* Peter Lawford. *Phyllis Brubaker:* Sally Kellerman. *Potter*

Original ad for *The April Fools.*

180

He has a wife. She has a husband.
With so much in common they just have to fall in love.

Jack Lemmon and Catherine Deneuve in "The April Fools"
Also starring Peter Lawford, Jack Weston, Myrna Loy and Charles

Title song sung by Dionne Warwick. Title Music by Burt Bacharach and Lyrics by Hal David. Music by Marvin Hamli
Music from original sound track on Columbia Records. A Jalem Production. Technicolor.®
Screenplay by Hal Dresner. Produced by Gordon Carroll. Directed by Stuart Rosenberg.
A National General Pictures Release. A Cinema Center Films Presentation.

With Catherine Deneuve.

Shrader: Jack Weston. *Grace Greenlaw:* Myrna Loy. *Andre Greenlaw:* Charles Boyer. *Benson:* Harvey Korman. *Leslie Hopkins:* Melinda Dillon. *Don Hopkins:* Kenneth Mars. *Mimsy Shrader:* Janice Carroll. *Stanley Brubaker:* Gary Dubin. *Walters:* David Doyle. *Naomi:* Dee Gardner. *Singer:* Susan Barrett.

The Movie

In the history of the American cinema, the late Sixties—particularly 1968–69—will probably be recorded as the era of the New Wave, represented by such tense, gritty and relentlessly realistic flicks as *Midnight Cowboy, Medium Cool* and *Easy Rider.*

Film language came of age during those years, as well as dazzling camera techniques and fancy cinematics. Directorial neophytes were experimenting all over the place and—as a result—American movies became truly exciting.

Exciting as *Midnight Cowboy* and *Easy Rider* were in their day, they were equalled—but on an entirely different plane—by Stuart Rosenberg's rosy and old-fashioned *The April Fools,* a soothing Preston Sturges-like romantic comedy done up in mod trimmings.

While *The April Fools* did well financially

With Catherine Deneuve.

and managed to charm some of the critics, its soft, madcap ways unfortunately seemed unimportant and unimpressive alongside the freneticism of its peers.

Unlike its more daring contemporaries, the movie is alive with a lot of feisty, positive determination about its theme (i.e., love conquering all) and doesn't cop out or compromise its principles the way, say, *Bob and Carol and Ted and Alice* does.

Hal Dresner's original screenplay, written originally for Lemmon and Shirley MacLaine and then restructured beautifully to fit the Gallic dreaminess of Catherine Deneuve, is writing of uncommon distinction and charm, taste and affection.

His plot is slight, basically a two-character job. And like Sturges, he's surrounded his two perfectly normal, attractive leading characters with a score of zany screwball types, some last-minute complications and the frenzy of a count-down fade-out.

Lemmon plays Howard Brubaker, a Wall

182

Street broker, saddled with a pseudo-intellectual, amateur-decorator wife (Sally Kellerman), a son who doesn't talk to him and a dog that growls at him.

After being named Fourth Vice President of his firm, Lemmon drops by a cocktail party at the posh apartment of his tycoon boss (Peter Lawford), where he meets the strikingly beautiful Catherine (Catherine Deneuve), an unhappily-wed woman longing to go home to Paris.

Little does Lemmon know that Deneuve is unhappily wed to boss Lawford.

Both are bored by the party and abandon it for a night on the town, during which they meet an eccentric night person (Myrna Loy) who invites them to her home to meet her husband (Charles Boyer).

Lemmon and Deneuve spend the night walking and talking and laughing and dancing. Something magical has happened: They've fallen in love.

Deneuve announces plans to leave her husband and return to Paris, inviting Lemmon to share her adventure. He hesitates and then decides. Yes. He'll fly off to Paris with his dream girl, leaving wife, mortgage, job and tension behind.

Both Lemmon and Deneuve are hassled by their respective friends—he by his lawyer (Jack Weston) and drunken colleague (Harvey Korman), she by her neighbors, the tacky Hopkinses (Kenneth Mars and Melinda Dillon).

Lemmon, now aware that Deneuve is married to Lawford, feels crazily liberated by the

With Peter Lawford.

entire escapade. He makes a mad dash for Kennedy Airport and, together with Deneuve, zooms off for Paris.

The revisions made in Dresner's script continued well into the filming, mainly to comply with Catherine Deneuve's real-life personality.

For example, in one scene in the film, Lawford laughs about Deneuve's "romantic fits"— her long, solitary walks at night in search of wounded birds.

It's a fact that during the filming, Deneuve

With Catherine Deneuve (left), Charles Boyer and Myrna Loy.

With Catherine Deneuve.

did slip away unnoticed and take solitary walks. She also rescued an injured sparrow in Central Park and named it "Pauvre Petit." She kept the bird in her bathtub at the Sherry-Netherland Hotel.

For a long time prior to *The April Fools*, Deneuve had been hankering to do an American film. But she chose to make her stateside debut in this one in particular because she loved the story.

The film failed to establish her in American movies but still has her enthusiasm.

"I'm not bitter about not having become a great success in America. I'm disappointed but not discouraged. I don't know what went wrong. I believed in the picture and liked Jack Lemmon and working with him."

"You cannot photograph that girl from a bad angle," says Jack in return, "because she doesn't have one. You could shoot her from the toenails and she'd still be gorgeous. She has regality. You would imagine her a princess or queen."

About the film itself, he adds: "I'm glad so many people seemed to like it. But I always felt *The April Fools* needed one key scene.

"By that, I mean a scene that would have established the relationship between myself and Catherine as firm once and for all. Stuart Rosenberg did a very competent job directing it; I can't fault him.

"I like the picture, but I feel it could have been better."

With Jack Weston.

The Critics

Vincent Canby in *The New York Times:*

The April Fools, which opened yesterday at the Pasific East and New Embassy Theatres, is a sweet, sentimental comedy edged in farce.

Howard Brubaker (Jack Lemmon), a successful Wall Street broker married to a suburban witch (Sally Kellerman), is the kind of schnook who goes to a posh party and tries to make a phone call in a piece of sculpture shaped like a telephone booth.

Catherine, as the lovely, chic wife of the party's host, is, like Lemmon, convinced that life somewhere else might be beautiful. They meet and fall in love. And twenty-four hours later they elope to Paris.

The best things in the movie . . . are the extraordinarily good supporting performances . . . and there are lots of quotable lines.

The April Fools is not a comic masterpiece, but it has a nice, understated sense of the absurd.

Florence Fletcher in *Cue:*

Frothy it may be, and as romantic as a bunch of violets, but this enchanting surprise package hasn't a flippant or phony thought in its head. . . . The gorgeous Miss Deneuve glows, and as for Lemmon, he again proves that in this sort of role, he is simply a genius. The satirical touches in Stuart Rosenberg's direction and Hal Dresner's screenplay neatly balance the romantic mood.

Variety:

It's a Lemmon, not a lemon. He's excellent as the square trying to play it cool when the flames of uncertainty are licking around his knees.

Lemmon is both funny and touching as the mild-mannered stockbroker, tied to a nothing of a wife. Given a big promotion by his boss, he meets the latter's wife (Catherine Deneuve) at one of those huge, stultifying cocktail parties that you're led to believe goes on all the time.

When the girl says she's leaving her husband to return to Paris, Lemmon determines to go along. The most original touches in the plot are that they (1) don't bed down together first and (2) do go to Paris.

With Catherine Deneuve.

The Out-of-Towners

A Paramount Picture (1970)

The Production Staff
Producer: Paul Nathan. *Director:* Arthur Hiller. *Original Screenplay:* Neil Simon. *Cinematographer:* Andrew Laszlo. *Editor:* Fred Chulack. *Art Director:* Charles Bailey. *Music:* Quincy Jones.

Produced by Jalem Productions, Inc. A Paramount Release. MPAA Rating: G. Running Time: 98 minutes. In color.

The Cast
George Kellerman: Jack Lemmon. *Gwen Kellerman:* Sandy Dennis. *Women in Police Station:* Anne Meara. *TV Man:* Sandy Baron. *Airline Stewardess:* Ann Prentiss. *Murray, the mugger:* Graham Jarvis. *Looters:* Jon Korkes and Robert Walden. *Lost-and-Found Supervisor:* Billy Dee Williams. *Hotel Clerk:* Anthony Holland. *Cab*

Original ad for *The Out-Of-Towners.*

186

With Sandy Dennis.

With Sandy Dennis.

Driver: Ron Carey. *Cuban Diplomat:* Carlos Montalban. *Police Sergeant:* Dolph Sweet. *Waiter on Train:* Johnny Brown. *Plane Passenger:* Robert Nichols.

The Movie

Arthur Hiller's *The Out-Of-Towners* isn't, in toto, a very good film. Its plotline is near nonexistent— basically a series of frenzied comedy sketches that have been done better (and with funnier results) on TV by Carol Burnett and company.

And what's worse, the film's humor (Neil Simon concocted the superficially amusing shenanigans here) ceases to be enjoyable early on because it's based on victimizing, suffering and utter chaos.

The comedy is Simon's one-sided indictment against big-city living, stressing the inconvenience and the grime without ever noting the exciting cultural and entertainment happenings usually available at arm's length in metropolitan areas.

The jokes and situations here are sour and grumpy and jaded, all executed by Hiller at a high pitch and a fast pace; it's like a soap opera with the pacing of a musical. And it just doesn't work.

Lemmon and Sandy Dennis play a Dayton,

With Sandy Dennis.

188

With Graham Jarvis and Sandy Dennis.

Ohio, couple who journey to New York for a final interview which will mean a big, fat promotion for Lemmon. They are scarcely out of Ohio when chaos strikes.

First, their plane can't land in New York, and is rerouted to Boston, where they learn that their luggage is still in Dayton. Determined to stick to the meticulous schedule mapped out by Lemmon, they make a mad dash for the Boston train depot—and end up standing all the way to New York.

By the time they're finally seated in the dining car, the menu is limited to only peanut butter and olives.

They finally arrive in Gotham about 2 A.M. during a downpour, a sanitation strike and a transportation strike. No cabs or buses are available. To worsen matters, all the hotels are jam-packed with convention guests.

While walking the streets, they're mugged, looted of their Cracker Jacks by a greedy pooch and accused of child molesting.

The failure of *The Out-of-Towners* is unfortunate because, beneath all the exaggeration and junk jokes, it says something about the unreasonable frustrations that brave city people casually accept.

The film's sole motive force is the well-timed duet between Lemmon and Dennis, who come across as a veritable human version of Punch and Judy, padding their roles and the film with much-appreciated enthusiasm and gusto.

"It's impossible to tell what will be a success and what will not," says Jack. *"The Out-Of-Towners,* for instance, I love Neil Simon who wrote it. Sandy Dennis was quite good in it. And Arthur Hiller, the director, was a ball to work for.

"Unfortunately, he's no flaming genius as a filmmaker. There was a five-minute sequence in the film that Hiller chose to cut that was better than anything left in it. It was a terribly important scene in terms of character motivation."

The Critics

William Wolf in *Cue:*
Neil Simon has uproariously caught the truth of life collapsing around us. Hold onto your equilibrium, wallets and pocketbooks.

All of the harrowing, up-tight encounters you complain about or read about in Fun City are squeezed into less than twenty-four hours, and they all happen to one couple.

Arthur Hiller directs at a pace that will leave

189

you breathless. Lemmon is in great form as he is buffeted around by strikes, muggers, airplanes, hotels, etc. Whatever they paid Sandy Dennis was worth it just for her voice quality in expressing dismayed surprise.

Roger Greenspun in *The New York Times*:
Between Lemmon and Sandy Dennis there is no conversation—only bullying, mostly by him. I can't fault Lemmon's performance; I simply can't see the reason for it. Miss Dennis exercises, or has had imposed upon her, exceptional self-effacing restraint.

Although there are many bit appearances, Miss Dennis and Jack Lemmon essentially have the movie to themselves. Except that about two-thirds of the way through, in Central Park, a boomed microphone appears in the upper part of the screen.

It pretty much stays there, twisting and turning to catch each speaker, for the rest of the film. *The Out-Of-Towners* may thus rank as technically the sloppiest as well as the most witlessly uncomfortable movie for some time.

Judith Crist in *New York* magazine:
Lemmon is presented as an ulcer-ridden bundle of nerves, a terrible-tempered Mr. Magoo and a near-imbecile whom the wary would not employ as a minor clerk, let alone consider for a vice-presidency of even that current gag-subject industry, a plastics concern.

Miss Dennis seems to have lent Lemmon all her nose-twitching mouth-tensions for the duration of the film and (herself) undertaken a nasal whining-wail manner of speaking more germane to the Bronx than Ohio.

Time:
Simon is a careful comic craftsman who is at pains to draw belly laughs from basically realistic—and therefore emphatic—situations. His humor never becomes bizarre, even though it is a bit strained by director Arthur Hiller's nerve-racking pace.

Jack Lemmon, frantically trying to retaliate against the injustices of the big city by threatening all clerks, drivers and officials with lawsuits, is still adept at playing Felix of *The Odd Couple*.

The only trouble is that it is getting to be his only role.

(The Out-Of-Towners) is a lot of typical evenings shaped by Simon into a frantic, funny tale that frazzles the nerve ends.

With Sandy Dennis.

Kathleen Carroll in the New York *Daily News:*
Neil Simon, that playwright and sometime screen-writer with the Midas touch, has a genius for discovering rich lodes of comedy in the most catastrophic situations.

Lemmon and Dennis play off each other like vaudeville pros. The more horrifying their situation, the more desperately hilarious they are.

Gene Shalit in *Look:*
Somebody call a cop—Jack Lemmon has mugged Neil Simon's script. There's more to acting than making faces: And Simon deserves better.

Lemmon begins at the top of his voice with nowhere left to go. (Where was director Arthur Hiller?) Sandy Dennis is far better than usual: We are spared her synthetic stuttering and her repetitions.

With Sandy Dennis.

Kotch

An ABC–Cinerama Picture (1971)

The Production Staff

Producer: Richard Carter. *Director:* Jack Lemmon. *Screenplay:* John Paxton. *Based on the novel* Kotch *by* Katharine Topkins. *Cinematographer:* Richard Kline. *Editor:* Ralph Winters. *Music:* Marvin Hamlisch. *Song* "Life Is What You Make It": Marvin Hamlisch *(music) and* Alan *and* Marilyn Bergman *(lyrics). Art Director:* Jack Poplin. *Set Decorator:* Bill Kiernan.

An ABC Pictures Corporation Presentation (A Subsidiary of the American Broadcasting Companies, Inc.). Distributed by Cinerama Releasing. MPAA Rating: GP. Running Time: 114 minutes. In color.

The Cast

Joseph P. Kotcher: Walter Matthau. *Erica Herzenstiel:* Deborah Winters. *Wilma Kotcher:* Felicia Farr. *Gerald Kotcher:* Charles Aidman. *Vera Kotcher:* Ellen Geer. *Vincent Perrin:* Darrell Larson. *Dr. Guadillo:* Paul Picerni. *Miss Roberts:* Jane Connell. *Sissy:* Lucy Saroyan. *Duncan Kotcher:* Donald *and* Dean Kowalski. *Stranger on Bus:* Jack Lemmon.

The Movie

For his directorial debut, Lemmon elected to film

Quote-oriented advertisement for *Kotch*.

With Felicia Farr.

Katharine Topkins' novel, *Kotch*, about the triumphs and failures of old age as seen in relation to a youth-oriented, liberated society.

The movie was a family project almost from the very start: Lemmon's closest Hollywood friend, Walter Matthau, was ultimately selected to play the title role of an old man who needs to be needed; his actress-wife, Felicia Farr, signed on to play Matthau's daughter-in-law, and his long-time friend and press agent, Richard Carter, personally produced the movie.

What's more, Matthau's stepdaughter, Lucy Saroyan, was sought out to play a secondary role.

On set, during the filming, Lemmon exhibited his Billy Wilder influence, wearing a trademark Wilder hat. But the finished feature seems less like Wilder than one would have expected; surprisingly, it plays more like a Richard Quine movie.

"I was drawn to *Kotch*," reveals Jack, "first by the character and the individual spirit of the human being. I was fascinated by it.

"It raises a lot of questions that I think need to be raised, but I was not trying to make any kind of statement about old age. I merely wanted to do a nice little drama about a character who happens to be old.

"What do you do if you're seventy-five years old but young from the neck up? That's what troubles Kotch. His kids love him, but still, there he is underfoot all the time. You root for this garrulous old guy—and yet his children have a legitimate problem with him that imposes tremendous guilt feelings on them.

"Fredric March was our original choice for Kotch, but he was in ill health and it's an awfully demanding role. The character is in almost every scene. We weren't sure he'd be able to handle it, and it became difficult to get backing for the project due to his state of health.

"I stumbled on the idea of having Walter play it merely by chance. I hadn't considered using anyone younger for the part, but when Walter proposed it, the idea just started sounding better and better, until we decided to go with it.

"Walter will take direction well, I found, unless something goes totally against his instincts," adds Jack. "But I directed him mostly by leaving him alone. He's so inventive that when I was editing the film, I found he never did the same thing twice, and I wanted to kill him because it was almost impossible to cut.

"As far as directing Felicia, well . . . it's the first time she ever listened to me!

"Anyway, directing *Kotch* has been the single, unbelievably, most exciting and gratifying experience of my life. There has been nothing like it, nothing to approach it, in any way, both personally and professionally.

"What's more, I *like* the film. A New York critic called it 'sentimental.' I'm surprised we didn't get hit harder!"

Of Lemmon the director, Matthau says:

With Walter Matthau.

"He's a fantastic director because he has a most unique ability to communicate with the broad spectrum of personalities on the scene, a man with a magnificent command of all the integral parts of a script.

"He has taste, talent and imagination. And being an actor, he has the added advantage of understanding an actor's problems."

Plotwise, *Kotch* has to do with a seventy-two-year-old man (Matthau) no longer useful or needed. His daughter-in-law (Felicia Farr), convinced that he's incapable of tending to her year-old son, hires a babysitter (Deborah Winters).

Winters is dismissed after Matthau reports her on-duty sexual shenanigans with her boyfriend. Alone and pregnant now, she leaves school and goes off to live with "relatives."

Matthau feels guilty about her situation and, while on a bus trip, seeks her out and asks her to live with him in a rented house until the baby is born.

Life with Winters isn't easy; she's moody, disagreeable and generally ungrateful. But Matthau loves every minute of it. With responsibility, life has a totally new meaning.

Once the baby is born, matters change, however. Winters secretly packs up and leaves, leaving him alone. A few days later, he finds a note Winters had written to the baby at the time she was planning to give it up.

The note eloquently described the old man and his foibles, his faults and his very human virtues: "Absent a few marbles, maybe, but conditions being more favorable, he'd have made you one hell of a grandfather."

194

Walter Matthau (left), Donald Kowalski and Felicia Farr.

After reading this, Matthau splashes water in his face, fixes his hair and goes off to have a beer with an old crony.

The Critics

Judith Crist in *New York* magazine:

Small doubt that *Kotch* is sentimental, but with Walter Matthau in the title role and Jack Lemmon making a most auspicious directorial debut, the charm predominates and the result is nice, neat and touching.

The outgoing, convivial old man and the uptight introverted girl make an odd couple, but Matthau, refreshingly non-star and totally in character right down to the teeth-sucking tics of senility, and Deborah Winters, give the relationship a shining authenticity.

Matthau shows a new dimension to his art and Lemmon proves his abilities behind the camera match those he has shown out front.

Vincent Canby in *The New York Times:*

Kotch, the first film to be directed by Jack Lemmon, takes what is essentially a desperate situation—what to do with a lonely, garrulous old man who is a nuisance to his son and daughter-in-law—and transforms it into a nice, sentimental, Life-Can-Be-Beautiful comedy of the second order. Its theme song is called "Life Is What You Make It," which is about as equivocal as the movie ever gets.

Lemmon's ability as a director must be judged, I think, as much by the material with which he chose to make his debut, as by the end product. Both are so unadventurous as to be downright depressing.

Time:

(Deborah) Winters is one of the few young actresses with comic timing, and Matthau gives a carefully detailed impersonation of a Californian slipping into his anecdotage. He is both abetted and hindered by his director, a new boy named Jack Lemmon.

Matthau and Lemmon first worked together as fellow actors in *The Fortune Cookie* and consolidated their partnership in *The Odd Couple.* Lemmon obviously has great affection for his sidekick; in 114 minutes, the star is hardly ever off-screen.

But in his incessant concern to keep Matthau beautiful, Lemmon takes away dimension from everyone but Winters. Kotch's children are Punch and Judy, and his neighbors caricatures.

What's more, the soupy conclusion tends to weaken all that went before. *Kotch* is "family" entertainment, but in its anxiety to please, it eventually cloys. It is a yes-man of a movie that Joseph P. Kotcher would have disdained.

William Wolf in *Cue:*

Actors in the business long enough frequently yearn to direct. It is Jack Lemmon's turn, and his film is about what one might have expected would grow from his movie experience—a very commercial mixture of comedy and homey pathos. Audiences who don't demand depth or special talent may find the superficial film warm and enjoyable.

I admired the way Lemmon and Matthau isolate moments of loneliness, but was turned off by corn, contrived sentimentality, and songs with lyrics like "Smile, the world is sunny—your Easter bunny."

With Barbara Harris.

The War Between Men and Women

A Cinema Center–National General Picture (1972)

The Production Staff

Producer: Danny Arnold. *Director:* Melville Shavelson. *Original Screenplay:* Melville Shavelson and Danny Arnold. *Inspired by the writings and drawings of* James Thurber *(including "The Last Flower," a parable in pictures). Cinematographer:* Charles F. Wheeler. *Editor:* Frank Bracht. *Music:* Marvin Hamlisch. *Song "You and Me":* Marvin Hamlisch *(music) and* Howard Liebling *(lyrics). Sung by* Barbara Harris *and* Jason Robards. *Production Designer:* Stan Jolley. *Set Decorator:* Robert Benton. *Animation Supervisor:* Robert Dranko.

A Cinema Center Films Presentation. A Shavelson–Arnold Production. Released by National General Pictures. MPAA Rating: PG. Running Time: 110 minutes. In color.

The Cast

Peter Wilson: Jack Lemmon. *Terry Kozlenko:* Barbara Harris. *Stephen Kozlenko:* Jason Robards. *Howard Mann:* Herb Edelman. *Linda Kozlenko:* Lisa Gerritsen. *David Kozlenko:* Moosie Drier. *Caroline Kozlenko:* Lisa Eilbacher. *Doctor Harris:* Severn Darden.

The Movie

"The script was a damn sight better than the

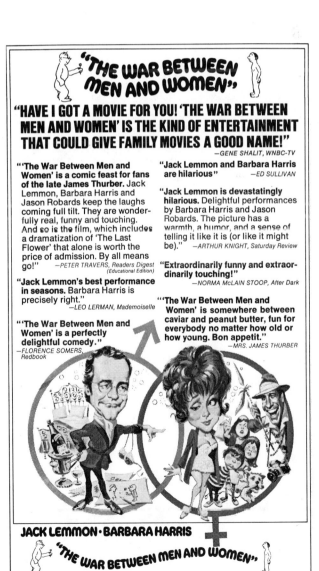

Quote-oriented advertisement for *The War Between Men and Women.*

With Jason Robards.

film," says Jack of this James Thurber-inspired comedy. "All I can say is sometimes you read a script and then you see the final result on film and you wonder what the hell went on during the making of it.

"Well, maybe you were just plain dead wrong in your initial appraisal of the script. Who knows?

"At the time, it was my first film in two years. I took a breather after *The Out-Of-Towners* to direct *Kotch*. There wasn't a stinking script in those two years that was worth doing.

"No, I'll qualify that. I read some outrageous things that I wanted to do but nobody would touch them. Then the very best thing I read—and I'm not just saying that—came along and the deal was made in forty-eight hours.

"What kicked me off is what always kicks me off: When I read a script and finish it, and I go all the way through it in one sitting because I'm so excited by it and then I realize that I don't know how to play the part."

The War Between Men and Women is a lot of dewy-eyed old muck about a starchy writer-cartoonist (Lemmon) who hates kids, dogs and especially women. It matters little to him that his fabulous career is based on his exploitation of females or that he seduces them regularly. To him, they're beneath contempt.

Naturally, the contrived script has Lemmon going out and marrying a flip divorcee (Barbara Harris) and settling down with her three—count 'em—three kids and ever-pregnant pooch.

The "fun" subsides momentarily for the purpose of introducing some heart-tugging sentiment: Lemmon, it seems, is slowly going blind. His career is doomed and he's too proud to live off Harris or her successful ex-husband (Jason Robards).

Since *The War Between Men and Women* was designed to be a family film, it ends on an upbeat note with Lemmon not only accepting his fate, but also curing Harris's second daughter (Lisa Gerritsen) of her stammer.

The release and eventual disappointment of

With Barbara Harris.

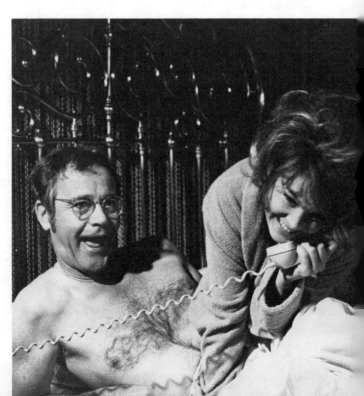

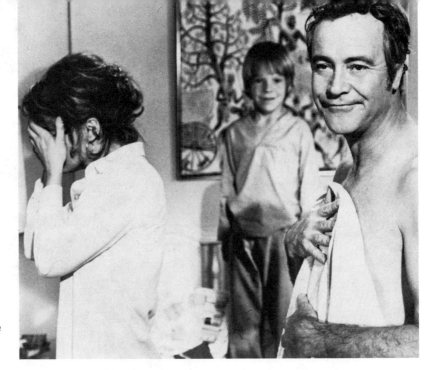

With Barbara Harris and Moosie Drier.

The War Between Men and Women had one yearning for the Jack Lemmon of yore—the Lemmon of *The Apartment, The Notorious Landlady, The Fortune Cookie* and *The April Fools*. The creatively subtle Lemmon.

There are a few scattered moments when this old Lemmon shines through in *War* but these come all too sporadically and fail to survive the deadening effect of the surrounding sentimentality, ineptness and, yes, vulgarity.

The War Between Men and Women proved to be something new in movies: an unwholesome family movie, replete with smutty jokes and smuttier situations.

The Critics

Paul D. Zimmerman in *Newsweek:*

The War Between Men and Women is a warm, human comedy about going blind. Jack Lemmon plays a curmudgeonly cartoonist and satirist who is, in fact, a lightly camouflaged stand-in for the great James Thurber. As Lemmon goes blind, he discovers that life can be beautiful and that women, dogs and children aren't agents of the devil after all.

This is the kind of tribute that makes you want to throw up. Once again, Jack Lemmon plays his specialty—the harried modern Everyman

With Barbara Harris.

as chump and victim—and once again he is mired up to his raised eyebrows in celluloid manure.

The movie (is) muddle-minded, sloppy and the sappy antithesis of everything the tough-minded Thurber held dear.

Liz Smith in *Cosmopolitan:*
The movie has the noise and quarrelsomeness of an old Terrytoon cartoon.

Yet otherwise Lemmon is his dry, wry old self; Barbara Harris is undoubtedly the most enchanting absentminded goof around; and Jason Robards is solidly in there as her ex-husband. You'll also see the best child actor in years—Lisa Gerritsen—who makes her stutter an art form.

Judith Crist in *New York* magazine:
All of this is garnished by the charming presences and ardent performances of Jack Lemmon and Jason Robards, as the husbands present and past, and Barbara Harris, as the absolutely char-

acterless woman in the middle. Each of their roles is so loaded with slickery, inconsistency and low-brow intellectualisms that the waste of talent is depressing.

Vincent Canby in *The New York Times:*
Watching *The War Between Men and Women* is like being in a haunted house in broad daylight. . . . However sunny it looks, it is really eerie, something all wrong and out of joint, a comedy about a man going blind, and about a child with a traumatic stammer.

Lemmon is not terribly funny, but he is vigorously myopic and looks ageless, neither young nor old, though a bit beat.

Although she hasn't the unbaked-cookie shape to be completely convincing as a Thurber woman, Miss Harris is so lovely and intelligent that I believed her completely. I also believed some other small moments in the film, like the little boy who, when asked what he is afraid of, answers desolately: "Everything."

Arthur Knight in *Saturday Review:*
(Jack Lemmon) is devastatingly hilarious when he drafts his agent to pretend to his wife that he is going off to Cape Cod to finish a book instead of into the hospital for an eye operation, touching and sympathetic when he remembers, belatedly, that he can't swim after diving off a pier to save a child, and when he knowingly makes another become angry enough to forget her habit of stammering.

With Juliet Mills.

Avanti!

A United Artists Picture (1972)

The Production Staff

Producer: Billy Wilder. *Director:* Billy Wilder. *Screenplay:* Billy Wilder *and* I. A. L. Diamond. *Based on the play of the same title by* Samuel Taylor. *Cinematographer:* Luigi Kuveiller. *Editor:* Ralph E. Winters. *Music:* Carlo Rustichelli. *Conducted by* Gianfranco Plemizion. *Art Director:* Ferdinando Scarfiotti.

A Phalanx-Jalem Production. A Mirisch Corporation Presentation. A United Artists Release. MPAA Rating: R. Running Time: 144 minutes. In color.

The Cast

Wendell Armbruster: Jack Lemmon. *Pamela Piggott:* Juliet Mills. *Carlo Carlucci:* Clive Revill. *J. J. Blodgett:* Edward Andrews. *Bruno:* Gianfranco Barra. *Anna:* Giselda Castrini.

The Movie

Billy Wilder's *Avanti!* is one of those unfortunate

Original ad for *Avanti!*

With Juliet Mills.

to Italy to claim the remains of his father, who was killed in an auto accident.

While there, the son learns that the old gent did not die alone; his English mistress was with him. Apparently, the couple had been carrying on every summer for over ten years.

The mistress's daughter (Mills) is also on hand and before long—you guessed it—the offspring are mimicking the romantic shenanigans of their elders. And that's it.

Lemmon pretty much groans and moans his way through the film, but he grows on you and his character eventually experiences a kind of liberation which makes it more agreeable by the end of the story.

Pudgy little Juliet Mills (she gained weight for the film), however, is a smashing delight, stealing the film as the English miss with an incurably romantic nature.

All in all, the contents of *Avanti!* are all pleasure. It's too bad that it takes more than one viewing to fully realize this fact.

The Critics

Judith Crist in *New York* magazine:
Romantic comedy from another time is offered

rarities that seems like a cinematic mishap after the first viewing (and hence is panned) but gets progressively better with each viewing (and hence never receives the favorable recognition it fully deserves).

The movie has everything going for it—a clever, romantic plot, some good ideas and dialogue, beautiful scenery, the fetching Juliet Mills and, of course, Lemmon.

It's a film whose parts are greater than its whole—but whose whole, even though it's lacking, is a good deal greater than other film comedies around.

Based on an unsuccessful Samuel Taylor play, *Avanti!* is a wistful throwback to Wilder's *Love In the Afternoon*, possessing the same cleverness, sophistication and high-style fun.

Substantial in length (it runs a longish 144 minutes), its plot is engaging: An uptight, middle-aged, married American (Lemmon) journeys

With Juliet Mills.

204

With Juliet Mills.

by Billy Wilder and I. A. L. Diamond, who chose to resurrect Samuel Taylor's *Avanti!*, a 1968, twenty-one-performance Broadway disaster.

The moment the stage is set, we can creak our way to the ending, which arrives an eternity of 144 minutes later.

Jack Lemmon, as the chap who thaws within his own limits; Juliet Mills, as the charmingly womanly girl with an endearing (at least to me) weight problem, and Clive Revill, as the all-understanding hotel manager, are all admirable and there are fine bits.

Donald J. Mayerson in *Cue*:
It is hard to believe that this sour chianti has come from the rich vineyards of Billy Wilder and

I. A. L. Diamond. Those masters of comedy have reconstituted the ingredients of an unsuccessful Samuel Taylor play; ecco—a movie flatter than a pizza.

Jack Lemmon strains and puffs his way through the role of an American business executive summoned to Italy to bring home the remains of his deceased father.... The proceeding drags on and on. It all has the air of a funeral, which I suppose is appropriate.

Juliet Mills is acceptable as (a) pudgy British girl, and Lemmon should be paid to keep his clothes on.

Jay Cocks in *Time*:
The topical dialogue by Wilder and I. A. L. Dia-

With Juliet Mills.

205

With Juliet Mills.

mond—Kissinger jokes, Billy Graham jokes, etc.—gives this passingly pleasant movie the sound of a Bob Hope TV special.

But Miss Mills is fresh and winning, and there is a deft performance by Clive Revill as the unflappable hotel manager who treats the problems of the tourist season, from overcrowding to murder, with style and resource.

A. H. Weiler in *The New York Times:*

Intermittently funny, charming, cute and, unfortunately, overlong . . . (Wilder and Diamond) have warped some parts of the playwright's plot to give us a fairly reasonable flow of giggles and an occasional guffaw.

Lemmon handles it all in satisfyingly familiar, confused, frenetic style, despite lead coffins and ransom for the bodies snatched by a local vintner, who know a good touch when he sees one.

Archer Winsten in the *New York Post:*

It is not possible for a Billy Wilder movie to be without some sharp asides, but this one is not his best by a long shot. Jack Lemmon's face seems to be hardening into something more given to fury than finesse.

Juliet Mills, with twenty-five pounds of meat padding her bones in this particular role, is still a charmer, but no one will resent her going back to her original 107 pounds.

With Juliet Mills.

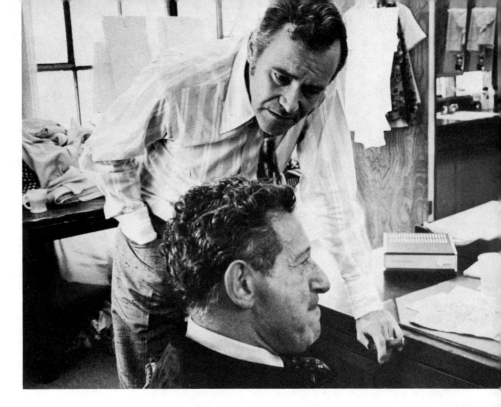

With Jack Gilford.

Save the Tiger

A Paramount Picture (1973)

The Production Staff

Producer: Steve Shagan. *Executive Producer:* Edward S. Feldman. *Director:* John G. Avildsen. *Original Screenplay:* Steve Shagan. *Cinematographer:* Jim Crabe. *Editor:* David Bretherton. *Music:* Marvin Hamlisch. *Art Director:* Jack Collis. *Set Decorator:* Ray Molyneaux.

A Filmways–Jalem–Cirandinha Production. A Paramount Release. MPAA Rating: R. Running Time: 100 minutes. In color.

The Cast

Harry Stoner: Jack Lemmon. *Janet Stoner:* Patricia Smith. *Phil Green:* Jack Gilford. *Myra (the hitchhiker):* Laurie Heineman. *Fred Mirrell:* Norman Burton. *Margo (the prostitute):* Lara Parker. *Meyer:* William Hansen. *Rico:* Harvey Jason. *Charlie Robbins:* Thayer David. *Sid Fivush:* Ned Glass. *Box-Office Cashier:* Pearl Shear. *Tiger Man:* Biff Elliott.

The Movie

"It's an absolute ripper!"

Original ad for *Save the Tiger.*

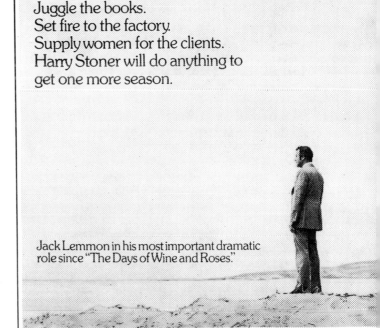

So says Jack Lemmon of *Save the Tiger,* the stunning character study which won him his long-awaited and well-deserved Oscar as Best Actor.

"I just thank God that it came along when it did. It's terribly difficult—no matter what your position in the industry may be—to find a script of real substance with a part that truly excites you and challenges you.

"I just hope it isn't another decade before it happens again."

Defining *Save the Tiger* is a problem. The problem at hand is to define an intensely personal reaction with a certain amount of self-control, honesty, finesse and economy—the very same ingredients that characterize the movie itself.

Essentially, as written by Steve Shagan and directed by John G. Avildsen, the movie stands as a dazzling one-character showcase about a well-married, successful businessman—Harry Stoner—who is unable to reconcile himself with the prospects of either failure or middle age.

The focus is almost solely on Harry during a telling thirty-six-hour period in his life.

The period brings Harry face to face with the sudden realization of middle age, imminent fail-

With Jack Gilford.

ure and his role in a sick society. It forces him to analyze and reevaluate himself through memories and fading dreams.

Harry is a prominent dress manufacturer. His business is now in trouble. A planned fire is his only way out—a fire in one of his warehouses.

The idea of this crime clashes with the ideals Harry held high as a young man—and

therein lies the point and the fascination of *Save the Tiger*.

It's a penetrating, powerful theme, and Lemmon and company give it a tough, uncompromising reading.

It's a joy to watch Lemmon's foremost performance as Harry and to share the actor's realization that he's reached the pinnacle of his career.

His dramatic ability has been nicely displayed in the past *(Days of Wine and Roses, Cowboy* and *The Fortune Cookie)*, but never so overwhelmingly.

His natural dramatic potential is at long last realized here—in a performance that's daring, resourceful, bittersweet and joyously memorable.

Shagan's dialogue—rich with raw, anguished outbursts and gems of wisdom—rates high among the screen's finest. Many lines are of classic stature. Lemmon agrees.

"Purely from an actor's point of view," notes Jack, "it's a strong, good dramatic piece, and one that's terribly pertinent.

"When I was doing it, I kept crying all the time. I'd be driving along and start crying. I'd see an old lady and start to cry. I still can't shake it.

"It's positively the best part I've ever had, and the best film I've ever done.

"You see, the film goes beyond the character of Harry and what he is; it shows the society has bred a man that can commit a felony. A basically decent man.

"Like the tiger, Harry is an endangered species. He's no Sammy Glick. Harry Stoner is a decent man who's changed, whose values are lost, whose world has changed since he was a kid. There's a part of Harry in everyone out there.

"*Save the Tiger* deals with the misuse of the American Dream. It offers no solutions, no answers. Art doesn't have to do that. What it does is make you see things in a bigger light.

"The movie says a lot of valid and important things. In this respect, it's a thinkpiece, but not a message film. It offers opinions in the form of an entertainment. Primarily, it's an entertainment—a dramatization with some high drama and even good bits of comedy.

"We're not preaching here; at least, I hope we're not. We're merely showing how hard it is today to stick by our principles and how easy it is to rationalize everything.

"John Avildsen—the choice of Steve Shagan, incidentally—is an intense young man. I think he brought more to the film than any more experienced director ever could. He avoided 'Hollywood gloss,' providing the film instead with a realistic, sometimes crude look."

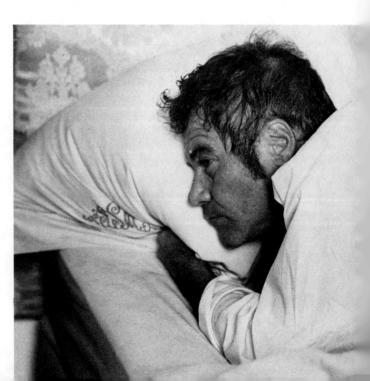

In winning his Oscar for *Save the Tiger*, Lemmon defeated one contemporary, Marlon Brando *(Last Tango in Paris)*, and three relative newcomers, Al Pacino *(Serpico)*, Jack Nicholson *(The Last Detail)* and Robert Redford *(The Sting)*.

The Critics

Judith Crist in *New York* magazine:
There are, for the audience as well as for the actor, those moments of perfect conjunction, when the actor and the role are suddenly one in a unique yet universal creation. . . . This rare and essential union is one of the hallmarks of *Save the Tiger,* John G. Avildsen's new film that, despite its flaws, stands as a remarkable achievement for its writer, its director, and above all, its star.

Lemmon's Harry Stoner is Ensign Pulver grown up—and ground up in the survival struggles of the past twenty years. He is the Everyman of the pre-World II generation that had ballplayers as heroes.

(The film's flaws) are overshadowed by the literacy of the screenplay, the excellent supporting performances and the superlative achievement of Lemmon.

This is Shagan's first script, Avildsen's best film to date and, for Lemmon, a triumphant celebration of his twentieth year in films.

Vincent Canby in *The New York Times:*
Save the Tiger is not a very good movie but it's a rather brave one, a serious-minded examination of some of the least interesting aspects of the failed American Dream.

In spite of very good performances by Mr. Lemmon, who projects a lightweight bitterness that is a sad fact of homogenized American culture, and by Jack Gilford, *Save the Tiger* never succeeds in disassociating itself from the self-pity it details."

Arthur Knight in *Saturday Review:*
Lemmon is always right as Harry. (The character) goes through twenty-four hours of accelerating tension, and at each point Lemmon lets us see not only the toll of those tensions but the basically decent guy underneath, the one we are sympathizing with and rooting for.

In one of the film's final sequences, (the character) launches into a litany of all the famous names that are meaningful to him. At that mo-

With his Oscar for *Save the Tiger*.

ment all role-playing ceases. Harry Stoner and Jack Lemmon are fused as any actor ever can be with the character he is creating.

Donald J. Mayerson in *Cue:*
An Arthur Miller world of the middle class is re-created by director John G. Avildsen in this pre-tentious film which deals with a day in the life of a middle-aged Los Angeles dress manufac-turer. The struggle for success and survival and the conflicts about morality remind one of early Miller, but author Steve Shagan's hero is such a hollow, charmless heel that his marital and busi-ness problems leave one unmoved.

   Avildsen does particularly well in handling the milieu of his people. Jack Lemmon gives an intricate, incisive performance as the hero, Jack Gilford catches the full flavor of his role as the business partner. Unfortunately, their expertise could not save the film.

Norma McLain Stoop in *After Dark:*
Seeing such a fine actor as Jack Lemmon with the opportunity of showing what he can do with a rewarding role is much to be grateful for. When the part is a complex characterization in a most interesting story, as in *Save the Tiger*, one can be doubly grateful.

   Save the Tiger is a deeply felt testament to American values—past and present—and it is a joy to see such an unusually fine production.

With Marv Kupfer.

Wednesday

An American Film Institute Picture (1974)

The Production Staff

Producer: Marv Kupfer. *Director:* Marv Kupfer. *Original Screenplay:* Barbara Witus *and* Marv Kupfer. *Cinematographer:* Irv Goodnoff. *Editors:* Michael Jablow *and* Barbara Noble.

Sponsored by the American Film Institute's Center for Advanced Film Studies. Running Time: 17 minutes. In color.

The Cast

Jerry Murphy: Jack Lemmon. *The Engineer:* Biff Elliot. *The Husband:* Ron Gold. *The D. J.:* Gene Weed. *The voices of the women on the telephone:* Selette Cole, Sarah Jean Frost *and* Carmelita Mann.

The Movie

Wednesday, an amazing first film by student filmmaker Marv Kupfer, is a highly professional and proficient vignette based on an original eighteen-page script about a show-bizzy, irresponsible disc jockey who invites housewives to call in and confess (on the air) their secret sins and vices.

Lemmon came into the production when Kupfer submitted his script to the actor for his perusal and opinion.

Always an active supporter of the American Film Institute and its programs, Lemmon read the script and was so impressed with its theme and contents that he offered to appear in it—in the role of the disc jockey, Jerry Murphy.

He received no money for his participation, but if *Wednesday* is ever made available for commercial engagements or televising, he'll be paid the minimum scale.

To date, the film's exposure has been limited to campus showings and film festivals, including the 1974 Atlanta Film Festival where it won the Gold Medal.

"I don't care—or know—whether it will be seen by the public," says Jack. "The important thing is that this kid now has a film to show what he can do. AFI is the one great hope for the movie industry."

Filmmaker Kupfer is one of the active members of the Fellows of the American Film Institute's Center for Advanced Film Studies. He holds a BA in journalism from the University of Missouri and worked briefly with the *Chicago Tribune* and *Newsweek* after foregoing a scholarship award to the Yale Drama School.

Kupfer's film—co-authored with Barbara Witus—has been given a bright, sunny look, courtesy of Irv Goodnoff's cinematography, a look which nicely counterpoints the disturbing theme.

Jack Lemmon as disc jockey Jerry Murphy.

The plot has Jerry Murphy probing his female listeners' sex lives—primarily for the sheer fun and ego-gratifying challenge of it. It's also good business, ratingwise.

On one particular day, a Wednesday, a silly, itchy woman telephones and foolishly reveals all about her husband, her lover and their respective lovemaking techniques. Jerry gleefully forces more and more information out of her.

Meanwhile, the camera picks up a car driving along. The driver—is it the woman's husband?—hears the conversation and promptly makes an irrational and threatening call to Jerry.

The film ends with the disc jockey making a nervous, tacky on-air apology.

Lemmon's performance here is especially efficient—a neat little character study of a screwed-up man.

"I came away from the experience," says Jack, "impressed with the knowledge and approach of the AFI students. The only difference I felt was that the shooting took a little longer than usual."

For the filming of *Wednesday*, the crew of students took over a small radio station for five nights. Their overall accomplishment is highly commendable, especially their avoidance of any sort of self-indulgence.

An occasional lack of subtlety in the writing is the only visible flaw in *Wednesday*.

The Critics

Variety:

Judging from Lemmon's excellent performance, the script's complex sophistication and the film's technical assurance, Kupfer is ready to direct a major feature tomorrow.

215

The Front Page

A Universal Picture (1974)

The Production Staff

Producer: Paul Monash. *Executive Producer:* Jennings Lang. *Director:* Billy Wilder. *Screenplay:* Billy Wilder *and* I. A. L. Diamond. *Based on the play of the same title by* Ben Hecht *and* Charles MacArthur. *Cinematographer:* Jordan S. Cronenweth. *Editor:* Ralph E. Winters. *Music:* Billy May. *Song* "Button Up Your Overcoat": B. G. DeSylva, Lew Brown *and* Ray Henderson. *Sung by* Susan Sarandon. *Song* "That Old Gang of Mine." *Sung by* Jack Lemmon and male chorus. *Art Director:* Henry Bumstead. *Set Decorator:* James W. Payne.

A Billy Wilder Film. A Universal–MCA Release. MPAA Rating: PG. Running Time: 105 minutes. In color and Panavision.

The Cast

Hildy Johnson: Jack Lemmon. *Walter Burns:* Walter Matthau. *Peggy Grant:* Susan Sarandon. *Earl Williams:* Austin Pendleton. *Mollie Malloy:* Carol Burnett. *Sheriff Hartman:* Vincent Gardenia. *Bensinger:* David Wayne. *Rudy Keppler:* Jon Korkes. *Dr. Eggelhofer:* Martin Gabel. *The Mayor:* Harold Gould. *Kruger:* Allen Garfield.

Original ad for *The Front Page.*

Murphy: Charles Durning. *McHugh:* Dick O'Neill. *Wilson:* Noam Pitlik. *Schwartz:* Herbert Edelman. *Jacobi:* Cliff Osmond. *Endicott:* Lou Frizzell. *Jennie:* Doro Merande.

The Movie

Billy Wilder's colorful remake of the celebrated Ben Hecht–Charles MacArthur theatrical piece, *The Front Page*, was released during the 1974 Christmas holidays and, appropriately enough, came bearing the joyous gifts of laughter, happiness, a warm heart and overall cinema perfection.

The film fairly oozes with opulent dash and loving care.

Its setting is Chicago, circa 1929. Its subject is big-city news reporting at its most flamboyant. And its focus is on those wonderful Damon Runyon denizens—American newspapermen—hardboiled, wisecracking, whiskey-guzzling and irreverent.

Newspaper people are a dedicated, colorful lot, to say the least—a fact beautifully realized in Wilder's picture-perfect casting.

The cast here is alert, attractive and fastidious, headed by Lemmon and Matthau, reteamed for the third hallelujah time.

The actors miss neither a beat, a mannerism nor an inflection. And the marvelous, driving dialogue couldn't be in better hands.

In this go-round, Lemmon (bright and sassy) plays reporter Hildy Johnson and Matthau (cagey and harried) is managing editor Walter Burns. Both are the backbone of the Chicago Examiner.

The Wilder–I. A. L. Diamond adaptation is faithful to the original play.

With Susan Saradon.

Burns is in desperate need for a scoop, preferably one concerning the notorious Earl Williams, a convicted cop-slayer. He isn't beneath creating a scoop if he has to—and Hildy, his top boy, is the one guy clever enough to concoct one.

Trouble is, Hildy has sworn off journalism (and the "politics and poker" that go with it) for good. He plans to turn respectable, marry, relocate in Philadelphia and join an ad agency.

Or so he thinks. The press room of the Chicago Criminal Courts building is alive with chaos: Earl Williams has escaped—and only Johnson knows where he is. What a scoop!

What follows is a mad scramble, with just about everybody chasing down the story, double-

With Austin Pendleton and Carol Burnett.

217

crossing everybody else and—all in all—running amuck.

Outstanding among the supporting performers here are Vincent Gardenia as the corrupt Sheriff Hartman; David Wayne as Bensinger, the prissy reporter for the rival Tribune and, most especially, Austin Pendleton, perfection as the sickly Earl Williams.

The distaff side is well-represented by Susan Sarandon as Peggy Grant, Lemmon's working-girl fiancee, and talented Carol Burnett as Mollie Malloy, Williams' prostitute-girlfriend.

The various reporters are played to the hilt by actors recruited from both Broadway and Hollywood (and all provide the film with a raucous, Runyonesque festal atmosphere): Allen Garfield, Jon Korkes, Charles Durning, Dick O'Neill, Noam Pitlik, Herb Edelman and Lou Frizzell.

They all do well by newsmen and pulp alike and also manage to keep *The Front Page* moving with the swift, smooth and mellifluous flow of a carousel—set to nickelodeon music, natch.

(One final note: The Wilder–Diamond screenplay includes an original Lemmon witticism that goes, "May the wind at your back never be your own!")

The Critics

Judith Crist in *New York* magazine:
Billy Wilder's remake of *The Front Page* is a re-

Hirschfeld caricature of director Billy Wilder (far right) with Carol Burnett, Jack Lemmon and Walter Matthau.

freshing refurbishment for our times. (He) has brought the bite and cynicism that is the hallmark of so much of his comedy to the 1928 Ben Hecht–Charles MacArthur stage play, wherein the Twenties were made more roaring by the Chicago Examiner's managing editor, Walter Burns, and star reporter, Hildy Johnson.

(Burns and Johnson) now come to us in that fail-safe team of Walter Matthau and Jack Lemmon, first linked by Wilder in *The Fortune Cookie*.

With Cliff Osmond and Walter Matthau.

Matthau and Lemmon cannot be faulted, with Susan Sarandon charming as the fiancee, Vincent Gardenia properly despicable as the sheriff, Austin Pendleton absolutely delightful as "the screwball who had the rotten luck to kill a colored cop in an election year," and Martin Gabel the ultimate Freudian to end all psychiatrist takeoffs.

Vincent Canby in *The New York Times:*

It had to happen sooner or later that Billy Wilder, one of the most astringent wits of the American cinema, would make a movie out of *The Front Page*. The property is a natural for Mr. Wilder and his screenwriting collaborator, I. A. L. Diamond, who, despite all their comparatively "nice" hits, have a special (and, to my mind, very appealing) appreciation for vulgar, brilliant con artists of monumental tackiness.

The Front Page displays (this) giddy bitterness that is rare in any films except those of Mr. Wilder. It is also, much of the time, extremely funny.

The Wilder–Diamond screenplay updates and makes somewhat rougher the original tough-guy dialogue and wisecracks, but the story has not been violated.

Singing *That Old Gang of Mine* with the press room boys.

The film contains at least two marvelous performances, Mr. Matthau's snarling, monomaniacal editor and Austin Pendleton as the condemned revolutionary.

Mr. Lemmon is comparatively reserved as the flamboyant Hildy, never quite letting go of his familiar comic personality to become dominated by the lunacies of the farce. He always remains a little outside it, acting.

Kathleen Carroll in the New York *Daily News:*
It is a juicy edition, full of the spark and the wit that Wilder and Diamond are most noted for. The comedy is perhaps too broad. And the movie seems unable to capture the more human qualities of the characters.

It is more a tabloid version of the play, but no matter, it is lively, refreshingly caustic and easily one of the funniest movies of the year.

Lemmon and Matthau are never better or more relaxed than when they are feeding each other lines and serving as foils for one another. Lemmon seems to lose that harried look and that nervous twitch, at least he certainly does in this case, a fact that makes his performance more appealing than ever.

Donald J. Mayerson in *Cue:*
Billy Wilder is at the top of his form. Taking Ben

With Carol Burnett.

Hecht's and Charles MacArthur's 1928 stage classic, Wilder has turned it into one of the funniest comedies of 1974. Lemmon and Matthau work and play together superbly. They are the top clowns in a terrific three-ring circus.

Archer Winsten in the *New York Post:*
It is very hard to see the picture as something fresh. Equally it is virtually impossible for the performers to add anything, and they don't. Walter Matthau, for the first time in memory, fails to thrill with his work, and Jack Lemmon simply goes through what he's supposed to do.

With Austin Pendleton.

With Anne Bancroft.

The Prisoner of Second Avenue

A Warner Bros. Picture (1975)

The Production Staff

Producer: Melvin Frank. *Director:* Melvin Frank. *Screenplay:* Neil Simon. *Based on his play of the same title. Cinematographer:* Philip Lathrop. *Editor:* Bob Wyman. *Music:* Marvin Hamlisch. *Art Director:* Preston Ames. *Set Decorator:* Marvin March.

A Melvin Frank Production. A Warner Bros. Release. MPAA Rating: PG. Running Time: 98 minutes. In color and Panavision.

The Cast

Mel: Jack Lemmon. *Edna:* Anne Bancroft. *Harry:* Gene Saks. *Belle:* Maxine Stuart. *Pauline:* Elizabeth Wilson. *Pearl:* Florence Stanley. *Charlie:* Gene Blakely. *Psychiatrist:* Ivor Francis. *Detective:* Stack Pierce. *Man Upstairs:* Ed Peck.

The Movie

In New York, just east of Central Park, lies the

Original ad for *The Prisoner of Second Avenue.*

fashionable, nouveau-riche district. The East Side. Particularly Second and Third Avenues, above 57th Street.

Swank high-rise apartments. Expensive restaurants. Neat little boutiques. And tension. Plenty of the latter.

Neil Simon's *The Prisoner of Second Avenue* —especially as translated on screen—is an amazingly perceptive, sad-funny examination of two people brutalized by the affluence and the comforts they slaved to attain.

Fifteen years earlier, in 1960, Billy Wilder wrote *The Apartment* for Jack Lemmon—the story of C. C. Baxter, an ambitious office clerk living in the West 60s but longing for Second Avenue.

The Prisoner of Second Avenue nearly shows the same man years later, "successful" in the way he wanted to be and now "comfortably" transplanted to the East Side. Only now his name is Mel.

While *The Apartment* is about striving for life at the top, *The Prisoner of Second Avenue* details the problems in *coping* with life at the top.

The two serve as veritable companion films, contrasting character studies of one man—then and now—made all the more fascinating because the character is portrayed by one actor, Jack Lemmon—then and now.

On stage, Simon's work seemed little more than an elongated comedy sketch, frenzied and high-pitched and in desperate need of revealing close-ups which only the camera could provide.

On screen, the work seems more refined

With Anne Bancroft.

and in control of itself—shorter, trimmer, less strained, less pretentious and, above all, substantially more dramatic.

There's also perfect chemistry between Lemmon and Anne Bancroft, who look and sound as if they might actually be married to one another.

They play Mel and Edna—and their situation is not particularly unique. Nor is it particularly funny. What's funny is their occasionally pointed reaction to it. And what's affecting about the whole thing is their stubborn determination to survive.

Mel is C. C. Baxter updated—a former Junior Executive who has worked his way up to the top. But the top is a pretty shaky place to be,

With Anne Bancroft.

224

With Gene Saks.

topheavy with discarded bodies of former colleagues.

The men around him in the office are losing their jobs right and left and, economics being what they are, Mel fears that he's next. This makes him nervous, to say the least, a problem that's compounded by the tormenting inconvenience of high-rise living.

Predictably, he loses his job, along with his sense of well-being and his rationality. So Edna takes a job. Meanwhile, Mel regresses.

Life is miserable for the next few weeks or so, with Mel reacting to his bruised ego with outbursts, insults and slurs—all directed at Edna.

Then Edna loses her job and—well, they don't exactly live happily ever after, but they do survive and eventually recover from their affluence.

Although Anne Bancroft nearly steals the film with her crackerjack stab at an atypical comedy role, Lemmon outdoes himself, mixing humor and pathos as he's never done before. This is one of his two or three best performances.

The Critics

Variety:

Neil Simon's *The Prisoner of Second Avenue* has been filmed, from a Simon adaptation, by producer-director Melvin Frank with Jack Lemmon and Anne Bancroft starred as a harried urban couple. The film is more of a drama with comedy, for the personal problems as well as the environmental challenges aren't really funny, and even some of the humor is forced and strident. The Warner Bros. release may therefore perform erratically.

Lemmon has done prior Simon plots on the screen, and he has the same basic character down cold. Bancroft is less familiar to filmgoers in this type of comedy, and she demonstrates a fine versatility in facing the script demands. Atop the couple's problems in their apartment comes Lemmon's axing after many years on the job. Gene Saks, Elizabeth Wilson and Florence Stanley do well as Lemmon's brother and sisters, while Ed Peck, the hostile upstairs neighbor, and Ivor Francis, Lemmon's taciturn shrink, head a good supporting cast.

With Anne Bancroft.

But maybe there have been too many films on the trials of urban existence to make yet another parade of big city woes laughable. And the job-displaced middle-aged population segments aren't exactly comedy material in light of current reality. Also, Simon's comedy is no better and no worse than it was in the Sixties; the trouble is, it's now the Seventies.

Technical credits are all professional. It is to Frank's credit that, given his proven empathy for human nature, the film comes off as well as it does.

Judith Crist in *New York* magazine:

Simon's is a comedy-drama, like most of his recent works, as filled with pain as with wow one-liners. And if, in the interim before its arrival on film, we have had a number of movies about the irritations, insanities, and inhumanities in the pressure cooker of Fun City life, we have had none so close to the upper-middle-class bone and none that offers a man and woman of such dimension and root.

Lemmon, of course, is complete master of

the harried ad-man character, adding the neuroses and uncertainties of the times to gnaw at his innards, the petty humiliations becoming outsized in the course of the major ones of job loss, of a home burglarized, of loving relatives who weigh the love.

Saturday Review:

The film, though it is largely comedic, has gained some relevance because of current events. . . . It's not quite so much of a joke. Almost as though realizing this, Mel Frank, the producer and director, has gotten an anguished performance from Jack Lemmon as Mel and a sensitive one from Anne Bancroft as his wife, Edna.

The compass of the story may be small, but what is given to us is made to work as entertainment with a certain amount of bite.

A. H. Weiler in The New York Times:

With a cast whose members appreciate what they're saying and doing, the gnawing problems of "Second Avenue" become a pleasure.

If Melvin Frank's direction is polished but not innovative, he is ably aided by Jack Lemmon and Anne Bancroft, who project forcefully natural characterizations that are as realistic as the authentic Second Avenue and other New York sites caught.

Mr. Lemmon and Miss Bancroft are simply an unromanticized, believable team as recognizable in their comic and serious give-and-take as many of New York's scrambling millions.

Al Hirschfeld caricature of Jack Lemmon and Anne Bancroft as Mel and Edna Edison in *The Prisoner of Second Avenue*.

Ann Guarino in the New York Daily News:

Neil Simon has effectively converted to the screen "The Prisoner of Second Avenue," his hilarious comedy-drama about the problems of city living.

Jack Lemmon is excellent as the frenetic hero. He is at his neurotic best plotting revenge on the man upstairs who dumped a pail of water on him. Anne Bancroft is warm, witty and a good comic foil as the wife.

Glamour:

Lemmon is, as always, marvelous, bitter, angry,

With Anne Bancroft.

227

With Anne Bancroft.

raging and funny, a sort of curdled Caspar Milquetoast, who has lost his job and is in the process of losing his mind to the city. It is a deft, funny movie and contains . . . Lemmon's incomparable ability to make one laugh.

Norma McLaine Stoop in *After Dark:*

Jack Lemmon handles the varied moods of his role with awesome expertise, and Anne Bancroft, as his talented, loving wife, gives a performance of surpassing artistry. (The film) is an absolute gold mine of entertainment with deep lodes of poignancy, sparkling nuggets of humor and won-

derful acting that polishes the product to a high gloss.

William Wolf in *Cue:*

Jack Lemmon gets a fair share of laughs as he rages against the frustrations of neighbors, noise, dirt, unemployment, growing older—just about everything.

But the attempt by Simon as screenwriter and Melvin Frank as director to make the film more dramatic and touching only makes it maudlin and unconvincing as tragedy.

Lemmon and Bolger.

The Entertainer

A Robert Stigwood Organization, Inc. Picture (1976)

The Production Staff

Producers: Beryl Vertue *and* Marvin Hamlisch. *Director:* Donald Wrye. *Screenplay:* Elliott Baker. *Based on the play of the same title by* John Osborne. *Cinematographer:* Jim Crabe. *Editor:* Ralph Winters. *Music:* Marvin Hamlisch. *Lyrics:* Robert Joseph. *Theme Song Lyrics:* Tim Rice. *Choreographer:* Ron Field. *Art Direction:* Bob Mackichan. *Set Decorator:* Sam Jones. *Costumes:* Dick Bruno *and* Marie Brown.

A Stigwood Production, in association with Persky-Bright Organization. No MPAA Rating. Running Time: 105 minutes. In color.

The Cast

Archie Rice: Jack Lemmon. *Billy Rice:* Ray Bolger. *Phoebe Rice:* Sada Thompson. *Jean Rice:* Tyne Daly. *Frank Rice:* Michael Cristofer. *Bambi Pasko:* Annette O'Toole. *Mr. Pasko:* Mitch Ryan. *Mrs. Pasko:* Allyn Ann McLerie. *Lilly:* Rita O'Connor. *Charlie:* Dick O'Neill. *Charlene:* Leanna Johnson.

The Musical Numbers

"The Only Way To Go"	Jack Lemmon
"Bend Over Backwards" and chorus girls	Jack Lemmon
"Can't Stop Horsing Around" and Ray Bolger	Jack Lemmon

Advertising art for U.S. telecast; film was theatrically presented in Europe.

Mobil Showcase presents

JACK LEMMON in THE ENTERTAINER

In 1944, when America was fighting for her life, Archie Rice was doing two shows a day for his.

starring RAY BOLGER and SADA THOMPSON
based on the John Osborne drama
original music by Marvin Hamlisch
WED. MAR. 10 9-11 PM NBC   Mobil

Three views of Lemmon as Archie.

The Movie

Elliott Baker's Americanized version of the celebrated West-End John Osborne play, *The Entertainer*—shown on TV in America, but presented theatrically throughout Europe—is a property which affords Lemmon the opportunity to essay a role created by one of his acting heroes, Sir Laurence Olivier, and also to sing on-screen on a full scale for the first time since *You Can't Run Away From It* (1956).

Baker's superficial and revamped screenplay pretty much destroys the point and purpose of the original Osborne piece and the situations in Baker's script (still basically British in texture and mood) prove to be hardly compatible with the new California backdrop.

But for Lemmon, the movie is a dazzling showcase for his versatility and acting depth and, professionally, serves as a good shot-in-the-arm for his career.

As Archie Rice, a failed vaudevillian, Lemmon takes center stage early on in the piece and holds on to it with the same command that Olivier exhibited in the earlier version. Within a scene, within a moment, Lemmon goes from desperately cruel to pathetically funny, all with razor-edge timing and an acting expertise wherein everything speaks—his eyes, his facial expressions, his body movements.

Lemmon insists that he modeled his interpretation of the role after "at least 100 different actors that I know." This makes sense, because in the end, *The Entertainer* emerges as Lemmon's own highly personal homage to the talents, hopes and frustrations of all actors and performers.

Prominently featured in the movie as Archie's father, a once-celebrated king of the vaudeville circuits, is the venerable Ray Bolger, making his first film appearance in ten years.

With Tyne Daly and Bolger.

Cast as Archie's long-suffering wife, Phoebe, is Sada Thompson and completing the ensemble for *The Entertainer* are Tyne Daly, Dick O'Neill, Annette O'Toole, Mitch Ryan and Allyn Ann McLerie.

Set in an American seaside resort in 1944, the piece recounts the efforts of Archie Rice (Jack Lemmon) to capture an audience's laughter, applause and approval. A middle-aged vaudevillian, he seeks the spotlight and the limelight, two entities never rightfully his.

Unhappy and unsatisfied in his role of husband and father, and forever caught in the shadow of his top-banana father (Ray Bolger), Archie has been reduced to a man of broken promises, idle dreams, cutting accusations and haunting snatches of song.

He berates his wife (Sada Thompson) when really his own weaknesses are to blame, ignores

Lemmon with Sada Thompson.

his children's need for him and forever and desperately seeks celebration as a star.

An unfortunate involvement with an unlucky show (and an affair with a girl younger than his grown daughter) forces Archie to seek out his father for both tangible and intangible aid.

To help keep his desperate son afloat, Archie's father agrees to perform with his son. There's magic in their on-stage antics—and also tragedy. The routine kills the aged Mr. Rice.

Again, Archie is left on stage alone. There's only one positive response from the audience. It comes from Phoebe, Archie's wife.

Archie plays to the sound, like a dying flower turning to the rain.

He could always leave Phoebe laughing—if no one else.

Supplementing and complementing all of this are several original songs penned by co-producer Marvin Hamlisch and some aptly tacky choreography by Ron Field.

The Entertainer marks the theatrical directorial debut of Donald Wrye, who replaced the project's original director, John G. Avildsen, at the last minute. Wrye's previous credits include such acclaimed and controversial TV movies as *Death Be Not Proud* and *Born Innocent*. Under Wrye's direction, Lemmon earned an Emmy nomination for his performance as Archie.

The Critics

Variety:

As a whole, the screenplay seems stronger than the Osborne original, although there is more schmaltz and it appears less symbolic. Lemmon gives a fine performance as Archie. Sometimes though, in his stage performances he is not so awful as he should be, giving the impression that he needs a better scriptwriter.

Pauline Kael in *The New Yorker:*

Language may be the only true glory that England has left, and so it seems just about the final insult to Americanize *The Entertainer*. A California-set *Entertainer* is like *A Streetcar Named Desire* laid in Edinburgh. Actually, it's even more of an act of cultural vandalism than that would be, because in Osborne's metaphor the decay of the music hall stood for the decay of England.

Here, Lemmon has got his talent in control again. He begins uncertainly, but he hits some new notes and does some very sure line read-

ings, without falling back on Jack Lemmonisms. There's no tender-heartedness, no asking for sympathy.

Considering the magnitude of Lemmon's attempt, it's a considerable achievement that he doesn't disgrace himself. Archie Rice's pain gives Jack Lemmon a new dignity. He's best in his thoughtful, quiet moments offstage.

Lemmon provides the rhythm for most of his scenes—and they're the only scenes that have any rhythm.

Jack Lemmon as Archie Rice, a would-be music-hall performer reduced to judging seaside beauty contests.

233

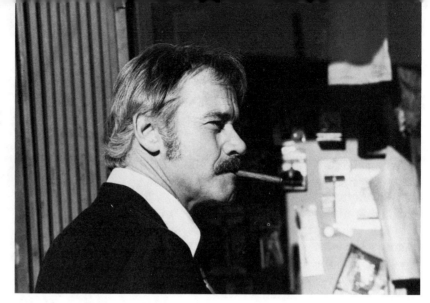

Jack Lemmon as a slightly rumpled, slightly weary California bail bondsman.

Alex and the Gypsy

A 20th Century-Fox Picture (1976)

The Production Staff

Producer: Richard Shepherd. *Director:* John Korty. *Screenplay:* Lawrence B. Marcus. *Based on the novella,* The Bailbondsman, *by* Stanley Elkin. *Cinematographer:* Bill Butler. *Editor:* Donn Cambern. *Music:* Henry Mancini. *Art Director:* Bill Malley.

A Richard Shepherd Production. A 20th Century-Fox Release. MPAA Rating: R. Running Time: 100 minutes. In color.

The Cast

Alexander Main: Jack Lemmon. *Maritza:* Genevieve Bujold. *Crainpool:* James Woods. *Judge Ehrlinger:* Robert Emhardt. *Morgan:* Joseph X. Flaherty. *Hammond:* Ramon Bieri. *The Golfer:* Gino Ardito. *Roy Blake:* Todd Martin. *Mr. Sanders:* Victor Pinhiero.

The Movie

A sophisticated and very adult comedic love story, *Alex and the Gypsy* went through several titles before it was finally released, not unlike Lemmon's earlier film, *It Happened To Jane* (1959).

Advertisement for *Alex and the Gypsy.*

In "The Days of Wine and Roses," he so effectively portrayed a man caught between love and despair that the role has become a classic.

He brilliantly displayed his genius for comedy in such hits as "Some Like it Hot" and "The Odd Couple."

His versatile career culminated in his outstanding performance in "Save The Tiger," which earned him a long-deserved Academy Award.

Now Jack Lemmon teams with one of today's most arrestingly beautiful stars, Genevieve Bujold, in a story as warm and touching as it is unique.

JACK LEMMON
GENEVIEVE BUJOLD
ALEX &
THE GYPSY
A RICHARD SHEPHERD—JOHN KORTY PRODUCTION
Produced by RICHARD SHEPHERD · Directed by JOHN KORTY · Screenplay by LAWRENCE
Based upon the Novella THE BAILBONDSMAN by STANLEY ELKIN
Original Music HENRY MANCINI · Color by Deluxe®
R RESTRICTED

Included among its various monikers were *The Gypsy and the Phoenician*, *The Main Man and the Gypsy*, *Skipping*, *Tattoo* and the most promising and best-sounding of all, *Loves and Other Crimes*.

The studio was pretty much set on the latter title until audiences at several advance trial screenings reacted negatively to it.

The title, however, is unimportant. What matters here are the superb individual performances of Lemmon and Genevieve Bujold and their fiery chemistry together, John Korty's light direction (certainly his most assured direction to date) and, most importantly, Lawrence B. Marcus's amazing screenplay.

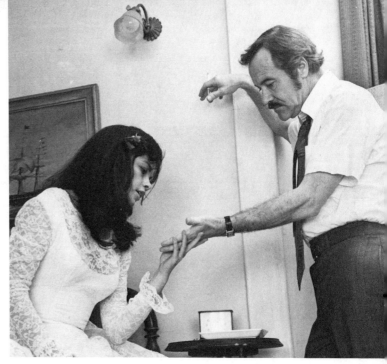

Bujold and Lemmon.

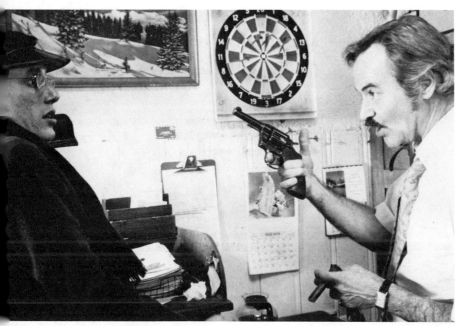

Lemmon with James Wood.

Bujold and Lemmon.

Stylistically, Marcus's script is reminiscent of Stanley Donen's *Two For the Road*, what with the way it tears into a wild love affair and conveys the incidents of it in an exhilarating unchronological format. The action skips around, bouncing back and forth in time, revealing bits and pieces that add up to a colorful, multifaceted, three-dimensional whole.

Plotwise, however, *Alex and the Gypsy* is highly original, resembling nothing that's ever been done before. Certainly not *Two For the Road*. Even though both films move in much the same way, and even though both films are very literate and mature in their respective examina-

Bujold and Lemmon.

Lemmon and Bujold.

tions of love, their tone, feel and situations are miles apart.

You might say that *Alex and the Gypsy* is the "black" counterpart to *Two For the Road*. While the Donen film is rather bright and romantic, *Alex* is strictly a black comedy—gritty, grim and unconventionally realistic. What's more, unlike *Two For the Road*, it boasts offbeat casting that makes for some unexpected delight.

Both Lemmon and Ms. Bujold are cast against type here—he as a slightly rumpled, slightly weary California bail bondsman (a kind of middle-aged Elliott Gould), she as a troublesome, eccentric, excitable gypsy. The combination is irresistible.

Alexander Main (Jack Lemmon), a bail bondsman slightly jaded by his associations of the past eighteen years, is knee-deep involved in a wild love affair with one of his "clients," a headstrong gypsy named Maritza (Genevieve Bujold).

A typical day in the life of Alexander Main goes something like this: He reports daily to his battered little office where he gleefully keeps his assistant (James Woods) enslaved in a way that

Lemmon with Bujold in studio publicity shot.

smacks of Dickens. It turns out that Alex once posted bail for his duty-bound assistant and, as a form of repayment, keeps the young man in veritable servitude.

Next, Alex arranges to post bail for an underworld mobster, even though the Mafia intends to execute the chap so that his case can never come to trial. If Alex doesn't take the business, some other bail bondsman will. So why the hell not?

Also, there's Maritza, imprisoned for stabbing the man she married after running out on Alex. He's hesitant about posting her bail; after all, she'll probably do her customary skipping and leave him responsible for the money. However, Alex recalls the wonderful year that he spent with this "crazy gypsy" and impulsively decides to arrange for her bail.

There's a catch, however. Maritza must go home with Alex and spend the four days before her trial making love with him. She agrees. It's better than spending four days in jail, she rationalizes.

Meanwhile, Alex does some sniffing and digging and discovers that Maritza is innocent. More flashbacks of their love affair help verify Alex's feelings for the girl: He loves her.

To make a long story short, Alex discovers his love too late. Maritza eventually skips on Alex. As the plane she chartered takes off, Alex chases it in ecstasy.

"Who the hell is that?," the confused pilot asks Maritza. "Oh him," she replies, "he's just a crazy gypsy!"

Maritza has probably paid Alex the greatest compliment she could conjure up.

The Critics

Pauline Kael in *The New Yorker:*
Alex and the Gypsy is off the beaten track, but that's just about the only thing you can give it points for. Whoever had the idea of turning Stanley Elkin's short novel *The Bailbondsman* into a romantic comedy by giving Alex, the bailbondsman (Jack Lemmon), a love affair with a gypsy (Genevieve Bujold) doesn't seem to have thought out how this love affair would "play."

Alex is still mostly Elkin's creation. Here's one of those reveling-in-their-own-exacerbated-cynicism characters whom authors show off with.

He's barely tolerable on the printed page

Lemmon and Bujold.

and outright offensive on the screen, where he expresses himself in torrents of cleverness. (Jack Lemmon shouts the words.)

If Lemmon trusted himself as an actor, and relaxed and did less, we might be able to see the necessary contrasts in Alex's character. But Lemmon is always up, and working desperately hard. And Bujold, who's meant to be the vibrant, tempestuous one, has to fight him for every bit of audience attention, and what should be a love story is a shouting match—ersatz D. H. Lawrence and ersatz Billy Wilder.

Where was the director, John Korty, on this picture? Lemmon needs a director who will unearth his talent by challenging him—forcing him to explain and justify each specific thing he does.

Kathleen Carroll in the New York *Daily News:*
As Genevieve Bujold's leading man, Lemmon fails to generate any real chemistry, much less warmth or interest.

The worst of it is that he appears to have gone stale as an actor. He can play only one character—the insufferably self-centered, bitterly resentful menopausal male—and it's reached a point where, in almost every movie, he suffers from frequent hot flushes of anger and carries a perpetual chip on his shoulder for no apparent reason.

That's just about the size of the irascible bailbondsman he plays in this film, in which the character is so irritating that one can hardly wait to see the last of him.

239

Frank Rich in the *New York Post*:
I really think we could live without another movie about a tired, emotionally hardened middle-aged man who falls in love with a free-spirited young woman who leads him to rediscover the joys of life. *Alex and the Gypsy*, now at the Sutton, is the latest example of the genre, and even if it were well done (which it is not), it would be emotionally banal, predictable and cloying.

Alex and the Gypsy is all of these things and rather spectacularly numbing besides.

Lemmon—who has grown a mustache, let his hair grow, and is always lit so that we can see every line on his face—plays Alex at an abrasive pitch, except when he reminisces about his late saint of a father, at which point his eyes have a faraway look that's meant to indicate introspection and remorse.

Variety:

Jack Lemmon, in a terrible lapse of career judgment, stars as a burned-out bailbondsman still hung up on the gypsy girl, Genevieve Bujold, who long ago jilted him.

Bujold is in that unique category of actress who can be forgiven any botched job of casting and performance. But it's quite another matter when Lemmon comes on as a man from whom nobody would accept for free a used car.

It's a cynical, distasteful film, full of grubby characters and situations.

William Wolf in *Cue Magazine*:
Director John Korty invades unusual territory, the odd world of the bailbondsman, with an unusual love story graced with sparkling performances by Jack Lemmon and Genevieve Bujold.

Looking different with mustache and longer hair, Lemmon projects toughness and cynicism. His milieu in California is populated by losers, one of whom is an attractive but troublesome Gypsy.

Accepting the plot requires the utmost stretching of the imagination. However, Bujold is extraordinary as the Gypsy and Lemmon surprisingly convincing as the bailbondsman.

Like most of Korty's work, this must be approached with an eye for an experience that is

Lemmon and Bujold (in plane).

different. For my taste it works, and both Lemmon and Bujold merit special applause.

Lemmon on *Alex and the Gypsy:*
"I must say that I'm very happy with the film in the sense that, by and large, the result was as I envisioned it—which is certainly not always the case. I haven't the foggiest notion if it will have a wide appeal, but I do think that it's a very good, honest, intimate love story with interesting and offbeat characters.

"In other words, honest unto itself, and I'm proud to be part of it."

Lemmon with James Booth.

Airport '77

A Universal Picture (1977)

The Production Staff

Executive Producer: Jennings Lang. *Producer:* William Frye. *Director:* Jerry Jameson. *Screenplay:* Michael Scheff *and* David Spector. *From a story by* H.A.L. Craig *and* Charles Kuenstle. *Inspired by the novel,* Airport, *by* Arthur Hailey. *Cinematographer:* Philip Lathrop. *Editors:* J. Terry Williams *and* Robert Watts. *Music:* John Cacavas. *Special Visual Effects:* Albert Whitlock. *Production Design:* George C. Webb. *Set Decorator:* Mickey C. Michaels. *Costumes:* Edith Head. *Lee Grant's Wardrobe:* Burton Miller.

A Jennings Lang Production. A Universal Release. MPAA Rating: PG. Running Time: 113 minutes. In color and Panavision.

The Cast

Don Gallagher: Jack Lemmon. *Karen Wallace:* Lee Grant. *Martin Wallace:* Christopher Lee. *Eve Clayton:* Brenda Vaccaro. *Emily Livingston:* Olivia De Havilland. *Peter Stevens:* James Stewart. *Nicholas St.*

Advertisement for *Airport '77.*

Jack Lemmon as pilot Don Gallagher.

III: Joseph Cotten. *Stan Buchek:* Darren ̶ ̶ ̶. *Eddie:* Robert Hooks. *Ralph Crawford:* ̶ ̶ ̶ ooth. *Banker:* Monte Markham. *Chambers:* ̶ ̶ ̶bert Foxworth. *Steve:* Tom Sullivan. *Julie:* Kathleen Quinlan. *Lisa:* Pamela Bellwood. *Patroni:* George Kennedy.

The Movie

"It should have sunk along with the airplane."

A critic on *Airport '77*? No, its star.

"I did it because I thought it might be fun to do a blatantly commercial 'cartoon,' which is something I felt I hadn't done, and try to play a practically nonexistent character of no depth whatsoever."

The snag, of course, is that the film more or less turned out to be exactly what Lemmon had set out to make. The problem is, it was embarrassing on a grander scale than he ever imagined.

But there was a bright side.

"I think I was also influenced by feeling the need to be in a commercial hit so that I could remain in a position of enough clout to get projects off the ground that would be of real interest to me. I was right."

Airport '77 also stars, among others, Lee Grant and James Stewart in leading roles. It is not a good movie, but then neither is it unwatchable—not with that cast. In fact, about the only thing wrong with it can be traced to a screenplay of dialogue and characters that has more clichés and corn than the telephone book has Smiths and Joneses.

However, since for my money Lemmon, Grant and Stewart could just stand there and *read* the telephone book, well, who's to quarrel with the material?

And for those moviegoers who like their action diluted by schmaltz, or their schmaltz spiced with some action, *Airport '77* more than effectively fills the bill.

TV veteran Jerry Jameson, directing his first and only theatrical feature here, shows a sure hand with the choreographing of the action, the mounting of the schmaltz and the balancing of his predictably varied cast of characters: There's someone for everyone's taste in *Airport '77*.

Amazingly, just about every performance in *Airport '77* is competent, in spite of the one-dimensional stereotypes, the pat, potboiling situations and the purple dialogue provided in Michael Scheff and David Spector's script. The phrase, "Oh my God!," for example, is uttered just about every five minutes and by just about every character.

However, Scheff and Spector are to be recognized—even applauded—for at least some genuine adventure. Unlike other films of this ilk, *Airport '77* serves us a full-fledged disaster here: The airplane

Christopher Lemmon (son of Jack) makes his film debut in a cameo role in his dad's *Airport '77*.

actually crashes (yes, it does), and the aftermath is several degrees more graphic and grueling than what's been offered in previous airplane/disaster flicks.

Despite its pervasive silliness and corn, *Airport '77* delivers everything it promises, giving it the dubious distinction of being the first disaster flick to quench our morbid interest in such "entertainments."

Furthermore, the production boasts an atypically perverted sense of humor. The writers here have sympathy for just about no one. *Everyone* gets it, from a kindly, self-effacing black maid to a couple of freckled types. And when Robert Hooks (as the plane's bartender) lies helplessly in pain, he's literally trampled by the coach's other passengers.

Much of this humor, however, is dampened—again, literally—by the pat situations. The plot has millionaire James Stewart deciding to transport his art collection to a Florida museum and inviting friends and close associates to travel along in his privately-owned 747 jumbo jet, a knock-out plane that's piloted by Lemmon.

Sabotage is inevitably introduced to the plotting, leading to a crash that sinks the craft. It splashes underwater. Everyone panics and confesses secret sins. Then comes the rescue. The End.

As previously noted in this book, Lemmon can make sense from even comic-book nonsense of this type. He's actor enough to do surprisingly well John-Wayning it in the gung-ho, change-of-pace hero role, investing it with an unusual amount of dignity and humanity.

He is supplemented by a fine supporting cast, most notably Grant as an outrageously alcoholic passenger; Christopher Lee as her stolid, do-gooder husband; Brenda Vaccaro as Lemmon's stewardess-girlfriend; and two (at the time) neophyte actresses who work beyond the call of duty giving excellent performances in small roles—Pamela Bellwood as Stewart's daughter and Kathleen Quinlan as a junior stewardess.

In 1979, NBC-TV televised a substantially longer version of *Airport '77* (75 minutes' worth of outtakes added) over a two-night period, and in this three-hour version, the characterizations are more fully fleshed out, especially those of Bellwood and Quinlan. On TV, this version ran four hours, including commercials.

The network subsequently televised an in-between version (running about 150 minutes, a full three hours with commercial breaks), as well as the official theatrical print.

I prefer the really long version. At three hours, *Airport '77* is positively lush—and positively ridiculous.

The Critics

Kathleen Carroll in the New York *Daily News:*

Fasten your seat belts, and brace yourself for a bumpy ride with *Airport '77*. This latest disaster movie could only have been assembled by a salesman of used airplane parts.

Instead of coffee, tea or a willing stewardess, one is served some priceless pieces of dialogue, which I feel should be recorded. Here goes:

Lee Grant, who can't decide whether she should try to save her marriage or continue to add to her collection of miniature whisky bottles, informs pilot Jack Lemmon of her displeasure at finding herself under 300 feet of water: "How could you let a thing like this happen to us?"

Joseph Cotten asks if there is something he can do to help Darren McGavin. Answers McGavin, brave and confident: "How's your breast stroke?"

A grateful Brenda Vaccaro to her rescuer, Jack Lemmon: "I love you."

William Wolf in *Cue:*

If your flight to Florida should be interrupted by an inconvenient plunge into the ocean, don't panic when you see water outside your window. Think of *Airport '77* and the frogmen who will arrive to float the fuselage to the surface before it springs too many leaks and the air supply gives out.

As you can see, they are straining for plot material to keep the sequels coming according to formula.

At least the focus on personal lives is minimal, with director Jerry Jameson paying most attention to the mechanics of the rescue operation. But the basic situation is irredeemably ludicrous.

Lemmon with Darren McGavin.

Archer Winsten in the *New York Post:*

If you can buy this kind of melodrama, *Airport '77* can be a very suspenseful exciting cup of strong tea. If not, it is equally possible to sneer at it as another of those disaster compilations, each one bigger and better and worse than the last. If you really want to, you can spend the whole picture wondering how they make that 747 do all those things without disintegrating. Technically, it's a dilly.

Vincent Canby in *The New York Times:*

The film was directed by Jerry Jameson, most of whose experience has been in television, but *Airport '77* looks less like the work of a director and writers than like a corporate decision.

Molly Haskell in *New York* magazine:

Airport '77 is a disaster movie that suffers from arrested development: It is a disaster all right, but it never quite makes it to being a movie....

I am not saying that something as profoundly worthless as *Airport '77* could have been saved

Lemmon with Brenda Vaccaro.

simply by having the valiant pilot, Captain Gallagher—or, if you prefer, Jack Lemmon—drown while trying to save lives. After all, even if Jack Lemmon died horribly, say, drawn and quartered by four rampaging horses, the film would still be a farce, because there is something deeply farcical about Lemmon's every expression and intonation, indeed about his very face, however much he may wrinkle it up in heroic self-abnegation. Comical, too, is Brenda Vaccaro, who plays his girlfriend, and whose sincere agonizing comes out unmistakably as campy mugging.

John Huddy in the *Miami Herald:*

It is an extremely funny movie—for all the wrong reasons. People will be talking about *Airport '77* for months to come—again for all the wrong reasons.

Desmond Ryan in the *Philadelphia Inquirer:*

The real perils of the friendly skies are not the hockey-puck steak and ptomaine lettuce served with plastic knives, Muzak, bores and so on, but an idea that is utterly incredible in its execution by every hand involved in it...Jack Lemmon at least appears to be having a good time amid the gadgetry.

The China Syndrome

A Columbia Picture (1979)

The Production Staff

Executive Producer: Bruce Gilbert. *Producer:* Michael Douglas. *Director:* James Bridges. *Screenplay:* Mike Gray, T.S. Cook *and* James Bridges. *Cinematographer:* James Crabe. *Editor:* David Rawlins. *Music:* Stephen Bishop. *Production Design:* George Jenkins. *Set Decorator:* Arthur Jeph Parker. *Costumes:* Donfeld. *Special Effects:* Henry Millar, Jr.

A Michael Douglas/IPC Films Production. A Columbia Release. MPAA Rating: PG. Running Time: 122 minutes. In color.

The Cast

Jack Godell: Jack Lemmon. *Kimberly Wells:* Jane Fonda. *Richard Adams:* Michael Douglas. *Herman De Young:* Scott Brady. *Ted Spindler:* Wilford Brimley. *Bill Gibson:* James Hampton. *Don Jacovich:* Peter Donat. *Evan McCormack:* Richard Herd. *Mac Churchill:* James Karen. *Pete Martin:* Stan Bohrman. *Hector Salas:* Daniel Valdez.

The Movie

Let's not mince any words.

James Bridge's *The China Syndrome* is that rare, topical thriller that mixes entertainment with a message, thereby working on a dual level.

Michael Douglas, Jack Lemmon and Jane Fonda.

While it comments harshly on the codes, morality and ethics of our society and on the commitment and courage of a precious few, it does so with an emotional pitch, lively good humor and fine performances.

Initially, it looks slick, like an engaging melodrama, but then—pow!—it catapults the viewer into a pounding suspense drama inspired by our machine-age paranoia.

The movie is about power—literal and symbolic power, both equally paralyzing and dangerous, and both out of our control. That's the scary part. *The China Syndrome* is a savage indictment against those who control, suppress and manipulate our world and our lives.

And what for? Money, for one thing. It's the root of all rationalization. Destruction, chaos, even death are easy to live with when large figures are involved.

Bridges' plot is simple, stark and ingeniously designed, an Orwellian warning about our bleak tomorrow. We're presented with an electronic personality (a TV newswoman), the electrician who records her (her cameraman) and the engineer who supplies the electricity. They all are prisoners of technology brought together by an unexpected catastrophe; they all learn the truth about "power" (the film's working title).

These three are controlled by power—the kind that makes it possible for us to watch TV and use our hair dryers at the same time, as well as the kind that controls our income and job security. Big-buck consciousness on the part of those in control and the compromises that the working person has to make for career reasons create a climate for power.

Kimberly Wells (Jane Fonda) is one of those perky, shrill TV reporters hired because of her good looks and winning, assertive personality. The management of her TV station thinks she's just right for happy news and soft stories. Kimberly can do better. She knows it; we know it (after all, that's Jane Fonda up there on the screen). But she settles for less because she wants to make it big and she can't do that if she loses what she already has. She cooperates—by smiling coyly, crinkling her nose, looking pretty, always looking pretty.

One day, while filming a tour through a nuclear power plant—an outing designed by her station to be a soft, educational story—Kimberly stumbles onto a big story. Something catastrophic is happening, although she's not really sure what it's all about. The engineers, particularly one named Jack Godell (Jack Lemmon), are in a snit. This "accident," meanwhile, is being photographed surreptitiously by her cameraman (Michael Douglas).

The footage turns out to be hot stuff, revealing that the plant is faulty and should be closed down. The "accident," had it not been contained by Godell, could have released a deadly ratioactive stream.

Pressured by the plant's officials, Kimberly's bosses—supposedly paid to inform the public—refuse to televise the film. Her cameraman manages to sneak it to a group of anti-nuclear activists, and with Godell now on her side, Kimberly fights for her story, her career and, to a degree, for herself.

Bridges neatly creates a feeling of paranoia by clinging to highly technical verbiage. We're never sure what the problem is, but we know it affects us—and that makes it all the more unnerving.

More important, his razor-sharp editing adds intensity to this paranoia, and visually his movie is stunning. As photographed by James Crabe, *The China Syndrome* is bright and sunny—appropriately deceptive, just like the evil forces at work in the film. He achieves a pleasant eerieness—the Hitchcockian ideal of sunlit terror.

Admidst this eerieness and the harsh realities of the film, Bridges never forgets the heartbeat, the mind and the anguish of the people caught up in it.

Jack Lemmon as nuclear engineer Jack Godell.

And he's helped by his able cast. Fonda is wonderful in the complicated role of an ambitious, talented woman forced to kowtow to inarguably inferior men in order to get her way. We understand her plight, what she might lose, but we don't start to truly admire her until she starts pushing.

Douglas, in his best role to date (and that includes *Romancing the Stone*), smoothly complements Fonda as the independent freelance cameraman who doesn't have to work for or worry about job security and, therefore, gets the ball rolling.

Best of all, however, is Lemmon, in a self-abandoning, emotionally draining performance as a dedicated professional who cannot settle for the cheap or leave the problem unsolved. He's the star of the movie, its hero. And with closely cropped gray hair, worry lines across his face and weary posture, well, what a regular hero Lemmon makes!

"Like some other films that have been vitally important to my career," says Lemmon, "*The China Syndrome* was a project that nobody in Hollywood wanted to touch. I waited a year and a half before we could get it off the ground, and the longer I waited the more I felt as I did when I was involved in the preproduction of *The Days of Wine and Roses* and *Save the Tiger*—that no matter how long it takes, it's worth it.

"And the satisfaction, of course, is not primarily because they were financially successful but because I felt that I was a part of something of genuine substance. They all were properties that did not just entertain, they enlightened. They all were exciting to me because they were very well written and provocative screenplays and because they afforded me marvelous and varied parts to play. It's like having your cake and eating it, too.

"Also, in my opinion, in each instance, I was working with wonderful fellow actors and fine directors. In other words, each experience was a total joy."

The Critics

David Denby in *New York* magazine:

The China Syndrome, a sensationally effective thriller about an accident and attempted cover-up at a nuclear-power plant, has been released with such devastating timing that one almost suspects the Columbia publicity people of going beyond the call of duty. To wit: A week before the movie opened, a jury was impaneled in an Oklahoma trial investigating the death of Karen Silkwood, a plutonium worker and persistent critic of nuclear power who died in suspicious circumstances in 1974; a similar "accident," based on the Silkwood death, occurs in the movie.

And a mere three days before the opening, the Nuclear Regulatory Commission closed down five nuclear-power plants as unsafe in the event of an earthquake; it's an earthquake that sets off the trouble in *The China Syndrome*.

The movie has thrust itself into a continuing public debate with a directness that's unique in American movie history, but few of us have the competence to say whether the technical stuff in the movie is accurate and responsible.

In *The China Syndrome*, the actors' histrionics make us believe in the gravity of the various crises. His facial muscles collapsing in despair, hunched back, eyes darting to left and right, Lemmon, though overacting as usual, gives us the physical detail necessary to cue in our reactions when we get left behind by the technical lingo.

William Wolf in *Cue*:

The rare combination of an urgent message and vigorous entertainment has been smashingly realized in *The China Syndrome*, a sizzling, nerve-shattering thriller about individual conscience and the danger of nuclear accident. Lemmon, in a shaded, passionate performance that is the best of his career, projects the qualities that throughout history have made some individuals withstand pressures and threats and refuse to go along with wrong-doing.

Using authentic-looking sets, director James Bridges packs the film with detail about both the nuclear and broadcasting operations, and keeps the story crackling at a feverish pace reminiscent of Z.

Arthur Knight in *The Hollywood Reporter*:

When television people refer to "happy news," they are talking about those side-bar tid-bits of heartwarming human interest that keep the nightly news from becoming an hour long recital of death and disaster, plus sports and weather. The happy news about *The China Syndrome*, however, is that it manages to puncture the glib, superficial façade of TV journalism and shows us what can happen when a "happy news" reporter manages to sink her teeth into a hard news story. It makes for tense, tingling drama, especially since the "story" is one that fills all of us with dire forebodings—the threat of an accidental nuclear holocaust.

It is Lemmon who dominates *The China Syndrome* as the harassed chief engineer of the plant, a man devoted to his work and convinced of its importance. Lemmon conveys with full intensity the mental anguish of a man who risks forfeiting his life's work—and eventually life itself—as a matter of conscience. Enter the first candidate for "Best Performance by a Leading Actor" in the 1979 Academy Awards sweepstakes.

Director Bridges with Fonda.

Kathleen Carroll in the New York *Daily News:*

The China Syndrome is a thriller of such incredible force and such terrifying ramifications that it leaves one absolutely shattered. It is one of those rare movies that manages to be intensely serious about its subject matter, while remaining an electrifying piece of entertainment. It is Fonda, Douglas and most particularly Lemmon who are the movie's main source of energy.

Gene Shalit on *The Today Show* (NBC):

Jane Fonda is smashing as the newswoman, Douglas is appealingly stubborn as the uncompromising cameraman, and Jack Lemmon gives a scorcher of a dramatic performance.

Vincent Canby in *The New York Times:*

Smashingly effective, very stylish....The film is as topical as this morning's weather report, as full of threat of hellfire as an old-fashioned Sunday sermon and as bright and shiny and new-looking as the fanciest science-fiction film. Jack Lemmon has the best role he's had in a long time. The three stars are [all] effective and splendid, but maybe Miss Fonda is just a bit more than that. Her performance is not that of an actress in a star's role, but that of an actress creating a character that happens to be major within the film. She keeps getting better and better.

Tribute

A 20th Century-Fox Picture (1980)

The Production Staff

Executive Producers: Lawrence Turman *and* David Foster. *Producers:* Joel B. Michaels *and* Garth H. Drabinsky. *Director:* Bob Clark. *Screenplay:* Bernard Slade. *Based on his play. Cinematographer:* Reginald H. Morris. *Editor:* Richard Halsey. *Music:* Ken Wannberg. *Songs:* "We Still Have Time," *music by* Barry Manilow *and lyrics by* Jack Feldman *and* Bruce Sussman; "It's All for the Best," *music and lyrics by* Jack Lemmon *and* Alan Jay Lerner. *Production Design:* Trevor Williams. *Art Director:* Reuben Freed. Set Decorator: Rondi Johnson. *Costumes:* Suzanne Grace.

A Joel B. Michaels-Garth H. Drabinsky Production. A 20th Century-Fox Release. MPAA Rating: PG. Running Time: 123 minutes. In color.

The Cast

Scottie Templeton: Jack Lemmon. *Jud Templeton:* Robby Benson. *Maggie Stratton:* Lee Remick. *Gladys Petrelli:* Colleen Dewhurst. *Lou Daniels:* John Marley. *Sally Haines:* Kim Cattrall. *Hilary:* Gale Garnett. *Evelyn:* Teri Keane. *Nurse:* Eileen Lehman. *Nurse:* Jennifer Goldie.

The Movie

Contrary to popular beliefs, not all of our contemporary movies are being made for 14-year-olds and antisocial adults with the tastes of 14-year-olds.

Some are being made by another kind of retarded adult, the kind whose taste veers towards Broadway-style, bitch-and-quip dialogue and death accompanied by glycerin tears and a drippy Barry Manilow theme song.

Lemmon's film version of his stage triumph, *Tribute,* is an excruciating example of the latter—a film in which snappy ping-pong style repartee is mixed uncertainly with "death therapy," making for a movie which is at best dubious—and at its worst, vulgar.

This movie lacks the less tangible ingredients that made the Broadway edition so appealing—i.e., genuine warmth and an unassuming modesty. On stage, it was a one-man show, a sad tribute to a foolish man who never managed to learn how to balance responsibility and discipline with his frivolous good times, a man of wretched priorities.

The man was, of course, played by Lemmon who, on stage, from a distance, seemed small and fading and powerfully affecting, something like a memory. On stage, Lemmon rarely exaggerated his

Lemmon.

expressions, but when he did, it fit the medium involved.

It was as if Lemmon's Scottie Templeton—a press agent, alienated from his grown son and now dying of cancer—was desperately trying to reach out to us. By the end of the play, he succeeded. He touched us.

On screen, however—and in close-up, no less—he's pathetic but not at all likable or sympathetic. Dialogue that seemed small and true on stage now comes off as diatribe and pontification. "When you're best friend dies," sighs Scottie, "you lose a friend. But when you die, you lose all your friends."

I loved that line when it was spoken on the stage of the Brooks Atkinson Theater, and I awaited it on film. I squirmed on cue.

It's easy to see why middle-aged movie people—studio heads and publicists—liked this film. It's a celebration of their priorities and wasted lifestyle. Scottie has been made into such an unworthy hero for the film and the son (Robby Benson) has been turned into such a revolting little prig, that there's no question whose life-affirming values the film's makers want us to applaud.

The film *Tribute* is rigged.

The son may be a snide kid but the fact is that Scottie Templeton was a lousy, irresponsible father who thought more of swapping corny jokes with his cronies at Jack Dempsey's than in spending time with his family. Now that he's dying, we're supposed to see him as some misunderstood saint and view his jokes as words of wisdom.

The son, Jud, never laughs at the jokes, and because of this, he's supposed to be a creep. But the jokes aren't funny, and Scottie's aggressive delivery of them are offensive. We come away scratching ourselves, instead of laughing.

On stage, in a theatrical setting (the show was literally a tribute), the jokes took on a kind of burly (as in burlesque) quality that worked. On screen, they only serve to make one feel embarrassed for Jack, who is otherwise fine in the role.

Tribute the film may be a dull, dreary, undistinguished male-oriented soap opera. It may have a hackneyed plot and clunky jokes (and a couple of clunky performances by Canadian starlets Kim Cattrall and Gale Garnett), but it also has Jack Lemmon.

The rumor that Lemmon can do no wrong is verified by his performance here. Any other actor would have died a thousand times over in this movie. There's no center to the human being he's playing. I'm not even sure you can call Scottie a human. But Lemmon firmly negates all of his character's deadly qualities whenever he's freed from the bad jokes and pretentious dialogue and allowed to register the relaxed knowingness of a man who's dying.

Lemmon has said that it has been a dream since his teens to have a Broadway hit and then recreate it on film. "I thank God that I still was able to appreciate it so fully when it finally happened." But, still, there are some regrets.

"Like most people that I know who saw both the play and the movie, I felt that the theatrical version was infinitely better than the film. For one thing, I don't think I fully succeeded in reducing a very flamboyant outgoing personality down to 'film size.' In the theater the portrayal demanded a bravura performance. But what worked in the theater may have been a bit too 'bravura' on the screen.

"That's nicer than saying somebody else f_____ it up, isn't it?"

Lemmon's supporting cast in the film come off like wrangling automatons. They're dreadful, particularly Benson in what should have been his breakthrough role. His idea of playing the repressed, stuffy son is to recite all of his dialogue through clenched teeth and with a spirit of somnolence.

This territory—the parent-versus-child bit—was covered around the time of *Tribute's* release by *Ordinary People* and *The Great Santini,* and to better effect.

By the end of *Tribute* the film, I was hoping that both father and son would die and be done with it all.

Lemmon with Benson.

I was even willing to settle for it amidst the gallons of free-flowing tears.

No such luck. Instead we get the kissy-kissy, quasi-happy ending that worked better on stage.

Incidentally, following *Tribute*, director Bob Clark made the infamous *Porky's* which, in essence, is about a lot of teenage Scotties. Some day, the two films will make a perverse double-bill.

The Critics

Andrew Sarris in *The Village Voice*:

In the case of the Jack Lemmon stage-and-screen vehicle entitled *Tribute*, the only tension in Bob Clark's direction of Bernard Slade's screenplay-adapted-from-his-play arises from the ancient Hollywood problem of taking a play "outdoors."

On the stage, Lemmon's performance was built around the "tribute" itself, a stylized theatrical device by which the players could address the audience directly with bit batches of bare-faced exposition. The movie obliterates all traces of the stylization for the sake of a more realistic approach that emphasizes only how dramatically threadbare the basic material happens to be.

Curiously, Lemmon strikes deeper chords of feeling on the screen than he did on the stage, and he is aided by more talented supporting players, notably Lee Remick as his wife, Robby Benson as his son, John Marley as his partner, and Colleen Dewhurst as his doctor-friend. What has been lost is the lightness and verve and playful rhythm that kept a maudlin story of a repentant, terminally ill bon vivant father reaching out one last time to his dull, bitter, rejected son from becoming a turgid evening in the theater.

Lemmon's performance was more than the uninspired calculation of Slade's play deserved, but Lemmon created an evening of levitation nonetheless. The misplaced reverence of the movie for the sentimental core of the play has drastically reduced the redeeming prankishness at the periphery. Mind you, this was not a decision imposed upon the playwright by a movie mogul, but a decision into which the playwright had full input. Even so, Lemmon, Remick, Benson, Marley and Dewhurst share more than the conventional number of exquisitely tender moments in this so-far joyless season, cinematically speaking.

Variety:

When Jack Lemmon opened *Tribute* on Broadway, people said it would be impossible to imagine any other actor in the role and sure enough, the show shuttered when he departed. It's equally impossible to imagine anyone but Lemmon in the film version, which can obviously be around forever—and proba-

bly will be.

The complex role of Scottie Templeton has been tailored for Lemmon's oft-proclaimed talents for both comedy and heavy drama. On the one hand, he must be a flippant, shallow ne'er-do-well; waster of his life; and, most importantly, be both willing and unwilling to change.

Working from his own stage script, and with an able assist from director Bob Clark, writer Bernard Slade uses film to deepen and enrich Templeton's story, which begins with his learning of his illness just as the young son he hasn't seen for years arrives for a visit.

Robby Benson is excellent in the equally complex part of the intellectual, introspective boy, both repelled by his father's superficial, even pimpish, existence as a Broadway press agent and attracted, as everyone is, to his charm. Most of all, he's resentful of the years lost since Lemmon divorced Lee Remick.

In the smallest of the three major parts, Remick nonetheless turns in a solid performance as the ex-wife who still loves him but learned long ago he wasn't worth putting up with.

There is a minority around that initially saw Slade's play as thinly obvious melodrama and Lemmon on the edge of overacting. It's not likely they will

Lemmon with Remick.

like the film any better. But they'll also still be in the minority.

David Denby in *New York* magazine:

Tribute, the film version of Bernard Slade's 1978 stage hit, is an insensitive and inept piece of moviemaking, and people who dislike being brow-beaten should stay away from it.

Bob Clark doesn't bring much life or temperament of his own to this project, and his faithfulness winds up exposing what was mechanical and gross in the play. Here we have two characters synthesized from a dozen Broadway hits of the past 35 years: Scottie Templeton, middle-aged theatrical press agent, a man who ratted on his talent, loused up his marriage, alienated his son, and is now dying of cancer; and his son, Jud, an "intellectual" young prig who judges his father too harshly.

No one has bothered to make a movie out of this play....Jack Lemmon was relatively subdued and therefore quite effective in *The China Syndrome*, but he now seems to have forgotten everything he has ever learned about performing for the camera. Every muscle in Lemmon's face acts—cheeks, eyebrows, lips, chin, brow, nose. He makes snaky movements with his hands and wrists to punctuate Scottie's anecdotes. He slips in and out of trick voices, drops his pants, thrusts his neck forward and bellows.

Lemmon gives us so much pain and anguish that he's unwatchable. He pushes so hard that he turns the playwright into a liar: All of Scottie's friends describe him as charming, irresistible, a born entertainer, yet this Scottie is so overbearing and manic he makes you hide under the seat.

If you resist the emotional blackmail of this movie, you are supposed to feel as priggish as Jud was before he realizes that his father was a great guy. Millions may weep at *Tribute*, but I'd rather be one of the prigs.

Buddy, Buddy

A United Artists/M.G.M. Picture (1981)

The Production Staff

Executive Producer: Alain Bernheim. *Producer:* Jay Weston. *Director:* Billy Wilder. *Screenplay:* Billy Wilder *and* I.A.L. Diamond. *Based on a story, play and movie (L'Emmerdeur/A Pain in the A———) by* Francis Verber. *Cinematographer:* Harry Stradling. *Editor:* Argyle Nelson. *Music:* Lazlo Schifrin. *Production Design:* Daniel A. Lomino. *Set Designer:* William Durrell, Jr. *Set Decorator:* Cloudia. *Costumes:* John A. Anderson *and* Agnes G. Henry.

A Bernheim/Weston Production. An M.G.M. Release. MPAA Rating: R. Running Time: 96 minutes. In color and Panavision.

The Cast

Victor Clooney: Jack Lemmon. *Trabucco:* Walter Matthau. *Celia Clooney:* Paula Prentiss. *Dr. Zuckerbrot:* Klaus Kinski. *Captain Hubris:* Dana Elcar. *Eddie (the bellhop):* Miles Chapin. *Assistant Manager:* Michael Ensign. *Receptionist:* Joan Shawlee. *Rudy "Disco" Gumbola:* Film Formicola. *Kowalski:* C. J. Hunt. *Mexican Maid:* Bette Raya. *Hippie Husband:* Ronnie Sperling. *Pregnant Wife:* Suzie Galler.

The Movie

"The greatest movie buddies of all time are back!"

Who? Laurel and Hardy? No, they're dead.

Martin and Lewis then. No, they rarely even speak to each other.

Then who? Jack Lemmon and Walter Matthau, according to the ads for *Buddy, Buddy*.

Look, I like Lemmon. I admire him. That's the reason for this book. And Matthau is lovable. There's no doubt about that. Individually they are wonderful, but in tandem, they are never quite what the ads promise.

Lemmon and Matthau worked extremely well in their debut film together, Billy Wilder's *The Fortune Cookie*, but hardly as a *team*. Their film version of *The Odd Couple*, deemed an instant classic back in '68, has pretty much faded over the years, and few people (with the exception of me) seem to even want to remember their remake of *The Front Page*, their second film with Wilder.

This leaves us with the boys' last reunion, Wilder's *Buddy, Buddy*, an affable, unfunny comedy that not only reveals their failings as a so-called team, but also sadly illustrates how both men (and Wilder, as

Advertisement for *Buddy, Buddy*.

254

Jack Lemmon, as the suicidal Victor Clooney, with Walter Matthau.

well) have lost their sharp comic timing.

Sitting through *Buddy, Buddy,* which is akin to sitting through a funeral, I thought about how fortunate it is that Lemmon has opted to play mostly dramas these days. This movie proves that he has gone beyond comedy, or, perhaps, vice versa.

Although it is based on (and is very faithful to) the hilarious Lino Ventura/Jacques Brel comedy, *A Pain in the A——* (*L'Emmerdeur*), in terms of pacing and the quality of its humor, *Buddy, Buddy* is closer to an inane *Get Smart* episode. Its humor is slightly dated, what with Wilder wasting time poking fun at hippies and (wow!) sex clinics, '60s-style.

Buddy, Buddy, Lemmon has bravely noted, "is one of those enigmas in which Billy Wilder, Jack Lemmon and Walter Matthau made a film that didn't work at all. I really can't pinpoint any one reason for its failure beyond the fact that those things just happen now and then. It is akin but not quite as disasterous as top producers, directors, writers and stars becoming involved in a Broadway production that closes in one night. One wonders how so many talented and experienced people can all be so wrong at the same time about the same thing."

The plot of Wilder's film still reveals its roots as one of Paris' most popular plays: A suicidal shlemiel (Lemmon, with annoying mannerisms) in the next room continually prevents a hired killer (Matthau, pleasingly low-keyed) from assassinating a political official from a hotel window.

You're in trouble when a "comedy" opens with Matthau killing off several people with cool dispatch, and asks us to *laugh.* As I recall the original French film, Ventura's hit man was much more humane and also humorous.

Anyway, for added laughs, Lemmon plays a TV censor upset because wife Paula Prentiss has run off with the head psychiatrist at a sex clinic, essayed with a sly wink by Klaus Kinski.

Kinski is obviously standing in for Wilder regular Martin Gable here. He plays the kind of shrink who calls his patients "fruitcakes," the very word used by Gable in Wilder's *The Front Page.*

How sad to see Lemmon, let alone Wilder and Matthau, strike out with such a thump. This one is in competition as Lemmon's worst film. *Buddy, Buddy* is from hunger.

The Critics

Andrew Sarris in *The Village Voice:*

Billy Wilder...deserves a great deal of indulgence. After more than half a century of productive effort in the industry, there is virtually nothing left for him to prove. In any event, *Buddy, Buddy* was not a project he initiated. Jay Weston and Alain Bernheim had secured the rights to a recent French farce entitled variously *A Pain in the A_____* and *A Pain in the Neck,* and had obtained Walter Matthau and Jack Lemmon for the parts originated on the screen by Lino Ventura and Jacques Brel. Then apparently Matthau and Lemmon brought Wilder into the package, and then Wilder and Diamond set out rewriting this typical sub-Feydeau French Boulevard farce.

The original French movie was performed with more energy and finesse on the slapstick level, and the casting of Ventura and Brel was more effective in establishing a conflict of ill-suited-to-each-other types. By comparison, Matthau and Lemmon seem to have settled into comparatively familiar Odd Couple routines. Also, Ventura could play the role of the professional hit man fairly straight whereas Matthau has to resort to a very stylized deadpan to keep the overly comic side of his persona from slopping over the part.

Lemmon's problem is subtler and more interesting. A much more resourceful actor than Brel, he nonetheless runs the risk of seeming too much the burnt-out wimp to project the horrible egocentricity the part demands. In this respect, Brel's clumsiness as an actor worked in his favor because he actually got extra laughs by functioning as the world's foremost nonlistener.

What Wilder and Diamond have done to overcome the appearance of fatigue in their two aging stars is to freshen up the verbal contexts for the two characters.... The price that Wilder pays for the greater emphasis on verbal rather than physical humor is a predominance of quiet chuckles over noisy belly laughs. I cannot really think of one sight gag that works as it should in *Buddy, Buddy.*

David Denby in *New York* magazine:

The odd couple have grown a great deal odder. In *Buddy, Buddy,* Walter Matthau is a vicious professional assassin with a steel jaw, a mean Detroit snarl, and a purposeful stride that looks strong enough to carry him through walls. Standing at the window of a California hotel, Matthau calmly sets about screwing together the parts of a high-powered rifle, but as soon as Matthau gets the rifle trained on his target across the way, the man in the next room, a pathetic wretch whose wife has left him, tries to commit suicide.

That wretch, of course, is Jack Lemmon. Doubling over in gastric agonies, his face a woebegone rubber mask, Lemmon has become a cringing, sniveling ham. His effects are so broad that he's passed beyond, or beneath the traditions of film acting in this country—he squats and stares like a road-company Kabuki player. Every time Matthau slugs him or tricks him, you rather enjoy it.

The latest collaboration between director Billy Wilder and writer I.A.L. Diamond, *Buddy, Buddy* has little going for it but the standard farce situation of the interrupted murder attempt. Yet the extreme contrast between the two actors is often funny—Matthau is as rigid as a stone basilisk, while Lemmon disintegrates before your eyes. And the congealed sadomasochism of the story becomes oddly fascinating.

Wilder and Diamond are not young, and their cynicism has long lost its power to startle. Grumpily, they strike out at decade-old straw men—slovenly hippies and sex clinics and the type of woman (frantic Paula Prentiss as Lemmon's wife) who boasts of her new "cosmic orgasms."

Buddy, Buddy is a pretty terrible movie, but Wilder and Diamond are so far out of touch that they sustain their own kind of sour-stomached purity. The only character they approve of is the implacable hit man serenely going about his business, wanting nothing, asking nothing, just trying to get through an honest day's work.

Variety:

The unhappy news is that *Buddy, Buddy* is undoubtedly the weakest of Billy Wilder's 25 Hollywood pictures, a comedy of sustained mirthlessness.

Reteamed Jack Lemmon and Walter Matthau try very hard...but it bears all the earmarks of having been made without a definite audience in mind and will therefore have trouble finding one.

This is one of the few projects not initiated by [Wilder], and a certain lack of care and even thought permeate the effort, from script to casting to execution. The tone is so off and comic imagination is so surprisingly absent that one must wonder what the rationale for the package was beyond an attractive-sounding idea.

To be sure, certain themes and motifs mark this as a Billy Wilder film—the pairing of an innocent schnook and a cyncial s.o.b., the caustic, nose-thumbing but nonetheless obsessive preoccupation with death, sex jokes and leech-like nature of certain central relationships. But the ugliness in the little world depicted here is not meaningfully realized. All the relationships are of a distinctly unhealthy nature, and there's a desperate quality to the attempted friendships which is not compensated for by any overriding artistic aims.

Lemmon and Matthau are at a loss to put the essentially fraudulent material over with anything more than momentary success. The tries at comedy seem forced and heavyhanded.

Missing

A Universal Picture (1982)

The Production Staff

Executive Producers: Peter Guber *and* Jon Peters. *Producers:* Edward Lewis *and* Mildred Lewis. *Director:* Constantin Costa-Gavras. *Screenplay:* Costa-Gavras *and* Donald Stewart. *Based on the book by Thomas Hauser. Cinematographer:* Ricardo Aronovich. *Editor:* Francoise Bonnot. *Music:* Vangelis. *Production Design:* Peter Jamison. *Set Decorator:* Linda Spheeris. *Costumes:* Joe I. Tompkins. *Visual effects:* Albert Whitlock.

A Polygram Presentation. An Edward Lewis Production. A Universal Release. MPAA Rating: PG. Running Time: 122 minutes. In color.

The Cast

Ed Horman: Jack Lemmon. *Beth Horman:* Sissy Spacek. *Charles Horman:* John Shea. *Terry Simon:* Melanie Mayron. *Captain Ray Tower:* Charles Cioffi.

Lemmon with Sissy Spacek.

Consul Phil Putnam: David Clennon. *U.S. Ambassador:* Richard Venture. *Colonel Sean Patrick:* Jerry Hardin. *Kate Newman:* Janice Rule. *Frank Teruggi:* Joe Regalbuto. *David Holloway:* Keith Szarabajka. *Carter Babcock:* Richard Bradford. *David McGeary:* John Doolittle.

The Movie

Today's filmmakers are in a quandary about how to encourage reluctant audiences, ruined by fictional trash, to sit still for movies on contemporary issues and truths that are serious and often unpleasant.

The ingenious and talented Greek filmmaker, Constantin Costa-Gavras, surmounted this problem in his explosive political movie, *Missing,* by dealing with a timely issue circuitously.

His film's unqualified success hinged on its director's penchant for dual-level filmmaking. The core of *Missing* may be a news event—an unrelenting political probe and revelation—but it works primarily as a sad, wrenching domestic drama.

In *Missing,* we get a very accessible story about a family irrevocably tangled with larger events sur-

rounding the 1973 right-wing coup that overturned Salvador Allende's government in Chile and brought Augusto Pinochet's regime to power. That's the news event reported here.

What sets it in motion and gives it dramatic thrust, however, and makes it such a harrowing experience of depressing power, are the people that it touched.

Gavras's movie chronicles the disappearance of a young displaced American named Charles Horman (newcomer John Shea) from his home in Santiago and the subsequent attempts by Horman's father and wife, Ed and Beth, to locate him and to initiate an investigation of the incident. Horman, a writer/filmmaker with political interests, vanished on September 16, 1973, at the height of the military coup, and he was never found.

I doubt if *Missing* can be considered the truth. Its creators have their own view of the truth. This viewpoint examines government-approved organized violence and inverted moralities that stamp out humanity for the sake of Humanity.

In *Missing*, the U.S. government is depicted as one whose "business interests" (i.e., the 3,000 American businesses reportedly in Chile) make it necessary to support a coup that promises to overthrow an unwanted leftist government. Officious lies and perhaps authorized violence against its own people are strictly a matter of course.

Although it does not directly identify Chile by name, *Missing* alleges that the American Embassy there both supported and willfully concealed the executions of American nationals like Horman, a fringe that threatened the success of the coup.

Working from Thomas Hauser's 1979 book, *The Execution of Charles Horman: An American Sacrifice*, and eschewing his usual near-documentary style, Gavras has come up with an incredibly human, involving movie, another that borrows on the tradition of John Ford's *The Searchers* and its story of one man's obsessive search for a loved one.

Ernest Hemingway once observed that *Huckleberry Finn* is the book from which all American literature stems. The same could be said of *The Searchers* and movies. Thematically, it has inspired such diverse films as *Hardcore, Close Encounters of the Third Kind, the Deer Hunter, Taxi Driver,* Chuck Norris' *Missing in Action* films, *Rambo—First Blood II* and, of course, *Missing*.

Gavras's film works largely because it is tied not to an engaging and enraging news event but to a simple, noble story of family devotion and determination, steeped in everyday heroism.

And the shrewd casting of two very American and very sympathetic performers—Lemmon and Sissy Spacek in naturalistic, deeply-felt performances as

Lemmon with Sissy Spacek.

Horman's father and wife—certainly doesn't hurt. These stars guarantee the emotional connection so important to the film's success.

Not that *Missing* treats the characters of Ed and Beth Horman with too much reverence. The movie is astute enough to question Ed's naivete and see it for what it is—the result of a comfortable, insulated, uninformed lifestyle. (This is called dramatic license, as the real Ed Horman is a well-read, informed, active man.)

Most of *Missing* is about the evolution of Ed Horman, as it pits a citizen against bureaucratic liars. When Ed finally sees through the governmental double-talk, he's efficiently zapped by an embassy official who, sadly, speaks the truth.

"We have interests here to preserve," the official explains, "business interests that assure us of our way of life. If it wasn't for this unfortunate situation, you'd be home now, as complacent as ever and oblivious to what's happening here."

Costa-Gavras is abetted by Lemmon, whose subtle combination of naiveté and irony, although very human and likable, only makes the ordeal all the more painful, and by Spacek's feisty, enlightening performance as the no-nonsense daughter-in-law.

Lemmon has said that the fact that *any* Hollywood studio would touch this material floored him.

"You might as well have told me that Walt Disney was going to produce it."

He has revealed that he wore a hat in just about every scene in the movie to convey the quality of a man keeping a lid on himself. "I feel that I more or less succeeded in depicting a man who did not display his emotions except in the few scenes where he could no longer, thus making those scenes all the more important.

"I doubt that an actor is ever fully satisfied with his work, certainly I am not, but my performance in *Missing* is personally very satisfying to me from one point of veiw—I felt that I more or less succeeded in keeping the character contained, and in keeping the performance very simple."

Simple, but great—Lemmon's best to date.

The Critics

Pauline Kael in *The New Yorker:*

When Jack Lemmon puts his finger under his stiff collar and twists his neck—the familiar tic of his which he uses to show that the character he's playing is writhing in discomfort—he puts me in mourning for the lost evening. The Italian actor Ugo Tognazzi often has the same effect on me. It's not that they're bad actors, exactly—it's that they're sweaty, loyal and hollow. They're actors through and through; they're nothing but actors.

Spacek with John Shea.

When they're in realistic roles—as Lemmon is in Costa-Gavras's *Missing* and as Tognazzi is in Bernardo Bertolucci's *Tragedy of a Ridiculous Man*—they're busy being realistic. The more they try to become Everyman, the more actorish they are. They're lightweights—gifted comedians—who get soggy when they try to fill the screen in heavyweight, tragicomic roles.

Jack Lemmon is so eager to have depth that he looks on a serious role as a chance for redemption—gazing at it with the wide-eyed-kid enthusiasm of a Jesus freak. Subdued and dolorous as he is in *Missing*, he's still hyperactive, and when he walks down a corridor clutching his stomach the screen oozes boringness.

[In *Missing*], Jack Lemmon is playing a variant of the role that Jane Fonda has been playing in films such as *Coming Home* and *The China Syndrome*; he's the naive, protected, nonpolitical conservative who is radicalized (or, at least, reeducated) by what he learns.

For the sake of this demonstration, the actual Ed Horman, a cultivated man who married a painter and was a devoted father, is presented as a rigid conformist who believes what the American Embassy officials tell him and thinks that if his son got into trouble it was his own fault. It's by turning Ed Horman into Costa-Gavras's notion of a Middle-American Everyman that the film hopes to make an impact on the mass audience.

Why is *Missing* receiving so much praise? Maybe because it's such a cornball virtuous melodrama about closing the generation gap and because Lemmon is there exuding all that heartfelt sincerity and learning how misguided he was.

Vincent Canby in *The New York Times*:

Whether or not its facts are verifiable, *Missing* documents, in a most moving way, the raising of the political consciousness of Ed Horman who has, until this devastating experience, always believed in the sanctity of his government and accepted its actions and policies without question.

Mr. Lemmon and Miss Spacek are superb, and their increasing respect and fondness for each other as the story unfolds gives *Missing* an agonizing reality.

A bit disingenuous [however] is the way the film never bothers to give a good answer to the question of why the Chilean—and possibly the American—authorities found it necessary to liquidate Charles Horman while allowing the safe departure from Chile of Terry Simon. Also, Mr. Costa-Gavras takes care not ever to identify Chile by name. [This is] a bit disingenuous. The cities are clearly named and identified.

Lemmon.

These are valid questions to raise about a film that is so fine that one wants it to be above reproach.

David Denby in *New York* magazine:

One image in *Missing* is unforgettable—a naked man, having been "interrogated," is led down a brightly lit tunnel in the depths of a large stadium; at the end of the tunnel, also in bright light, lie five, six, seven bodies, yet the man keeps walking because there's nothing else to do. This is Costa-Gavras's poetry. Yet the director, who can rival Eisenstein at moments, is only half an artist. The other part of him is a calculating melodramatist—obvious, overinsistent and narrowly obsessive.

I'm afraid that Costa-Gavras doesn't want the audience to think. By casting Jack Lemmon as the father, he has made a grab for the politically unawakened Americans who, he imagines, can be reached only through the gut. When Lemmon's Ed Horman arrives in the capital, he's disgusted with his son, whom he regards as an idle, unproductive flake—a hippie. He's such a sour, censorious prune that he's cruel to Beth, who loved her husband and may very well be his widow.

But we know that Jack Lemmon cannot be bitter for long and, sure enough, as Ed pursues his inquiry, he begins to admit that he's always loved the boy, and eventually he's reconciled to him and to Beth as well.

Maybe another actor could make this affecting, but with Lemmon playing Ed, the role is just a wheeze—utterly predictable. We know every crevice of Lemmon's face, every tremor in his voice, every swallow of the lump in his throat. While Lemmon doesn't do anything outrageous, he doesn't discover anything new, he doesn't work against the grain of what's easy.

Variety:

Lemmon is superior as a man facing up to issues he probably never thought of and certainly never wanted to confront personally.

Mass Appeal

A Universal Picture (1984)

The Production Staff

Executive Producer: Joan B. Kroc. *Producers:* Lawrence Turman *and* David Foster. *Director:* Glenn Jordan. *Screenplay:* Bill C. Davis. *Based on his play.* *Cinematographer:* Don Peterman. *Editor:* John Wright. *Music:* Bill Conti. *Production Design:* Philip Jeffries. *Set Designer:* Don Woodruff. *Set Decorator:* Robert Checchi. *Costumes:* Shari Feldman *and* Bruce Walkup. *Technical Advisor:* Father Joseph Battaglia.

An Operation Cork Presentation. A Turman-Foster Company Production (in association with Jalem Productions). A Universal Release. MPAA Rating: PG. Running Time: 100 minutes. In color.

The Cast

Father Tim Farley: Jack Lemmon. *Mark Dolson:* Zeljko Ivanek. *Monsignor Burke:* Charles Durning. *Margaret:* Louise Latham. *Mrs. Hart:* Alice Hirson. *Mrs. Hart's Mother:* Helen Heigh. *Mr. Jennings:* John C. Becher. *Father De Nicola:* James Ray. *Marion Hart:* Sharee Gregory.

The Movie

At this moment in time, the film version of *Mass Appeal* stands as "possibly the biggest single disappointment" in Jack Lemmon's career—"and it has absolutely nothing to do with my performance or the finished product."

Lemmon's disappointment stems from the fact that the film never received a general release because of contractual problems between Universal Pictures, the releasing company, and Joan Kroc's company, which completely financed the film.

Based by Bill C. Davis on his successful play, *Mass Appeal* was released in a few major cities, most notably Los Angeles and New York, in December of 1984 in order to qualify for the Academy Awards. "It was booked in a few major theaters," Lemmon explains, "for only a few weeks on purpose, the theory being that after it received some nominations, it would then go into general release the following spring.

"Universal spent a considerable amount of money for those limited openings on the theory that they would recoup when it went into a broader release later on. But two unfortunate things occurred. Number one, it opened soft and its box office business was only fair. Number two, while everybody

Lemmon with Ivanek.

except yours truly assumed that it was a shoo-in for several major nominations, it ended up getting none.

"Universal then took a good look at its deal, and realized that the first $5 million of domestic gross would contractually go to Mrs. Kroc's company, and they decided not to take the chance of spending more money on prints, advertising, etc. and cancelled all plans for any further theatrical release domestically, figuring to get their money in foreign distribution and subsequent TV sales.

"In other words, with Monday morning quarterbacking, they decided they had made a lousy deal. Unfortunately, I got caught in the middle along with [producer] Larry Turman and everyone else who had spent over a year and a half trying to get the film made.

"It was more than just a bitter disappointment. I was in total shock. It's the only time that anything remotely like that has happened to me and I can only thank God that I have had so many other wonderful experiences that far outweigh *Mass Appeal* and the expectations for it that were never realized."

It's a pity that more people didn't get to see *Mass Appeal* on screen. You may not buy most of its chicken-soup homilies—about faith, conviction and commitment and their threat to survival—but the reading of them by Lemmon and newcomer Zeljko Ivanek makes you think.

I doubt if anyone would go home a convert to either Catholicism or a better way of living their life, but for at least 90 minutes or so the film makes you a believer.

Mass Appeal is an easy entertainment with a few deep-dish ideas hedged in between the jokes about the confrontation between an old-guard, show-bizzy priest who has put his parish performance on automatic pilot, and a radical upstart, offended by the old priest's comfortable, paint-by-the-numbers complacency and his disregard for traditions and the basic demands of the job.

Jack Lemmon's Father Farley is a fat cat who drives a Mercedes-Benz and whose success in his community has been based on keeping his congregation entertained. He doesn't make waves for his people or point an accusatory, intimidating finger at them. He tells them what they want to hear, inviting them to approve out loud during what Farley calls "dialogue sermons," and then he passes the collection plate.

The money that Father Farley takes in is looked on by the priest as his Nielsen rating, and it's a high one. He's boffo at the B.O.

Mark Dolson (Ivanek), the feisty, insensitive seminarian assigned to Farley for "guidance," is not into consoling or babying his listeners, but making them feel mad and guilty. He wants to battle them in the same way that he's alienated the Church's hierarchy.

The drama that unfolds between these two men loses its petty personal edge after a while and evolves into an intense, ugly political slugfest and a wrenching fight for survival. It turns out that the Church (as represented by evil Charles Durning) doesn't want to reform the annoying Dolson; it wants him out—even if it means labeling the young priest an active homosexual to get rid of him.

Farley, who has honed his own survival skills, knows what's happening and ends up being both affected by the boy and enraged by the grand dark plan for him. Farley warns Mark, but it isn't enough. He has to get involved himself, and his own involvment could mean the end of a cushy lifestyle for Farley.

The movie, as directed by Glenn Jordan, moves with standard sitcom self-assurance. The jokes, gags and prefab pathos come on cue, pushing the narrative towards some of its darker truths. As it progresses, the comedy starts to subside and the film tries to cut deeper as both Farley and Mark painfully adjust.

The facile ending, strictly a sitcom device, assures us that goodness will win out, evil will be exorcised and everyone will live happily ever after, so long as there is some conviction in their lives.

Davis and Jordan are fortunate enough to have two attractive and intelligent actors whose combined performance is a miracle of comic timing and emotional precision.

Lemmon and Ivanek create the kind of accessibility and friendly warmth of which Father Farley would approve. Amen.

The Critics

Kenneth Turan in *California* magazine:

Every year, as Oscar time draws near, movie insiders speculate about "the Jack Lemmon slot," the best actor nomination that traditionally goes to a veteran performer doing a by-the-numbers star turn the spitting image of every other turn he's ever done. This year the suspense ends early as the gentleman himself puts a lock on the proceedings with *Mass Appeal*.

It's not that Lemmon's acting is lousy; bad actors usually don't manage eight Academy Award nominations. It's simply that it's too unadventurous, too pat, a performance that never goes anywhere unexpected. Even if it's played to perfection, a single note doesn't sound like a symphony.

In *Mass Appeal,* Lemmon's persona is more of a problem than usual because it blunts part of the point of the script, adapted by Bill C. Davis from his Broadway success. The lead character, Father Tim Farley, is a priest whose problem appears to be overexposure to Jack Lemmon movies, who believes being a facile entertainer is all a clergyman can manage these days. We're so used to seeing Lemmon in this sort of glib role that the crux of the piece—that a priest should be doing more—takes a long time coming into focus. Why should a Jack Lemmon character be doing anything more? One never has before.

Naturally flip Father Farley ends up working with an eager, idealistic young deacon, Mark Dolson, who is so gung-ho you expect him to accuse the pope of malingering. Though Zeljko Ivanek brings an interesting intensity to the role, and certainly does better in conflict with Lemmon than Robby Benson did in *Tribute*, the whole concept is directed in such a predictable way by Glenn Jordan that nothing can really budge it from its self-satisfied conventionality. Yes, the old padre finally learns that "what you believe has got to be more important than what your congregation means to you," and the young sprout sees that giving sermons on the order of "Jesus is not impressed with your mink hats, cashmere coats and blue hair" is not perhaps the most efficacious way to

Lemmon with Ivanek.   Lemmon with Charles Durning.

Two views of Lemmon as Father Farley.

console parishoners, but the battle has been too obvious for those victories to have any kind of impact.

David Edelstein in *The Village Voice*:

Jack Lemmon plays Father Farley, a snappy, lovably dissolute priest in *Mass Appeal*—a man who likes to keep his flock in stitches, and who regards the collection plate as the sermonistic equivalent of a Nielsen rating (hence, the title). One day a young seminary student, Mark Dolson (Zeljko Ivanek), shows up in a jogging suit at one of Father Farley's "dialogue sermons" and actually wants to have a dialogue. Hmmm, thinks Farley, peeping over his spectacles at the obstinate intruder: Who is this upstart?

Five minutes into *Mass Appeal*, it's all over except for the jokes. Mark Dolson, we perceive, is the brash, puritanical young idealist who'll provoke the slippery old man into recovering his congregation once more; the priest, meanwhile, will teach the abrasive boy a lesson in real-world diplomacy.

We're supposed to identify with Dolson, but Zeljko Ivanek, out of perverse integrity, plays him as an insufferable prig.

Lemmon's performance is echt Lemmon, with one exception: he doesn't massage the back of his neck in *Mass Appeal,* although he looks as if he should, because it appears to be retracting into his shoulders. As an actor, Lemmon has been folding in on himself for years. On talk shows, he boasts about how selective he is in choosing roles, and that's not hard to believe. He plays the same role in every movie, the jokester whose flip persona is a mask for cowardice and the inability to love. And all of them end with the character being shot down, exposed, made serious. (No wonder he loved Davis's play: it says that any priest who believes in the value of entertainment is a fraud.) These aren't perform-ances—they're grandstanding death rattles. From Lemmon's first weary look at the young deacon, he know's he's done for—it's like he's recognized his executioner from a prophetic dream. *This* is the man who should have played Kurtz in *Apocalypse Now.*

Variety:

Confrontation and growing rapprochement between a crafty, fat-cat priest and a fiery, idealistic seminary student are performed to a winning hilt by Jack Lemmon and Zeljko Ivanek. Performances of toplined duo are sufficiently special to tap Oscar nominations.

A pickup of a Turman-Foster production, shot for $7 million and change, and financed by San Diego millionairess Joan Kroc under her Operation Cork banner, pic is that comparatively rare instance of a film that improves upon its popular legit origins.

Going My Way the film is not. Nor, on the other extreme, does it flirt with that scalding legit satire, *Sister Mary Ignatius*.... Director Jordan has found a gratifying filmic context for what is essentially a three-character drama. And it's a film in which you lean into the dialogue.

The dialogue is crisp and frequently barbed.

Macaroni (Maccheroni)

A Paramount Picture (1985)

The Production Staff

Producers: Luigi *and* Aurelio De Laurentiis *and* Franco Committeri. *Director:* Ettore Scola. *Screenplay:* Fuggero Maccari, Furio Scarpelli *and* Ettore Scola. Cinematographer: Claudio Ragona. *Editor:* Carla Simoncelli. *Music:* Armando Trovajoli. *Production Design:* Luciano Ricceri. *Set Design:* Ezio Di Monte. *Costumes:* Nana Cecchi.

A Filmauro/Massfilm Production. A Paramount Release. MPAA Rating: PG. Running Time: 104 minutes. In color. Spoken in English and in Italian with English subtitles.

Lemmon with Marcello Mastroianni.

The Cast

Robert Traven: Jack Lemmon. *Antonio Jasiello:* Marcello Mastroianni. *Laura De Falco:* Daria Nicolodi. *Carmelina Jasiello:* Isa Danieli. *And with* Maria Luisa Saniella, Patrizzia Sacchi, Bruno Esposito, Marc Berman, Jean-Francois Perriere *and* Fabio Tenore.

The Movie

For his 44th movie project, Lemmon attempted a first—a foreign film. *Macaroni (Maccheroni)* was a "crossover" movie not only for Lemmon, but also for its Italian filmmaker, Ettore Scola (*Le Bal* and *A Special Day*), an interesting experiment that just didn't work.

A more apt title might have been *Missed Opportunities*.

At the core of its plot lies a lovely idea about the kind of man who, for reasons too complicated to unravel, reasons that go back in his personal history, lets life slip by. He lives to work and actually permits himself to be terrorized by the tension of it. Time flies, life goes by, opportunities are missed—or, at best, they are realized when it's too late.

What better way could there be to dramatize this very valid point than via an overworked American businessman—Lemmon, naturally—alone in *la dolce far niente* world of Italy?

And who could be better blatantly espousing the easy life than Italians? And so, with director Scola on hand to provide the native insights and observations and with Marcello Mastroianni on screen as his spokesman, *Macaroni* would seem to be a complete package, something surefire.

But this movie is about missed possibilities in more ways than one. *Macaroni* itself is a missed opportunity—a chance to team up two aging, graceful screen comedians in a story about what counts in life. And exactly what counts? Life itself, *living* it, that's all.

So why was this movie titled *Macaroni*? Don't ask. No one connected with the production seems to know and, if you look closely, you'll notice that the substance macaroni doesn't figure into the plot; it isn't even ingested. A title that doesn't make sense is usually a good indication of a bad omen.

With Lemmon cast as a former G.I. back in Italy after a 40-year absence, and with Mastroianni as the man who befriended him then and now, one would expect a leisurely film about drinking, reminiscing, occasional womanizing and stopping to smell the flowers. One would expect a holiday, a tiny vacation, but *Macaroni* is anything but.

In fact, more often than not, it is strangely unpleasant.

Lemmon's Robert Traven, a big-deal consultant to Aeritalia, is the problem. You're in big trouble when the first character you introduce is a surly, disagreeabler man, a man with family problems, drug and alcohol problems and, most important, an attitude problem. Traven seemingly has no redeeming qualities, and Lemmon does a disservice to the film by playing him too authentically.

You've heard of films that leave you with a bad aftertaste. Well, *Macaroni* conjures one up *right away*. Traven's first meeting with Mastroianni's Antonio Jasiello is actually a beautifully written and played scene of modern hostility and rudeness. It rings absolutely true, but it gets the film off to a disastrous start, from which it never fully recovers.

Antonio was an old friend of Traven's during the war. Traven romanced Antonio's sister, and Antonio has never forgotten his "American friend." (*My American Friend*, actually, would have been an apt title for this movie.) Traven, however, bad-tempered, preoccupied and self-absorbed, hardly remembers Antonio and, what's more, he couldn't care less. He coldly dismisses the man and then, when that fails, insults him.

Ettore Scola has so many family characters, relationships and conflicts to map out that it seems to take the entire film before Traven and Antonio finally get together to sort out *their* differences. Antonio, it turns out, is a would-be writer and dramatist and he's used these skills to turn the jaded, unappreciative American into something of a folk legend in Naples. Antonio not only remembers everything, he embroiders it; Traven, on the other hand, remembers nothing.

Actually, Traven is Antonio's greatest creation. For years, he has entertained neighbors and friends with tales about the daring exploits of his American friend. So, when Antonio is finally reunited with the prig, his world crumbles—but only momentarily.

Traven sees the light, goes out and drinks with his new friend, makes peace with him (well, kind of) and even attends one of Antonio's godawful plays (providing the movie with its funniest and best sequence). Here, in these few scenes, *Macaroni* finally comes alive and becomes the film that it's been struggling to be.

The nostalgia and sentiment of these moments, the bittersweet remembrance and desperate attempts to "hold on" and turn back the clock and to bring back the past, these moments are genuinely touching. But they go by too quickly and, before we know it, *Macaroni* is caught up in a yawn of a subplot about Mastroianni's son and his money troubles and then it ends on a jarring note that makes one glad, for once, that life is not like the movies.

Macaroni has a difficult time articulating its ideas, which may or may not have something to do with its international assemblage (everyone's voice in the film has been looped, everyone's except Lemmon's), but one thing is certain: It comes alive, fleetingly, in its middle section by finding sensuality and sensibility, a truly scintillating blend, in friendship.

Upon completion of *Macaroni*, Lemmon moved forward with his plans for a stage revival of *Long Day's Journey into Night* and he is still dickering with 20th Century-Fox about the possiblity of directing Wendy Wasserstein's adaptation of John Noonan's play *A Couple of White Chicks Sitting Around Talking*." Susan Sarandon and Jill Clayburgh are its tentative stars.

Jack Lemmon as businessman Robert Traven.

The Critics

Vincent Canby in *The New York Times:*

Ettore Scola's *Macaroni* is a gummy little comedy about a successful, physically exhausted, pill-popping, possibly alcoholic American businessman, Robert Traven (Jack Lemmon), who learns how to relax and live the good life during a three-day trip to Naples.

The instrument of Robert's salvation is Antonio Jasiello (Marcello Mastroianni), a somewhat down-at-the-heel archivist who takes life as it comes, writes plays on the side and regards the wasting of time as a kind of art. Antonio dearly loves his large, Neapolitan family while Robert, of course, is in the middle of a divorce.

It's one thing for Americans to make such movies about over-achieving Americans, but something else for Italians—it's as if they'd begun to believe the publicity we'd sent them in the form of movies like *Summertime* and *It Started in Naples.* One need not have read Henry James to find this view of Europe a little simple-minded.

Mr. Lemmon sputters and rages and suddenly sees the light, at which point he is likely to cry. Mr. Mastroianni, his coat draped over his shoulder, moves blithely through melancholy personal crises that would send his American friend reaching for his tranquilizers.

Macaroni...is a star vehicle, but it seems awfully out of date and joyless.

Catherine Rambeau in the *Detroit Free Press:*

It took Italian director Ettore Scola to put Jack Lemmon and Marcello Mastroianni in the same picture, and what an inspired idea it was.

Without them, *Macaroni,* a slight, loving tale of a casual friendship that blooms again after 40 years of separation, could hardly have worked so well.

Because of their specific talents—Lemmon's at portraying exhausted, frustrated businessmen, Mastroianni's at conveying a joie de vivre that transcends poverty, family troubles and bad health—*Macaroni* is a shining liittle bubble of pleasure that gleams with humor and glistens with charm.

The immensely popular *Cocoon* is a film about the old made by the young. *Macaroni* is a film about men in their 60s made by their peers: The film's

Lemmon and Mastroianni.

director, writers, stars and at least one of its producers are all 60-plus. *Macaroni* will undoubtedly have a smaller audience, but it has a sense of the years between middle and old age that is absolutely authentic.

Variety:

Macaroni is a mild comedy-drama teaming the formidable talents of Jack Lemmon and Marcello Mastroianni. Stronger in expression of honest sentiment than in its humorous component, the picture faces weak theatrical prospects via Paramount release as a pickup. It was originally scheduled to be an HBO Premiere Films presentation (a slot it would fill comfortably) until the pay-cable outfit dropped out of the project.

Macaroni rarely achieves the comedic heights of director Ettore Scola's previous work. There simply isn't an abundance of funny situations or witty dialog here. Best sequence has amateur playwright Mastroianni filling in as the villain in one of his monthly poverty productions. Mastroianni is genuinely funny in the brief skit acted with Italian dialog.

Lemmon and Mastroianni, reminiscing.

Elsewhere, this English-language film is hampered by the dialog, with merely okay readings by Mastroianni, artificial dubbing of Isa Danieli as his empathetic wife and rote, direct-sound speeches by Daria Nicolodi as Aeritalia's p.r. officer. Acting is okay but diluted by the language distraction.

Lemmon throws himself into his role with customary passion, pumping life into some routine scenes.

Andrew Sarris in *The Village Voice:*

Macaroni is an unusually coarse title for a movie of unusually crude contrivances. Jack Lemmon plays Bob Traven, a McDonnell-Douglas Aircraft vice president, who arrives in Naples to advise Alitalia [sic] on the most efficient way to use their recent purchases. This Via Veneto cafe-play on the name of the legendary author (B. Traven) of *The Treasure of the Sierra Madre* is never followed up or explained. I suspect it was good for a chuckle or two over Campari at a post-midnight pre-script conference.

From the moment Traven disembarks at the airport he assumes the dyspeptic demeanor of the Ugly American Capitalist abroad. You just *know* from his expression that his marriage in the States is on the

Mastroianni and Lemmon, eating "rum babas."

Lemmon and Mastroianni.

270

Marcello Mastroianni as Antonio Jasiello.

rocks, that he has no "real" friends, that his heart has been cold for so long that he carries his chill all the way to Naples, aided in no small measure by the oddly gloomy Eastmancolor cinematography of Claudio Ragona.

Traven is grouching off a hangover in his hotel room when he is beset by Antonio Jasiello (Marcello Mastroianni), a "friend" of 40 years before. After angrily rejecting the effusive overtures of Antonio, sending the Neapolitan archivist away in despair, Traven has second thoughts as long-dormant memories of the man he was years ago enter his reveries. The stage is set for a full-fledged buddy-buddy romance with varicose veins.

Both Lemmon and Mastroianni are likably talented enough to take much of the sting out of the ethnic stereotypes. Still, I was somewhat surprised to see an Italian filmmaker treating Neapolitans as vital, quaintly eccentric "life-givers" on the condescendingly colonial model of the stage-set Okinawans in *Teahouse of the August Moon.*

271

That's Life

A Columbia Picture (1986)

The Production Staff

Producer: Tony Adams. *Director:* Blake Edwards. *Screenplay:* Blake Edwards *and* Milton Wexler. *Cinematographer:* Anthony Richmond. *Editor:* Lee Rhoads. *Music:* Henry Mancini. *Song:* "Life in a Looking Glass," *music by* Henry Mancini, *lyrics by* Leslie Bricusse. *Set Design:* Tony Marando.

A Blake Edwards Production. A Paradise Cove/Ubilam Release Film. A Columbia Release. No MPAA Rating or running time (as of press date). In color.

The Cast

Harvey Fairchild: Jack Lemmon. *Gillian Fairchild:* Julie Andrews. *Holly Parrish:* Sally Kellerman. *Father Baragone:* Robert Loggia. *Madame Carrie:* Felicia Farr. *Megan Fairchild Bartlet:* Jennifer Edwards. *Larry Bartlet:* Matt Lattanzi. *Kate Fairchild:* Emma Walton. *Josh Fairchild:* Chris Lemmon. *Janice Kern:* Cynthia Sikes. *Steve Larwin:* Rob Knepper. *Dr. Keith Romanis:* Joordan Christopher. *Fanny Ward:* Dana Sparks. *Chutney:* Chutney Walton. *Honey:* Honey Edwards.

Jack Lemmon and Julie Andrews as Harvey and Gillian Fairchild in *That's Life.*

The Movie

As this book goes to press, Blake Edwards is completing the post-production work on an intensely independent and experimental project titled *That's Life* (formerly *Crisis*), a movie which also marks a reunion of sorts for the writer-director and Jack Lemmon.

Their paths have crossed several times during the past 30 years, beginning in 1955 with *My Sister Eileen* (which Edwards co-wrote with Richard Quine) and *Days of Wine and Roses* and *The Great Race*.

For the occasion, Edwards prepared a skeletal 13-page script with Milton Wexler, plus 36 pages of character descriptions of the 11 speaking roles in the planned film, and then gathered friends and family in supporting roles for a highly improvisatory film about a weekend in the life of one American family, the Fairchilds.

Edwards describes the film as being about "seventy-two dramatic, funny, hectic hours in the life of a successful Malibu architect, ex-boy-genius Harvey Fairchild (Lemmon), his equally successful singer-wife Gillian (played by Julie Andrews, Edwards's wife) and their three children (played by Lemmon's son Chris, Andrews's daughter Emma Walton, and Edwards's daughter Jennifer)."

Also in the cast, in the small role of a fortune teller, is Lemmon's wife, Felicia Farr.

"Being that *That's Life* is such a personal story," adds Edwards, "it seems only logical to have a 'personal' cast. Jack and I go so far back that we could be family."

The plot of *That's Life* reportedly chronicles the comings and goings of a family during a three-day weekend, and how each member treats his or her

The Fairchild Family in *That's Life* (from left)—Jennifer Edwards, Chris Lemmon, Jack Lemmon, Julie Andrews and Emma Walton.

Lemmon (second from left) with producer Tony Adams, writer-director Blake Edwards and co-author Milton Wexler on the set.

own crisis and the crises of fellow family members. It is Edwards's microscopic account of the life span of a family.

The father, Harvey, a life-long hypochondriac, is now actually on the verge of a nervous breakdown over his concern about his age and appearance. He is a seriously panicked man who can't understand why this—i.e., aging—is happening to him. And his sexually playful nature is strictly a defense.

Gillian, his wife, meanwhile, is having problems with her own health, but remains passive about it for the sake of her husband and his difficulties with his decline.

Other familial problems include those of Kate (Emma Walton), who has just broken up with her beau (Rob Knepper); Megan (Jennifer Edwards), who is pregnant and feels unattractive and unappreciated by her husband (Matt Lattanzi); and son Josh (Chris Lemmon), whose girlfriend (Dana Sparks) is attracting the attention of Megan's husband.

All of these people are self-absorbed with their own problems or, in the case of Josh, a lack of problems. They are quite oblivious to everyone else's crisis, particularly Harvey's.

Their trivialities all come to a head during the 60th birthday party that Gillian has planned for Harvey, and among the outsiders in attendance are the staple wacky neighbor (played by Sally Kellerman, Lemmon's wife in *The April Fools*), a priest and Harvey's old college roommate (Robert Loggia), and, of course, the family doctor (Jordan Christopher).

Part of the built-in appeal of *That's Life,* despite its obvious downer status, is the way that everyone in the cast will deal with one another, based on past histories, and, as a result, how much each one will bring to their respective roles.

The movie is somewhat autobiographical, says Edwards. "I just sat back and let Jack be me, to some extent."

"Blake developed the characters, the story, how the characters would behave," Lemmon reports, "but we put in the words. The characters speak as we feel they should. Blake is the referee, in a sense. And God, is it fresh and wonderful!"

In order to have total control necessary to be able to give everyone virtually free rein, Edwards filmed much of the story at his beach house in Malibu, using as small a crew as possible. This created a relaxed atmosphere that enabled the cast to come up with their own dialogue and, in some cases, to create hunks of major scenes at their own discretion.

But, in Lemmon's words, *That's Life* belongs to Edwards, completely. "He excites you. I have total faith in him. I think he's got terrific taste, and nobody has a better sense of humor."

That's Life is tentatively scheduled to be released in the fall of 1986.

Happiness Is...

An Afterthought by BILLY WILDER

"Happiness is discovering that your daughter is in love with an older man—Paul Getty.

"Happiness is having a doctor who smokes four packs a day.

"Happiness is working with Jack Lemmon."

—Billy Wilder

Billy Wilder, directing.

With Lemmon (rear) on set of
Irma La Douce, 1963.

Some of Lemmon's
Leading Ladies

With Judy Holliday in
It Should Happen to You, 1954

With Kathryn (Grant) Crosby in
Operation Mad Ball, 1957

With Shirley MacLaine in
The Apartment, 1960

With Doris Day in
It Happened to Jane, 1959

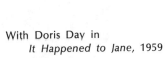

With Kim Novak in
The Notorious Landlady, 1962

With Shirley MacLaine in
Irma La Douce, 1963

With Lee Remick in
Days of Wine and Roses, 1962

With Carol Lynley in
Under the Yum-Yum Tree, 1963

With Romy Schneider and Dorothy Provine in
Good Neighbor Sam, 1964

With Virna Lisi in
How to Murder Your Wife, 1965

With Judi West in
The Fortune Cookie, 1966

With Elaine May in
Luv, 1967

With Catherine Deneuve in
The April Fools, 1969

With Sandy Dennis in
The Out-of-Towners, 1970

With Barbara Harris in
The War Between Men and Women, 1972

With Anne Bancroft in
Prisoner of Second Avenue, 1975

With Paula Prentiss in *Buddy, Buddy,* 1981

With Sissy Spacek in *Missing,* 1982